Ojibwe Discourse Markers

Ojibwe Discourse Markers

BRENDAN FAIRBANKS

UNIVERSITY OF NEBRASKA PRESS, LINCOLN AND LONDON

Sections 3.2.1.1 and 3.2.1.2 were previously published in "All about *Mii*," in *Papers of the Thirty-Ninth Algonquian Conference*, ed. Karl Hele (London: University of Western Ontario, 2008).

This book is published as part of the Recovering Languages and Literacies of the Americas initiative. Recovering Languages and Literacies is generously supported by the Andrew W. Mellon Foundation.

Library of Congress Cataloging-in-Publication Data
Names: Fairbanks, Brendan, author.
Title: Ojibwe discourse markers / Brendan Fairbanks.
Description: Lincoln: University of Nebraska Press, [2016] | Includes bibliographical references and index.
Identifiers: LCCN 2015040325 | ISBN 9780803299337 (hardback: alk. paper) | ISBN 9780803288232 (paper: alk. paper) | ISBN 9780803299368 (epub) | ISBN 9780803299375 (mobi) | 9780803299382 (pdf)
Subjects: LCSH: Ojibwa language—Discourse analysis. | Discourse markers. | Ojibwa language—Grammar. | Ojibwa language—Connectives. | Ojibwa language—Texts. | Ojibwa language—Spoken Ojibwa. | Ojibwa Indians—Social life and customs. | BISAC: SOCIAL SCIENCE / Ethnic Studies / Native American Studies. | LANGUAGE ARTS & DISCIPLINES / Reference.
Classification: LCC PM851 .F35 2016 | DDC 497/.3335—dc23 LC record available at http://lccn.loc.gov/2015040325

Set in Huronia by Tseng Information Systems, Inc.
Designed by Ashley Muehlbauer.

For the elders at Mille Lacs and for my son Mekethia

CONTENTS

PREFACE

In this book I describe the functions of a variety of discourse markers in the Ojibwe language, a language belonging to the Algonquian family of languages of North America.

Discourse markers have been defined by Schiffrin as "sequentially dependent elements which bracket units of talk" (1987a, 31) and as elements that, among other things, are syntactically detachable from a sentence (i.e., independent of sentential structure) and commonly used in initial position (1987a, 32, 328). This book shows that her initial characterization must be broadened in order to account for languages such as Ojibwe that show discourse markers occurring in both initial and second position, and for other languages that show discourse markers occurring in medial and final positions within utterances. Also, since many languages like Ojibwe and the Amazonian languages examined in this book make regular use of clitics and affixes as discourse markers, I show that not all discourse markers are "detachable" from their containing sentences. Based upon this and other cross-linguistic evidence, I offer a definition of discourse markers that essentially refines Schiffrin's characterization.

This book ultimately reveals the exploitive nature of language (and ultimately of its speakers) in regard to discourse. While languages show that individual words, particles, lexicalized phrases, clitics, and affixes may be "exploited" for their sentence-level functions for work at the discourse level, Ojibwe shows that entire inflectional systems may also be targets for discourse work. For example, Ojibwe exploits the sentence-level cohesive function of conjunct verbs in order to mark the eventline structure of a narrative. This accounts for the seemingly contradictive ability of conjunct verbs to serve as subordinate clauses at the sentence level but as independent clauses at the discourse level. Such behavior, termed "discourse marking" in this book, shows that the use of morphological forms must also be included within a viable definition of discourse markers.

ACKNOWLEDGMENTS

I am indebted to the elders of the Mille Lacs Band of Ojibwe, without whom this work would not have been possible, and thankful for their patience as I bombarded them with my endless questions. Miigwech gidinininim: Biidaaba-nookwe (Marge Anderson), Okaadaak (Elfreda Sam), Naawigiizis (Jim Clark), Zhaawanigiizhigookwe (Millie Benjamin), Wewenabiikwe (Dorothy Sam), Bebaamaashiikwe (Susan Shingobe), Biidwewidamookwe (Maggie Kegg), Mash-kawigaabawiikwe (Virginia Davis), Gimiwan (Raining Boyd), Asinigaabawiikwe (Carol Nickoboine), Amikogaabaw (Larry Smallwood), Obizaan (Lee Staples), and Naawigiizis (Frank Mason). All these elders allowed me free access to their brains and their intuitions about the language data contained in this book. I would especially like to thank Marge Anderson for letting me text and call her anytime I wanted to ask her a million questions and to pick her brain! This was invaluable. I would also like to thank Lillian Rice (Ogimaakwe) in helping me to understand many of the nuances existing with many of the discourse markers examined for this book.

I would also like to thank the members of my dissertation committee (super-visors Jeanette Gundel and John Nichols, along with Hooi Ling Soh and Nancy Stenson), who provided me with much-needed feedback and support with the original dissertation from which this book sprang. Their counsel and mentoring have allowed me to be a much better researcher.

I would also like to acknowledge my father for his speeches growing up about the importance of getting an education, my mom, who always said I was smart, and my grandmother, who has always inspired me by her love of education.

I also want to thank my friends and colleagues who have constantly encour-aged my research in the Ojibwe language. I want to thank Laura Pederson, Tony Drews, Marisa Carr, Amber Ruel, Karen McCall, Loanna Lynn Stainbrook, and Patricia Shepard, who have all been my traveling partners to Mille Lacs over the years. They have all kept me company on our long trips up to Mille Lacs.

ONE

Introduction and background

In this book, I identify and describe DISCOURSE MARKERS as they occur in Ojibwe, a language belonging to the Algonquian family of languages. The particular dialect that I investigate is the one spoken by people living at the Mille Lacs Band of Ojibwe reservation located in east central Minnesota. The topic of discourse markers in Ojibwe is largely unexplored, and many discourse markers in Ojibwe are either unknown or poorly understood. Also, discourse markers have not been the topic of much debate nor discussion within the Algonquian literature, let alone within the growing cross-linguistic literature surrounding discourse markers. This book fills some of that void.

Ultimately, this book will show that discourse markers have two major functions in Ojibwe: to add to the cohesiveness of a narrative ("discourse connectives") and to contribute an interpersonal nuance to an utterance ("mystery particles").[1] Discourse connectives show a tendency to exploit grammatical features, lexical items (i.e., words), or even whole inflectional paradigms (all which have functions at the sentence level) in order to accomplish work at the discourse level. In a way, discourse connectives in Ojibwe live double lives, in that they are part-time sentence-level elements (grammatical or lexical) and part-time discourse markers, doing work above the sentence level. Mystery particles, on the other hand, are full-time discourse markers, as they are *always* working at a level above that of the sentence, indicating a variety of interpersonal functions, such as denial of propositions, justification, reprimand, eliciting pity, correcting interlocutors, and so on.

In more theoretical terms, this book contributes to the literature an account of the use of second-position particles and preverbal elements as discourse markers, expanding the domain in which these elements are known to occur. This is significant, as the literature to date has been quite silent about the occurrence of discourse markers in second position, as well as those occurring as preverbs (a common grammatical element in Algonquian languages). With the contribution of the Ojibwe data, the cross-linguistic data show that discourse markers may essentially occur in any position within the domain of a sentence (or in its vicinity, straddling sentence boundaries), showing that discourse markers cannot be defined by their location, as early characterizations have attempted to claim (e.g., Schiffrin 1987a). Nor can they be reliably defined by their linguistic form, since discourse markers appear to come in many forms, as we will see, for example, grammatical/lexical items, affixes, clitics, and particles, including entire inflectional paradigms. Therefore, the general behavior of discourse markers cross-linguistically suggests that the identity of discourse markers and their likely locations are largely constrained by the linguistic machinery already existing in the language. For example, if a particular language makes use of a lot of clitics, we might expect to find discourse markers that occur as clitics, as we will see with many of the Amazonian languages. The identity and the various docking spots of discourse markers are influenced not only by this already existing grammatical machinery but also by the grammatical options made available to speakers either in their own language or by language contact. This, I believe, shows the tremendous facility of the language mechanism within the brain to use many seemingly simple features in language to accomplish work at varying levels of discourse.

1.1   THE LANGUAGE

Mille Lacs elder Jim Clark once told me, "Anishinaabe means Indian, and Ojibwe is a type of Anishinaabe." I mention this because a couple of terms are commonly used in referring to the language under discussion in this book: (1) *Ojibwemowin* 'Ojibwe language', which is based upon the word *Ojibwe*, used to describe the people; and (2) *Anishinaabemowin* 'Indian/Ojibwe language', which is based upon the word *Anishinaabe* meaning 'Indian, human being'. The people at Mille Lacs and at other Minnesota reservations normally refer to their language as *Ojibwemowin*, or just *Ojibwe* when speaking English. Traditionally, though, the language has also been known as *Chippewa*, an anglicized variant of *Ojibwe* that has largely fallen out of use nowadays. For related dialects in Canada to the north and to the east, the language is typically known by its speakers as *Anishi-*

naabemowin (or some variant based upon this word), but many times as *Ojibwe* when referring to the same language in English. The practice of using the term *Ojibwe* as a blanket term to refer to the language in English appears to have become widespread among native speakers (especially among those involved with language revitalization efforts), even for native speakers who did not traditionally refer to their language as *Ojibwe* in past generations. For example, Patricia Ningewance (a native speaker and language activist from Lac Seul, Ontario) reports that speakers in her community never used to use the term *Ojibwe* in earlier times but do today when referring to their language in English (personal communication). This appears to be common out east too, in southern Ontario and some parts of northern Michigan, where the language is typically known as *Anishinaabemowin* when speaking the language but as *Ojibwe* when speaking English. For some in the east, *Anishinaabemowin* is pronounced *Nishnaabemwin* and is commonly known by linguists as the *Odawa* language. Valentine uses the term *Nishnaabemwin*, though, in his grammar of this language, since "that is the term that its speakers, the NISHNAABEG (singular, NISHNAABE), typically use to identify their language" (2001, 1). He notes, however, that Odawa has also gone by other names, such as *Ottawa*, *Chippewa*, and *Ojibway*.

The blanket use of *Ojibwe* (or *Ojibwa*) is also evident within the early literature. For example, Goddard, in the *Handbook of North American Indians*, lumps together various dialects spoken by Indian groups such as Ojibwa, Chippewa, Saulteaux, Ottawa, Mississauga, Nipissing, and Algonquin under the label *Ojibwa* (see Goddard 1978, 583).[2] More recent scholarly classifications, however, have tried to do away with the general *Ojibwa* label, preferring rather the term *Ojibwayan* (albeit it has not been widely adopted by Ojibwe scholars) to describe these various languages (Goddard 1996, 4). In his foreword to the reprint edition of Baraga's famous "Otchipwe" dictionary, Nichols states that the "Otchipwe" language (Baraga's term), or as he generally refers to it, "Anishinaabemowin," is genetically related to about twenty-five other languages within the Algonquian language stock and is one of the most widespread of North American languages, being "spoken today in the United States in Michigan, Minnesota, North Dakota, and Wisconsin and in Canada in Manitoba, Ontario, Saskatchewan, and Quebec" (Nichols in Baraga 1992, v–vi). The sister dialects that come under the umbrella of *Ojibwe* are: CHIPPEWA, spoken in North Dakota, Minnesota, Wisconsin, and Michigan; SAULTEAUX, spoken in northwestern Ontario and farther west into Manitoba, Saskatchewan, and Alberta; SEVERN OJIBWE, or OJI-CREE, spoken in northwestern Ontario; ALGONQUIN, spoken near the Quebec-Ontario border; NIPISSING, spoken in an area north of Lake Huron by Lake Nipissing; and ODAWA, spoken on the shores of Lakes Huron and Michigan (Valentine 1994, 1–6). Among these related dialect groups, not all refer to their language as *Anishinaabemowin*, however. Some Severn Ojibwe speakers, for example, call their language *Anishininiimowin*, and some Saulteaux speakers call their language *Nakawemowin* (Valentine 1994, 1; Ningewance 2004, xix).

Given that the term *Ojibwe* (and its various spellings) is most often used as a blanket term to speak about a wide variety of closely related languages within the Algonquian language family that are spoken across a wide geographical area within the United States and Canada, it is important to distinguish the dialect being discussed in this book from this blanket term. The descriptions of the discourse markers in this book are primarily based upon their usage by native speakers at Mille Lacs, located in east central Minnesota. Despite this limited description, however, the discourse markers discussed in this book are actually quite common among most, if not all, sister dialects that have come under the blanket term *Ojibwe*. Many of their functions and meanings, therefore, are going to be similar, if not the same, for most sister dialects in question. This means that language learners from related dialects will still be able to learn about the major functions of the discourse markers that they have in common with Mille Lacs Ojibwe while also learning local nuances common to their communities. Teachers, especially those who are native speakers, might find the descriptions in this book helpful in a pedagogical sense, in that they may find alternative ways in which to explain the various nuances and meanings of discourse markers to their students. Linguists interested in the general theoretical implications of discourse markers may also find these descriptions helpful in supporting current discourse theory, or in formulating new theories. At the writing of this book, the Ojibwe language is an endangered language (though we are making great strides in revitalizing it), and this book is a humble attempt to describe elements in the language that are probably the most difficult to describe and the most difficult to acquire by language learners. This is just the beginning.

1.2   WHY STUDY OJIBWE DISCOURSE MARKERS?

At the time I was doing research for this book in 2008, there were over 4,000 enrolled members of the Mille Lacs Band of Ojibwe. This includes 2,100 members who lived within reservation boundaries, 800 tribal members who lived in the Minneapolis–St. Paul metropolitan area, 500 tribal members who lived in other Minnesota towns, and 600 tribal members who lived elsewhere in the United States and other places (Mille Lacs Band of Ojibwe website, www.millelacsojibwe .org, 2008). Ojibwe as a spoken language is quite endangered at Mille Lacs. The elders at Mille Lacs stated to me that there were only an estimated eighty fluent speakers out of the four thousand enrolled tribal members, putting their fluency rate (i.e., number of fluent speakers) at about 2 percent (Marge Anderson, personal communication). At Mille Lacs, all native speakers of Ojibwe are over fifty years of age.

The current state of the language for other Minnesota Ojibwe reservations is similar. In a work published by the Minnesota Humanities Center, Treuer estimated in 2009 that there were 400 native speakers at Red Lake, 150 at Mille Lacs (notice that this is higher than the estimate above from the Mille Lacs elders), 90 at Leech Lake, 20 at Nett Lake, 15 at White Earth, 3 at Grand Portage, and none on the Fond du Lac reservation (Moose et al. 2009, 4). While it is not known to me how accurate these estimates are given the discrepancy in the estimates at Mille Lacs, it is clear that the Ojibwe language is nonetheless in an endangered state.

In response to a decline in the number of native speakers, there has been a recent movement to preserve and revive the Ojibwe language. This is evident in the many active community language classes and conferences, the publishing of language materials in various formats, and the recent move toward immersion education at both the preschool and elementary levels. The Ojibwe language is also taught at various universities and tribal colleges.

There is also a growing number of second-language speakers of Ojibwe. These are usually young people who are of Ojibwe heritage and did not grow up speaking Ojibwe but have attained an advanced level of fluency as adults. Many of these second-language speakers have become immersion teachers within the many emerging Ojibwe immersion programs across Minnesota and Wisconsin.

Incidentally, many of these young immersion teachers are now speaking to their own children in the Ojibwe language. This is *very* encouraging and exciting.

On the academic side, while a long history of Algonquianist linguistics has brought to light many complex insights about the Ojibwe language as a whole, especially in the inflectional system and historical developments, many aspects of Ojibwe remain unexplored and misunderstood. There is no academic research that focuses on the general area of discourse for Minnesota Ojibwe (but see Rhodes 1979 for his work on what he identifies as the Central Ojibwa/Ottawa dialect), let alone research on discourse markers. To my knowledge, discourse markers are also not commonly taught as part of Ojibwe language curricula at the university level, nor, from my vantage point, are they a significant part of second-language speech. Their proper use and function, for the most part, is just not known. For example, in evaluating the speech of many second language learners, I have noticed that discourse-structuring elements such as *izhi* 'and then, and so' (also to be discussed) and a whole slew of other discourse particles appear to be largely nonexistent in the speech of even the most advanced language learners. This is no surprise, however, since discourse markers are notoriously difficult for adult learners to acquire, especially when the target language has second-position phenomena, as Ojibwe does. Further documentation and new research in the area of discourse markers would serve to broaden our knowledge and the scope of the Ojibwe language as a whole.

In formal linguistic circles, a study of discourse markers in Ojibwe contributes to the area of discourse marker research in general, since the Ojibwe data present a number of problems for the current theoretical characterization of discourse markers. The description of discourse markers provided in this book ultimately broadens our knowledge of the behavior of discourse markers in general and contributes to an already growing cross-linguistic body of work on the subject. Therefore, while this book is intended to be primarily a descriptive piece with the intention of helping to preserve, document, and revive the Ojibwe language, it contributes to broader theoretic concerns as well.

1.3   METHODOLOGY

For an endangered language such as Ojibwe, there are not many sources from which to garner examples of discourse marker usage. For example, in Minnesota there are no radio broadcasts, television shows, or newspapers in Ojibwe, nor are there many books that are entirely published in Ojibwe (although recently there have been a growing number of children's books entirely in Ojibwe). There are, however, a multitude of published texts (i.e., stories and narrations by various native speakers, including Mille Lacs speakers) available in issues of *Oshkaabewis Native Journal* (an academic journal), *Omaa Akiing* (Treuer 2000), *Living Our Language* (Treuer 2001), and *Portage Lake* (Kegg 1993, edited and transcribed by John Nichols). For this book, I examined texts by Mille Lacs speakers published in the *Oshkaabewis Native Journal* and *Portage Lake* and unpublished texts that I personally collected from my consultants. I also consulted my field notes taken over a period of five years in meetings with my consultants. My notes include a number of recorded examples of discourse marker usage as they occurred in real time within interactions between speakers themselves, or with those of us visiting the elders.

For the texts published in the *Oshkaabewis Native Journal*, if an accompanying audio was provided with the transcription (which is common practice for the *Oshkaabewis Native Journal*), I relied heavily on the published audio rather than the published text to ensure that an accurate representation of discourse marker usage was obtained. When needed, I retranscribed select stories that I reviewed for the purposes of this book and worked out translations with my consultants at Mille Lacs. This provided a clear picture of discourse marker usage within those texts. The *Portage Lake* texts, though not accompanied by original audio, were quite reliable, as the editor of those texts vigorously worked out both the translation and transcription with the author of the stories. Examples from both sources are cited throughout this book. In regard to the discourse markers found either in stories or within my own notes, I queried my consultants as to their various meanings and usage. Many times my consultants were easily able to provide translations for certain discourse markers, but other times they were not. This is no surprise, since discourse markers are notoriously difficult to translate. In all cases, however, I gave great attention to the context in which each discourse marker was used, since many discourse markers can only be defined and understood within context. I have tried to incorporate these various contexts within the characterizations of each discourse marker appearing in this book.

The description of these elements, which one of my consultants described as "little bugs that are holding on for dear life" (James Clark, personal communication, 2008), and elements that I have analyzed as discourse markers should not be viewed as exhaustive. My goal was only to describe the functions of the most common discourse markers found within stories and narratives and within the speech patterns of my consultants, so as to illuminate their core functions, which to date have been either unknown, misunderstood, or unexplored. There are undoubtedly other nuances and functions for many of these discourse markers that remain unknown to me or are inadequately described in this book. This book, it is hoped, will provide a starting point for further research into the topic of discourse markers in Ojibwe.

1.4   ORTHOGRAPHY

The orthography used in this paper is the one devised by Charles Fiero for Ojibwe (commonly known as DOUBLE VOWEL ORTHOGRAPHY), a phonemic system now widely used by language teachers and linguists alike in both the United States and Canada (see also Nichols 1995, xxiii; Valentine 2001, 29). This system is quite commonly used and well known nowadays, and so I will provide only a very brief explanation of the writing system here for those who might be unaccustomed to its use.

Ojibwe has both short vowels (i.e., vowels said with short duration) and long vowels (i.e., vowels said with long duration). Vowel length in Ojibwe is distinctive. What this essentially means is that changing a long vowel to a short vowel, or vice versa, in an Ojibwe word can also change its meaning. For example, if you change long vowel *aa* in *maanaadizi* 'she/he is ugly' to short vowel *a* getting *manaadizi*, the meaning of the word changes to 'she/he is promiscuous, she/he is easy to have relations with'. So it is easy to see from this example how important it is to say your long vowels long, and your short vowels short. Fiero's system has the advantage of capturing this feature.

Generally speaking, the way the system works is that doubled identical vowels represent long vowels, and single vowels represent short vowels. The long vowels are: *aa, ii, oo,* and *e*; the short vowels are: *a, i,* and *o.* Note that because long vowel *e* has no short vowel counterpart, it is written as single vowel *e* as a matter of efficiency rather than as doubled vowel *ee.* Nasal vowels (vowels produced through the nasal cavity) in Ojibwe are represented by attaching *-nh* to the vowel, e.g. *aanh, enh, iinh, oonh,* rather than using the [˜] symbol often used in other languages to mark nasality. An example of a word containing a nasal vowel is *nandookomeshiinh* 'monkey'. In the Ojibwe word for *monkey*, long vowel *ii* is a nasal vowel and is so represented by the attached -*nh*. Some Ojibwe vowels occurring as nasal before consonants *s, sh, z,* or *zh* are usually followed by -*n*, rather than -*nh*, for example, *oshkanzhiin* 'his/her fingernail' as opposed to *oshkanhzhiin* (see Nichols and Nyholm 1995, xxv, for full discussion of this convention).

The Ojibwe consonants consist of six lenis (or "weak") consonants: *b, d, g, j, z, zh*; their six fortis (or "strong") counterparts: *p, t, k, ch, s, sh*; two nasals: *m, n*; two glides: *w, y*; and two glottal consonants: *h,* ' (Nichols and Nyholm 1995, xxvi–xxviii). The designation of *lenis* (i.e., consonants produced with less energy) and *fortis* (i.e., consonants produced with more energy) is a convenient linguistics label that attempts to characterize the nature of Ojibwe consonants as having weak/strong counterparts, such as the so-called lenis/fortis counterparts represented by the Ojibwe consonants: *b/p, d/t, g/k, j/ch, z/s, zh/sh*. The lenis (or weak) consonants *b, d, g, j, z, zh* are typically pronounced voiceless (i.e., with little or no vocal cord vibration) at the beginning and the end of a word, but inside words (especially when they occur between vowels) they are typically pronounced as voiced (i.e., with vocal cord vibration). The fortis (or strong) consonants *p, t, k, ch, s, sh* are actually long consonants, meaning that they are said with relatively longer duration than English consonants. Long consonants are probably more easily understood as being doubled themselves, especially when occurring in the middle or at the end of a word: *pp, tt, kk, chch, ss, shsh*, albeit they are written as singlets *p, t, k, ch, s, sh* for efficiency. For example, the Ojibwe word for *woman* is represented in the Double Vowel orthography as *ikwe*, but its pronunciation is more accurately written as *ikkwe*, since the *k* is said twice as long, stretching over a syllable boundary: *ik.kwe* 'woman'. Pronouncing *woman* as *i.kwe* with short consonant *k* actually sounds more like an English *k*, and it is a common challenge among language learners to stretch short *k* (which is English sounding) over syllable boundaries, thereby producing an Ojibwe-sounding long *k*.

With regard to the use of hyphens, it has been a common practice with the Double Vowel orthography to offset tense markers and other preverbal elements from their host words by the use of hyphens, such as in the verb phrase *gaa-izhi-wiisinid* 'and so she/he ate', which is made up of the past-tense marker *gaa* (changed form of past-tense marker *gii-*), the relative root *izhi* 'and so', and the verb *wiisini* 'she/he eats'. Since common interlinear glossing (i.e., the word-by-word analysis directly under example sentences) conventions in linguistics papers also utilize hyphens to offset morphological content within words, the use of hyphens in this book may be confusing to those unfamiliar with the use of hyphens in the Double Vowel orthography. Most of the interlinear glosses provided in this book, however, will be broad and will not utilize hyphens to separate content below the word level. The use of hyphens, for the most part, will reflect the normal use of hyphens within the Double Vowel orthography. In some cases where a narrow gloss is necessitated, hyphens may be used to offset morphological content below the word level. The gloss itself will be specific enough so as to make clear what is being offset. For example, clitics (i.e., words that are reduced to one syllable and attach to a neighboring word) that normally would not be explicitly marked in the gloss as clitics will be specifically marked as "CL" in narrow interlinear glosses. This practice will also be applied to other elements not explicitly marked or accounted for in broad glosses should the occasion arise when glossing below the word level is necessitated.

In regard to clitics, the common convention for Ojibwe has been to simply leave them unattached as separate words, rather than to use hyphens to attach them to their host words. For example, for the sentence *mii go ge-zhi-wawaabishkiganzhiiyan* 'you will have telltale white spots on your fingernails' (written in the conventional way), all preverbal elements associated with the main verb *wawaabishkiganzhiiyan* 'that you have telltale white spots on your fingernails', such as tense marker *ge* 'future' and relative root *izhi* 'and so' are offset by hyphens, but the particles *mii* and *go* are left unhyphenated. This is the normal practice, but because I analyze *go* as a clitic (its full form being *igo*), I normally adjoin clitics to their host words with a hyphen, getting *mii-go* rather than *mii go*. There is some evidence to suggest that such a practice is warranted. For example, one of my consultants, Millie Benjamin, used to adjoin clitics like *go* to their host words while also adjoining all tense markers and other preverbal content seamlessly with the main verb, yielding the following arrangement: *miigo gezhiwawaabishkiganzhiiyan* 'you will have telltale white spots on your fingernails'. Millie's arrangement shows that she, as a native speaker, intuitively preferred to adjoin clitic *go* to its host word *mii*, yielding *miigo* rather than *mii go.* Though she did not use hyphens, I use hyphens to show this native-speaker grouping and also to help language learners distinguish the play of host words and their clitics. If emphatic clitic *go* appeared in its full form *igo*, I usually opted to write it as a separate word, although Millie preferred to write the full form *igo* as adjoined, for example, *boochigo*, rather than separated as in *booch igo*.[3] The reason for leaving *igo* unattached stems from the fact that a minimal word in Ojibwe is bimoraic. In other words, the shortest content words in Ojibwe must be words consisting of either two short vowels, such as *ashi* 'put him/her there', or a word consisting of one long vowel, such as *miizh* 'give it to him/her' (see also Hayes 1995, 217, for a similar analysis for Eastern Ojibwa).[4] In the case of *igo*, its distribution (a full accounting of which is beyond the scope of this book) appears to suggest that *igo* is its full form, and its clitic form is the phonologically reduced form *go*. While it may be tempting to analyze the initial segment on *igo* as epenthetic *i* (i.e., inserted as a connective vowel between consonants), this appears to be negated by the fact that *go* may appear on words ending in a consonant without a connective vowel, such as in *wiin-go ogii-ayaan aw gwiiwizens ge-miijid* 'the boy always had something to eat'. This suggests that the initial segment on *igo* is not epenthetic *i* and that *igo*, when it occurs, is indeed the full form. Such a practice will also be extended to discourse markers that have full forms and clitic forms.

There are times when traditional convention takes precedence over the practice of using hyphens to connect clitics to their host words, and I break my own rule. For example, in the case where the particle *mii* combines with contrastive particle *idash* to get what is conventionally written as *miish* 'and then', strict adherence to the rule offered here demands that this be written as *mii-sh*. While I prefer *mii-sh* (because it more accurately represents the reduction and attachment of *idash* to host word *mii*), I chose to leave it as *miish* within sentences quoted from already published texts that utilized the Double Vowel orthography. I preferred not to change other scholars' conventional use of *miish* for the purposes of this book. If I had to rework any transcriptions, I used the convention of attaching clitics to their host words using hyphens in *my* version of the transcription provided in this book. In such cases, the audio is cited rather than the published text, but I still provide the page number so that readers may quickly find the original text (albeit my version of the transcription may differ from the published transcription). If I had to transliterate any transcriptions written in a different orthography, this was duly noted.

While hyphens most likely will have little benefit for the native-speaker reader, the use of hyphens in written Ojibwe serves to delineate for language learners the various levels of complexity existing in even the simplest of phrases or sentences. For this reason, I make regular use of hyphens in this book.

TWO

What is a discourse marker?

There has been a struggle in the literature to precisely define the elements that are widely known as DISCOURSE MARKERS (the term used in this book). The struggle has been compounded because these elements are known by many different names, for example (just to name a few): DISCOURSE MARKER (Schiffrin 1987a; Brody 1989; Jucker and Ziv 1998; Fraser 1990), PRAGMATIC MARKER (Brinton 1996), DISCOURSE PARTICLE (Schourup 1985; Massam, Starks, and Ikiua 2006; Davidsen-Nielsen 1996; Hakulinen 1998), UTTERANCE PARTICLE (Kwong 1989), CONNECTIVE (Park 1999; Sadler 2006), and DISCOURSE CONNECTIVE (Biq 1990).[1] The difficulty is also compounded by the many functions that discourse markers are said to have, such as: "discourse connectors, turn-takers, confirmation-seekers, intimacy signals, topic-switchers, hesitation markers, boundary markers, fillers, prompters, repair markers, attitude markers, and hedging devices" (Jucker and Ziv 1998, 1, 2).

Perhaps the biggest difficulty in pinning down a definition, or in delimiting these elements into some sort of distinct category, stems from the fact that linguistic items or expressions serving as discourse markers may be members of various distinct word classes "as varied as conjunctions (e.g., *and, but, or*), interjections (*oh*), adverbs (*now, then*), and lexicalized phrases (*y'know, I mean*)" (Schiffrin 2003a, 57). This also forces the question as to whether these are the only word classes from which discourse markers could be drawn (as noted by Schiffrin 1987a, 40).[2]

To further compound an already complex situation, there is also some disagreement in the literature about which particular linguistic expressions qualify as discourse markers and which do not. For example, while Schiffrin (1987a; 2003a, 66) characterizes expressions such as *y'know* as discourse markers, Fraser (1990, 392) does not. While Schourup (1985) includes interjections such as *aha* as discourse markers, Fraser (1990, 391) does not. These disagreements stem, no doubt, from the fact that the study of discourse markers is relatively new.

There were only scattered studies on these elements in the 1980s, when serious study of discourse markers in English began (Fraser 1990, 384). Since then, a vast amount of literature, including cross-linguistic studies, has appeared, leading Fraser to conclude that "the study of discourse markers has turned into a growth industry in linguistics, with dozens of articles, both theoretical and descriptive, appearing yearly" (1998, 301). While earlier scholarly works have produced various definitions for discourse markers (see Goldberg 1980; Schourup 1985; Blakemore 1987; Schiffrin 1987a; Fraser 1990; Redeker 1990, 372), the vast majority of literature on discourse markers to date relies heavily on the characterization made by Schiffrin (1987a) for English discourse markers, and most papers on the topic of discourse markers appear to cite her initial characterization. Because her framework provides, in my opinion, the most comprehensively descriptive view of the behavior of discourse markers, I will both utilize and expand her initial characterization to include findings from languages other than English, including Ojibwe. Even at the time of her initial characterization, Schiffrin admitted that she did not have the benefit of cross-linguistic data to inform her definition of discourse markers. In the following sections, I hope to tighten up this definition based upon such cross-linguistic evidence.

2.1   SCHIFFRIN'S DEFINITION OF DISCOURSE MARKERS

Much of the scholarly literature relies heavily upon Schiffrin's characterization of discourse markers. That initial characterization was made in her 1987 work, where Schiffrin operationally defined discourse markers as "sequentially dependent elements that bracket units of talk, i.e. nonobligatory utterance-initial items that function in relation to ongoing talk and text" (1987a, 31; 2003a, 57). Schiffrin analyzes the following items as discourse markers:[3]

(1)   English discourse markers (Schiffrin 1987a, 327)[4]

(a)	*oh, well*	(particles)
(b)	*and, but, or, so, because*	(conjunctions)
(c)	*now, then*	(time deictics)
(d)	*y'know, I mean*	(lexicalized clauses)

By "sequentially dependent elements," she means those elements that function at the discourse level (i.e., above the sentence) and that are not dependent upon their containing clauses, or smaller units of talk, but are sequentially dependent on the structure of the discourse (see Schiffrin 1987a, 39–40). For example, the coordinating conjunction *and* (in sentence-level grammar) may only link items of the same word class or sentence constituent, but when used as a discourse marker (above the sentence level, where it can bracket chunks of discourse), *and* may link distinct linguistic units. For example, in (2), discourse marker *and* links a declarative sentence with an interrogative sentence, showing dependence not upon smaller linguistic units (such as when sentence-level *and* connects two noun phrases or two verb phrases) but upon the discourse structure itself.

(2)   Discourse marker *and* linking distinct units (Schiffrin 1987a, 38)

Debby: I don't $\begin{bmatrix} \text{like that.} \\ \text{I don't like} \end{bmatrix}$ that. **And**, is he accepting it?
Zelda:

By "brackets," she means the marking of the boundaries of discourse units, or what she calls "units of talk" (Schiffrin 1987a, 31). The term "units of talk" is intentionally kept vague in this definition, since discourse markers do not demarcate only sentences but may mark other units of talk, such as propositions, speech acts, or tone units (see Schiffrin 1987a, 31). According to Schiffrin, "Metalinguistic brackets, for example, can mark a discourse unit as long as a conversation or as short as a word; they can mark units embedded within larger units, e.g. reasons within explanations, or answers within question/answer pairs" (1987a, 36). It is in this manner that the term "bracket" is being used in her operational definition.

Later in that work, her operational definition for discourse markers is refined into a more theoretical one, in which she tentatively ("tentative" because she admittedly did not have the benefit of cross-linguistic data to inform her formulation) specifies the conditions that would allow an expression to be used as a discourse marker.[5] Her conditions are given in (3).

(3)   Schiffrin's "tentative suggestions" (1987a, 328)

(a)   "it has to be syntactically detachable from a sentence"

(b)   "it has to be commonly used in initial position of an utterance"

(c)   "it has to have a range of prosodic contours (e.g., tonic stress and followed by a pause, phonological reduction)"

(d)   "it has to be able to operate at both local and global levels of discourse, and on different planes of discourse; this means that it either has to have no meaning, a vague meaning, or to be reflexive (of the language, of the speaker)"

In order to understand her theoretical definition, it is first important to understand her framework for discourse. This is the framework in which she embeds both her understanding and her characterization of discourse markers in general. In regard to understanding discourse markers, she states, "DMs function in relation to aspects of language that can be defined only through discourse per se (a linguistic unit larger than the sentence) and in relation to communicative processes underlying (and realized through) situated language use. Sometimes the unit being marked is a sentence; at other times, the unit is defined as an action, an idea unit, or turn at talk" (Schiffrin 2003b, 458). In other words, when we undertake a conversation with someone, we are trying to accomplish a multitude of things simultaneously. For example, we negotiate turns, make points, concede points, acknowledge receipt of information, request receipt of information, hedge, emphasize, signal speech acts, and initiate repairs, as well as convey the basic message to be communicated, all in the attempt to establish discourse coherence. In dialogic discourse, speaker and hearer jointly interact in the creation of discourse coherence using many of the devices just mentioned. Discourse coherence is thus achieved by the "joint efforts from interactants to integrate knowing, meaning, saying and doing" (Schiffrin 1987a, 29). In monologic discourse, she explains, the speaker is primarily burdened with the task of creating coherence, that is, opening a story, making points and proposals, and making sure that those proposals are understood in culturally appropriate ways. Schiffrin (2003b, 458) proposes that discourse coherence may be understood as an interdependency between differing levels or planes of discourse, planes that represent our cognitive, social, expressive, and textual knowledge. These discourse planes are given in (4).

(4)   Planes of discourse (Schiffrin 1987a, 24–29)

      EXCHANGE STRUCTURE   turns in talk

      ACTION STRUCTURE   speech acts

      IDEATIONAL STRUCTURE   propositional content, ideas

      PARTICIPATION FRAMEWORK   how speakers/hearers relate to each other

      INFORMATION STATE   organization and manage ment of knowledge and metaknowledge

It is against the background of this discourse model (which is a sociolinguistic one, as opposed to a purely semantic/pragmatic one) that Schiffrin identifies and characterizes the discourse markers observed in her data. Recall that the discourse markers that Schiffrin describes are: *oh, well, and, but, or, so, because, now, then, I mean, y'know.* These markers were all taken from a corpus of live conversations between herself and a group of Jewish neighbors in a Philadelphia neighborhood. Some examples of these markers from Schiffrin's data are provided in (5), with all markers provided in bold type. Note that commas in these examples mark brief pauses, and the absence of commas indicates that the marker in bold is part of the intonational unit of the following content.

(5)   Schiffrin's discourse markers (1987a)

(a)   ***Oh,*** *well they came when they were a year.* (73)

(b)   ***Well,*** *when y'get to the cemetery, y'make a right.* (122)

(c)   ***And,*** *he says, 'Well I don't know.'* (133)

(d)   ***But,*** *I went into the army.* (155)

(e)   ***Or*** *some good uh: . . . very good literature.* (179)

(f)   ***So,*** *yeh, she would hit kids with a ruler.* (199)

(g)   ***Because*** *the Jewish people are the most liberal minded people in the world.* (213)

(h)   ***Now*** *our street isn't that nice.* (231)

(i)   ***Then*** *when they went ho-off eh for their nap, I:-* (251)

(j)   ***Y'know*** *when you get older, you just don't keep socializing anymore.* (277)

(k)   ***I mean*** *let's get married!* (297)

Examining these various examples, it is easy to see that Schiffrin's criteria for what would allow an expression to be used as a marker are based upon the distribution of the markers occurring in her data. For example, her discourse markers all appear on the periphery of the sentence in such a manner that they remain "independent of sentential structure" (1987a, 32). According to her, this means that their removal from the sentence "leaves the sentence structure intact" (32). It is in this manner that Schiffrin's discourse markers are "detachable from a sentence."

Schiffrin's markers appear predominantly in initial position. The markers *then* and *y'know*, however, may also occur in other positions. For example, she notes that *then* may occur utterance initial and utterance final but states that "initial *then* has wider scope as a discourse marker than final *then*" (1987a, 247). She also notes that most of the tokens of *then* in her corpus were usually preceded by other markers (see 247 for discussion). For *y'know*, Schiffrin's examples show that while most occurrences appear in initial position, it may also occur in medial and final positions. Despite the distributional flexibility of these two markers, the overall pattern of the discourse markers occurring in her data clearly suggests that they have a strong proclivity to occur in initial position. This appears to be the reason why she characterizes her markers as "commonly used in initial position of an utterance" (328).

Schiffrin's markers also show that they may either occur with tonic stress (i.e., apparently meaning that they may occur with their own stress followed by a pause) or occur with the intonational contour of the containing sentence. Her data show that each one can appear with or without tonic stress. This is shown in the following.

(6) Marker *oh* (Schiffrin 1987a, 73)

(a) *Oh, well they came when they were a year.*   (with tonic stress)

(b) *Does he like opera? Oh maybe he's too young.*   (without tonic stress)

In addition to these markers' various prosodic contours, some of Schiffrin's markers appear as being phonologically reduced, such as the discourse markers *y'know* (which is lexicalized as phonologically reduced) and *cause*. This behavior is shown for *because* in the following examples.

(7) Marker *because* (Schiffrin 1987a, 197, 204)

(a) ***Because*** *we got too many of our old friends, y'know, that uh ...*

(b) ***cause*** *the younger one's gonna come for dinner.*

While the first three criteria in Schiffrin's characterization of discourse markers speak to syntactic or phonological features, the fourth criterion speaks to the multifunctionality of discourse markers, which, according to Schiffrin, is "one of the central defining features of discourse markers" (2003a, 67). This multifunctionality has two aspects to it. First, Schiffrin's discourse markers show that they are able to display relationships between both local and global levels of discourse. For Schiffrin, a local level of discourse is the relationship that a discourse marker displays between adjacent utterances, while a global level of discourse is the relationship that a discourse marker displays between wider spans of discourse. This can be seen in the following example, where discourse marker *because* operates on both a local and a global level of discourse.

(8) DM *because* at both local and global levels of discourse (Schiffrin 2003a, 57–58)

Debby: (a) Yeh. Well some people before they go to the doctor,
        they'll talk to a friend, or a neighbor.

      (b) Is there anybody that   [uh ...

Henry: (c)   [Sometimes it works.

      (d) **Because** there's this guy Louie Gelman,

      (f) he went to a big specialist,

(g) and the guy … analyzed it wrong.

[narrative not included]

(j) So doctors are — well they're not God either!

In (8a), Debby makes the statement that some people will talk to a friend or neighbor before seeing a doctor; Henry seeks to validate that statement by relating an experience of a friend of his. In (8c) he says *sometimes it works,* and then he proceeds to give his justification for his statement in (8d–g). As Schiffrin explains, *because* operates locally by linking Henry's statement *sometimes it works* in (8c) with Henry's opening justification *because there's this guy Louie Gelman* in (8d). But then *because* operates globally by linking *sometimes it works* with Henry's narrative of his friend's experience in (8f–j). It is in this manner that discourse markers may work on both local and global levels of discourse.

The second aspect of multifunctionality is the ability of markers to connect utterances either on a single plane or across different planes simultaneously. This multifunctionality is demonstrated in (9) with the markers *because* and *but.*

(9)   Multifunctionality of discourse markers (Schiffrin 2003a, 57)

(a)   On a single plane

Yeh, let's get back, **because** she'll never get home.

(b)   On multiple planes simultaneously

Jack: [The rabbis preach,   ["Don't intermarry"
Freda: [**But** I did-   [**But** I did say   those intermarriages
          that we have in this country are healthy.

In (9a), *because* connects two actions in a single plane of discourse (action plane): a request and the justification for that request. In (9b), however, *but* connects an utterance defined on several different planes of discourse simultaneously and thus relates (or anchors) the different planes of discourse to one another. As Schiffrin explains, Freda's *but* prefaces an idea unit (i.e., intermarriages are healthy), displays a participation framework (nonalignment with Jack's proposition), realizes an action (i.e., a rebuttal during an argument), and seeks to establish Freda as a current speaker in an exchange (opens a turn at talk). The discourse marker *but* thus locates an utterance "at the intersection of four planes of talk" (Schiffrin 2003a, 57). The usage of *but* in this example demonstrates quite nicely the anchoring ability that discourse markers have across different planes of discourse. This anchoring ability, according to Schiffrin, is due to their status as INDEXICALS (1987a, 322–25) or as CONTEXTUALIZATION CUES (2003a, 58; 1987a). This means that discourse markers (due to their meaning and/or grammatical properties) are able to guide the hearer as to how particular units of discourse are to be interpreted. As INDEXICALS, discourse markers propose, according to Schiffrin, contextual coordinates by anchoring simultaneously differing levels of discourse (1987a, 322–26). What this essentially means is that, as indexicals, discourse markers "index their containing utterance to whatever text precedes them (proximal), or to whatever text is to follow (distal), or to both. They either point backward in the text, forward, or to both" (1987a, 323). For example, the additive marker *and* indexes an utterance with both prior and upcoming talk, since its additive function is forward looking to the next idea or action, while the marker *but* only indexes an utterance with prior talk, since it seeks to contrast an utterance to prior talk (1987a, 323–24).

This indexical role, however, is partly delimited by the individual functions that markers may have. The meaning relations between utterances that they select (and consequently display, rather than create) are constrained by both their respective referential (semantic) meanings and their grammatical or lexical properties, if any. For example, conjunctions *and* and *but* (within sentence grammar), when used as discourse markers, are used in ways that reflect their sentence-level grammatical use as conjunctions and may have distributions at the discourse level that *do not* parallel their distribution in sentence grammars (as we saw previously with *and*).[6] The point here is that these discourse markers have a *primary function* as conjunctions in the ideation plane in conjoining idea or propositional structures, but they may also have *secondary functions* as discourse markers in other planes of discourse (see Schiffrin 1987a, 315–17). For example, all the conjunctions have their primary function within idea structures (propositional structures), but they are, in a sense, *borrowed* to accomplish more global functions at the discourse level.[7] Their functions at this level of discourse, because of their referential and/or grammatical usage as conjunctions, are largely mirrored in their use as discourse markers.

On the other hand, discourse markers *oh* and *well* have either no, or very little, referential meaning on their own. These types of discourse markers are much freer to have functions within other planes of discourse. Schiffrin notes that "if an expression used as a marker **does** have meaning, its primary use in discourse will be in the organization of referential meaning at a textual level—and that if a marker does not have meaning, its primary use will be elsewhere" (1987a, 319). This tendency is exactly what we observe in the behavior of discourse markers cross-linguistically, as we will see.[8]

So this naturally divides discourse markers into two groups: those that are primarily textual (e.g., connectives such as *and, but, or, so, because, now, then*) and those that are interpersonal in nature, or largely pragmatic (e.g., *oh, well*). Brinton (1996, 38) also suggests that discourse markers fall into two categories (having a twofold function): those which belong to the *textual* mode of language, and those which belong to the *interpersonal* mode of language.[9] According to Brinton (1996, 38), in the *textual* mode, the speaker structures meaning as text, creating cohesive passages of discourse. The *interpersonal* mode is the expression of the speaker's attitudes, evaluation, judgments, expectations, and demands, as well as the nature of the social exchange, the role of the speaker and the role assigned to the hearer. Brinton also notes that this twofold function of discourse markers is already recognized by Schiffrin, since Schiffrin recognizes discourse markers as providing "coordinates within their context by indexing utterances either to the participants (focus on the speaker is proximal and on the hearer is distal) or to the text (preceding discourse being proximal and the following discourse being distal)" (Brinton 1996, 39, summing up Schiffrin 1987a, 316–17; 1987b, 25). More recently, Schiffrin has stated, "[D]iscourse is defined both as structural—a unit of language larger than a sentence—and as pragmatic, that is, language in use. Thus it is not surprising that DMs [discourse markers], as terms that define units of discourse, can also be identified as both text- and speaker-based" (2003b, 459). The cross-linguistic evidence also speaks to this duality of function of discourse markers, but as we will see in section 2.3.4, the cross-linguistic data also show that some discourse markers may have both textual and interpersonal functions simultaneously.

2.2   RELEVANCE THEORISTS' VIEW OF DISCOURSE MARKERS

Before we examine the cross-linguistic evidence, it is perhaps worth mentioning the approach that relevance theorists have taken toward the characterization of discourse markers. Their view of markers is embedded within the framework of RELEVANCE THEORY (RT), a theory that characterizes human communication in terms of a communicator who *provides* evidence of his or her intention to convey a certain meaning and an audience (the interlocutor) who must *infer* what that meaning is based upon the evidence put forth (Wilson and Sperber 2004). The underlying principle here is that the communicator presents just enough evidence of his or her intention without putting the interlocutor through too much processing effort. To put this in RT terms, "[e]very ostensive stimulus conveys a presumption of its own optimal relevance" (Wilson and Sperber 2004, 612). Provided that the ostensive stimulus presented by the communicator is relevant enough for the interlocutor to process it, the interlocutor will then follow a path of least effort in computing cognitive effects (i.e., working out a relevant interpretation). Once the interlocutor's expectation of relevance is satisfied (i.e., once he or she figures out what the interpretation is), the interlocutor stops. In short, communication is achieved through an *inferential* process that culminates in the interlocutor's appropriate interpretation. According to Wilson and Sperber, this approach to communication (i.e., inferential pragmatics) is to be contrasted with the classical code model, which characterizes communication as the encoding of an intended message into a signal that then must be decoded by an interlocutor who has the same copy of the code. While utterances, they add, constitute linguistically coded evidence (necessitating interlocutor decoding), they represent only one type of input possible within a nondemonstrative inference process that yields an interpretation of the speaker's meaning. As they also point out: "The goal of inferential pragmatics is to explain how the hearer infers the speaker's meaning on the basis of the evidence provided" (2004, 607). A nonverbal example of this process offered by Wilson and Sperber goes like this: If someone leaves her empty glass in your line of sight, and you then notice it, you might conclude that she *might* want a drink. If, on the other hand, she deliberately waves it at you, you would then be justified in concluding that she *would* like a drink (611–12). In essence, you are able to infer that your guest (the person with the empty glass) wants another drink because she provides just enough evidence of her intention that your processing effort is minimal and worth your time. Your natural human tendency to search for relevance then allows you to infer what your guest's intention is. It is in this manner that relevance theorists strive to characterize discourse markers.

As Blakemore (2004, 236) points out, relevance theorists are not interested in the *behavior* of discourse markers (as Schiffrin and I are) in regard to their distribution or structure, but rather they are interested in what kinds of meaning they *encode* and how their functions might be pragmatically inferred by the search for relevance. For example, Blakemore argues in regard to Schiffrin's analysis for *but* that while *but* may be analyzed as functionally marking the continuation of a turn at talk (i.e., continuing a speaker's action), it is not clear whether *but*, or any other discourse marker for that matter, actually encodes information about turn taking. In other words, Blakemore has serious doubts whether *but* actually encodes a meaning of "turn taking" or whether the turn-taking function can be inferred from the encoded meaning of *but* (whatever that may be), taken together with the assumption that the speaker has been optionally relevant (Wilson 1994, cited in Blakemore 2004, 236).

A predominant idea in RT is that there are two types of linguistic meaning, CONCEPTUAL and PROCEDURAL. When a linguistic construction (i.e., an utterance) encodes conceptual representations (i.e., a concept, or what Schiffrin might term an idea unit), it is said to be conceptual. If an utterance encodes procedures for manipulating those conceptual representations, it is said to be procedural. Therefore, "[i]nferential comprehension involves the construction and manipulation of conceptual representations" (Wilson and Sperber 1993, 10). Applied to discourse markers, then, this approach holds that they aid in the search for relevance by guiding an audience to the appropriate contextual affects that ultimately lead to the appropriate interpretation of an utterance. While some have claimed that discourse markers encode only procedural information and are not truth-conditional in the sense that they do not affect the truth-conditionality of the expressions that contain them (see Andersen 1998; Jucker 1993; Fraser 1996, 1998, 1999), it is largely recognized now that discourse markers may encode both types of information (i.e., procedural and conceptual). For example, Ziv showed that the Hebrew marker *kaze* encodes procedural meaning while at the same time affecting truth conditions of its containing utterances (Ziv 1998; Blakemore 2004, 230). On the other hand, it has been argued that non-truth-conditional discourse markers such as *in contrast, in other words,* and *as a result* encode concepts rather than procedures (Blakemore 2004, 230).

One of those who has characterized discourse markers within the RT framework is Fraser (1990, 1999), and I will briefly describe his approach. Fraser's characterization assumes that sentence meaning is analyzable into two separate types of conventionally encoded information: content (propositional content) and pragmatic (signals of the speaker's communicative intentions). He calls the "signals of speaker's communicative intentions" pragmatic markers and further divides pragmatic markers into three major types: BASIC PRAGMATIC MARKERS, COMMENTARY PRAGMATIC MARKERS, and PARALLEL PRAGMATIC MARKERS. Basic pragmatic markers include expressions such as *please* and performative expressions such as *I claim* and *I promise,* which signal the force of the basic message. Commentary pragmatic markers include expressions such as *frankly, incredibly, amazingly, if I may be personal,* and *well* and signal the force and content of an entire message, rather than just the basic message. Parallel pragmatic markers include expressions such as *damn* as well as vocatives *sir* and *my friend* and encode an entire message, but one separate from and in addition to the basic and/or commentary message(s) (Fraser 1990, 386–87).

To Fraser, discourse markers are a type of commentary pragmatic marker that signals a sequential discourse relationship. In other words, discourse markers "impose a relationship between some aspect of the discourse segment they are a part of, call it S2, and some aspect of a prior discourse segment, call it S1" (Fraser 1999, 938). In short, they "signal how the speaker intends the basic message that follows to relate to the prior discourse" (Fraser 1990, 387). Examples of his discourse markers are given in (10) in bold type.

(10) Fraser's discourse markers (1990, 383)

(a)   *John can't go. **And** Mary can't go either.*

(b)   A: *I like him.* B: ***So** you think you'll ask him out then.*

(c)   A: *Did you like it?* B: ***Well,** not really.*

(d)   ***But** when do you think he will really get here?*

(e)   *I think it will fly. **Anyway,** let's give it a chance.*

(f)   ***Now,** where were we?*

Elements that do not relate some segment with some prior segment would not be considered discourse markers by Fraser. Therefore, expressions such as *frankly, obviously,* and *stupidly* are not counted as discourse markers, since they do not signal a two-place relationship between adjacent discourse segments. Rather, they are commentary pragmatic markers, as they "signal a comment, a separate message, that relates to the following segment" (Fraser 1999, 942). Excluded also are focus particles such as *even, only,* and *just,* pause markers such as *hum, well, oh,* and *ahh,* modal particles such as *indeed,* vocatives such as *sir, Mr. President,* and *Anyone?,* as well as interjections such as *Oh!, Wow!,* and *Shucks!*

Another stipulation that Fraser has for discourse markers is that "when an expression functions as a discourse marker, that is its exclusive function in the sentence." He explains that while discourse markers may have "homophonous" forms (one form analyzable as an adverb and one as a discourse marker) they do "not serve in both roles in the same sentence" (Fraser 1990, 389). In regard to positional distribution, Fraser characterizes discourse markers as typically occurring only in utterance-initial position but notes that there are also occasions when they are utterance-internal and utterance-final, such as with the marker *however.* Finally, Fraser considers discourse markers to have a core meaning distinct from the meanings of their homophones, noting that discourse markers are drawn not from a single grammatical source but from a variety of grammatical sources, including adverbials (*now, then, still*); literally used phrases (*to repeat, what I mean to say, similarly, overall*), idiomatic phrases (*while I have you, still and all*), verbs (*look, see*), interjections (*well*), coordinating conjunctions (*and, or, but*), and subordinate conjunctions (*so, however*), as well as terms such as *anyway* and OK. His points here are that "discourse markers are not adverbs, for example, masquerading as another category from time to time," that discourse markers (and not their adverb homophones) have a core meaning that "places restrictions on the details of the relationship between s2 and s1" (Fraser 1998, 308), and that "discourse markers should be analyzed as having a distinct pragmatic meaning which captures some aspect of a speaker's communicative intention" (Fraser 1990, 393).

In sum, the approach taken by Schiffrin (the approach used in this book, but expanded to include cross-linguistic details) and the one taken by relevance theorists are not really at odds with one another, since they are asking different questions in regard to the characterization of discourse markers. While Schiffrin, for example, is interested in describing the *behavior* of discourse markers within actual language use via a sociolinguistic model of discourse, relevance theorists attempt to explain *how* discourse markers encode meaning and *how* that meaning is interpreted by interlocutors to achieve some cognitive effect in the search for relevance. Having said that, each approach does have some bearing on which expressions are counted as discourse markers. For example, while Schiffrin considers expressions such as *oh* as discourse markers, Fraser does not. This is largely due to the fact that Schiffrin defines discourse markers as working not only to display discourse relations but to display interpersonal relations as well. Fraser, on the other hand, sees discourse markers as only displaying a discourse relation between s2 and s1, relegating the interpersonal marker *oh* to a separate designation as an interjection. Interjections, he admits, are a group of expressions that "share certain properties with discourse markers," but he argues that they are not part of a sentence but an entirely separate "sentence" expressing the emotional state of the speaker (Fraser 1990, 391). Since most researchers agree that discourse markers must be described at a level of discourse above the sentence level (see also Blakemore 2004, 221), it is odd that *oh* would be excluded as a discourse marker when *oh* serves a discourse function—to express the emotional state of the speaker. Others, such as Aijmer and Simon-Vandenbergen, have since followed Fraser by making a formal distinction between discourse markers and pragmatic markers: they consider discourse markers to be a *subclass* of pragmatic markers that function only to "mark coherence relations" and consider pragmatic markers to be the "signals in the communication situation guiding the addressee's interpretation" (see Aijmer and Simon-Vandenbergen 2006, 2–3).

What I find unattractive about Fraser's approach is that because he (and now others) does not include interpersonal type markers in his inventory of "discourse markers," he is forced to create various classes of "pragmatic" markers in order to account for a multitude of expressions that all appear to work at a level above that of the sentence. In short, since they all appear to serve some discourse function, why not call them all discourse markers? Also, one overarching consequence of his approach is that the "multiple functions of markers—including, critically, social interactional functions—are downplayed (if noted at all) and not open to linguistic explanation" (Schiffrin 2003a, 59). The result is that analyses such as those espoused by Fraser (and others) miss, I believe, the central defining characteristic of discourse markers: their multifunctionality on different planes of discourse. "It is this multifunctionality on different planes of discourse that helps to integrate the many different simultaneous processes underlying the constructions of discourse, and thus helps to create coherence" (Schiffrin 2003a, 58).

The purpose of this book is not to explain *how* discourse markers work but to describe their behavior within a sociolinguistic model of discourse developed by Schiffrin.[10] While her initial characterization lacked the benefit of cross-linguistic data, it provides the most comprehensive view of discourse markers and provides a framework in which to embed the exposition of Ojibwe discourse markers.

2.3   CROSS-LINGUISTIC DATA

Because Schiffrin did not have the benefit of extensive cross-linguistic scholarship to inform her theoretical definition of discourse markers, she was forced to qualify her initial characterization as "tentative." Though her initial characterization has often been quoted, even in recent literature, it is perhaps time for a definitional tightening up, to include observations about the behavior of discourse markers cross-linguistically. Since the 1980s, the body of cross-linguistic literature on the subject of discourse markers has grown, including studies that examine their use in Chinese (Biq 1990; Kwong 1989; Or 1997; Zhou 2013), Danish (Davidsen-Nielsen 1996; Jensen 2000), Finnish (Hakulinen and Seppänen 1992; Hakulinen 1998), French (Cadiot, Ducrot, Fraden, and Nguyen 1985; Hansen 1998; Vincent 1993; Dajko and Carmichael 2014), German (Abraham 1991), Italian (Bazzanella 1990; Bruti 1999; Catricala 2010), Portuguese (Silva and de Macedo 1992; Macario Lopes 2011; Cunha and Chaves Marinho 2012), Hungarian (Vaskó 2000), Indonesian (Wouk 1998), Japanese (J. Cook 1990; H. Cook 1992; Fuji 2000; Matsumoto 1988; Onodera 1994, 1995; McGloin and Konishi 2010; Katayama 2012), Spanish (Koike 1996; Schwenter 1996; Landone 2009, 2012), Latin (Kroon 1998), Korean (Park 1999; Do 2006; Hyun-Oak Kim 2011; Pak 2013), Andean Spanish (Zavala 2001), Bulgarian (Tchizmarova 2005), Hebrew (Ariel 1998; Maschler 1997, 1998; Ziv 1998; Shemesh 2006), Maya and Nahuatl (Torres 2006), Niuean (Massam, Starks, and Ikiua 2006), and Yagua (Payne and Thomas 1990) (see Schiffrin 2003a, 54, where she notes many of these works also). The cross-linguistic inventory is replete with an array of discourse functions, in-

cluding: attention getters and explanatory connectives (Finnish), sequential connectors (Portuguese, Tojolab'al Mayan), textual cohesion (Tojolab'al), emotional
intensifiers (Spanish), phatic connectives (Italian), agreement markers (Italian),
discourse coordination (Japanese, English), equivocation markers (Finnish),
softeners (Spanish), evidentials (Spanish), hedges (Hebrew, Spanish, Bulgarian),
explanations (Portuguese), clarification and confirmation devices (Andean Spanish), common understanding markers (Cantonese, Indonesian), reaction markers
(Danish), affirmative markers (Niuean), and requests for feedback (Portuguese),
just to name a few. While this body of work shows a large number of discourse
markers, all of which are in line with Schiffrin's analysis of discourse markers, the
cross-linguistic data also show that discourse markers may differ in their positional distributions, in what types of expressions are used as discourse markers,
and in what types of inflectional systems may carry discourse functions. Section
2.3.1 discusses the positional distribution of discourse markers across languages,
section 2.3.2 discusses the use of clitics and affixes as discourse markers, and section 2.3.3 discusses the use of TAM forms (tense-aspect-mood forms), or inflectional systems, as a way that some languages mark discourse.

2.3.1 Position

While a significant amount of the cross-linguistic literature shows discourse
markers occurring primarily in the sentence-initial (or utterance-initial) position, some studies show them occurring in sentence-final position, for example,
in Bulgarian, Hebrew, Quechua, Chinese, Maya and Nahuatl, Niuean, and Spanish, among other languages. Others show them occurring in both initial and final
positions, such as in Finnish, or occurring in initial, medial, and final positions,
such as in Italian.

(11) Sentence initial[11]

(a) Niuean (Massam, Starks, and Ikiua 2006, 197)

*mafola, fai nakai he magafaoa haau ne ne fai kitekiteaga hokulo lahi ke
hevagahau Niue tuga e pehē ka ha akoako faiaoga?*

'**okay**, is there anyone in your family who has an in-depth interest in the
Niuean language, like a pastor, teacher?'

(b)   Spanish (Schwenter 1996, 856)[12]

   mi tía Pepita viene el día 20.

   'My aunt Pepita is coming on the 20th.

   o sea el viernes que viene.

   O SEA, next Friday.'

(c)   Tojolab'al (Brody 1987, 512; Torres 2006, 616)

   Entonse ti = *wa yajni jaw* = *ʔi*

   '**And** that's how it was.'

(d)   Bulgarian (Tchizmarova 2005, 1149)

   Xajde *stiskajte zăbi ošte malko tam, dano neštata da se opravjat.*
   '**Come on**, hang on in there a bit more, let's hope things will get better.'

(12)   Sentence final[13]

(a)   Korean (Park 1999, 194)

   *cey -ka tayphyokito pwuthaktuli -lyekwu ha -**nuntey**:*
   'I wanted to ask you to do the representing prayer **nuntey**'

(b)   Andean Spanish (Zavala 2001, 1006)

   *Sí, en esa misma **pe***
   'Yes, in the same one **pe**'

(13)   Sentence initial, medial, and final

(a)   Italian (Bazzanella 1990, 633)

   (i)   **Insomma** *era una difesa mista [. . .]*
       '**After all/well** it was mixed defense [. . .]'

   (ii)   *[. . .] i pagani ormai erano stati eh scon-* **insomma** *distrutti totalmente.*
       'pagan were by now eh won- **after all/I mean** totally destroyed'

   (ii)   *Ma se mi dimettevo (chi) lasciavo, Zamberletti?* ABBIA *pazienza Padre Zanotelli* **insomma** *eh ((laughter)).*
       'If I resigned, whom was I leaving, Zamberletti? Don't be funny, Father Zanotelli **after all**.'

While this growing body of literature has expanded the distribution of discourse markers to include medial and final positions, little mention has been made of discourse markers that may occur in second position (or Wackernagel's particles).[14] Of all the works cited previously, only Payne and Thomas (1990) mention the existence of such a marker, *jį́įta* or *jį́į*, in Yagua, an Amazonian language.[15] Payne and Thomas hypothesize that as a discourse-structuring element, *jį́įta* shows "progression through a discourse. This may be progression along the main eventline (in narrative), or progression from one thematic paragraph to another" (1990, 427). An example of this usage follows.

(14) Yagua second-position discourse clitic *jį́įta* (Payne and Thomas 1990, 427–28)[16]

diíy rabyeejyérya ríicya jidyé rácą́ątą́ąsa
'There I set the fish trap yesterday in the afternoon in the middle (of the stream).'

ratyę́ę́ryąjay jį́įta rumusiy jiyu roorimyúją
'I returned here to the house from there.'

rą́ą́są́ąchą́ą́siy jį́įta
'This morning it dawned.'

rayą́ą́siy jį́įta ránaachǫ
'I went this morning towards it.'

2.3.2   Clitics and affixes

As it turns out, there is a significant amount of literature that speaks to the various discourse features of many indigenous languages of the Americas, which shows that the word classes from which discourse markers are drawn must also be expanded to include CLITICS and AFFIXES (see Brody 1989, which first made this point). For example, in Tojolab'al Mayan, Brody identified not only discourse markers of the type described by Schiffrin (i.e., syntactically detached items such as *ti* 'when', *entonse* 'then', *pwes/pwe/pes/pe* 'well', *este* 'um', etc.) but also those that occur as clitics (e.g., *-xa* 'now', *-ta* 'already', *-to* 'still', *-xta* 'durative', *cha/cho* 'repetitive'), as well as utterance-final clitics such as *-tak* 'emphasis, anyway', *-b'a* 'contrast, emphasis', *-ye7/ye7n* 'emphasis, anyway'. In Huichol, an indigenous language of western central Mexico, Grimes revealed that "both words like *mérí+kɹnte* 'well, then' and postfixes (suffix-like forms that follow enclitics) like *-rii* 'definitely'" (1975, 93) have functions in discourse. For the Ecuadorian language Cayapa and the Columbian languages Cubeo, Inga, Guajiro, and Ica, Longacre showed that both particles and affixes may serve as discourse markers, since they are "found to have a function which relates to a unit larger than the sentence, i.e., to the paragraph and the discourse" (1976, 468). In these languages, both particles and affixes that are used as discourse markers have largely a common function in marking the backbone structure of stories and narratives, which I will refer to from now on as the EVENTLINE. For one of these particles, *'cari*, for example, Longacre states that "if one copies out all the sentences from a discourse which have this particle within them, one gets a tolerably good abstract of the whole discourse" (1976, 468). In other words, these elements mark the backbone of the discourse. This backbone-marking function, led Salser and Salser. to label *'cari* as a "backbone tag" (Longacre 1976, 469; Salser and Salser 1976). Affixes, such as the Cayapa suffix *-ren*, may carry this function as well. Some of these elements may also show either digressions from the main event or that important events that entail role reversals are eminent or forthcoming. Longacre demonstrates the role-reversing function with the following example from Cayapa, in which the suffix *-n* shows up on a variety of words—verb, noun, conjunction, and adverbials—within a narrative to show that such a distant role reversal is coming later on in the narrative. In the example, strategic words in the story are marked by *-n* to preface the eventual downfall of a man who forgot to pay his bill.

(15)   Suffix *-n* as a discourse marker (Longacre 1976, 471)

"He was seated at a table eating, and since he was long **conversing** (-n), he arose and left without remembering to pay the bill. This man took a long time before he returned. Three years later he went to the same **place** (-n) and ordered another meal. Then he said to the owner, 'Godmother, long ago I **ate** (-n) a meal here but I forgot to pay for it and left. Now I want to pay for it: what do I owe you?' So the woman answered, 'You owe me seven pesos.' **So-being** (-n) the woman's son spoke to her, "Mother, why do you say seven pesos? That isn't right, Mother . . .'"

As Longacre explains, this story turns on the unpaid bill. When the son interceded and demanded an outrageous amount of money, difficulties ensued that eventually led to the man's death. Relevant events that led to this downfall are strategically marked by the role-reversing suffix -*n*. The -*n* on the verb *conversing* marks the fatal circumstance from which the whole ordeal originates. The -*n* on the noun *place* marks the relevance of the place where the man returned after three years to pay his bill. The -*n* on the verb *ate* marks the narrator's imposed point of view that trouble is coming (since the man at the time would not have known that these were fatal circumstances). And finally, the -*n* on the conjunction *so-being* 'then' marks that it is the woman's son speaking up that leads to the eventual trouble.

What is striking about the use of -*n* is that it also has a grammatical function in low-level structure (i.e., sentence level) showing contrast, much like the English *but*. This is shown in (16).

(16) Grammatical function of suffix -*n* (Longacre 1976, 472)

His father him to work ask (-n), the boy refused.
'His father asked him to work **but** the boy refused.'

The use of -*n* at the sentence level affirms the observed tendency for discourse markers in English (and as we will see, in Ojibwe as well) in which some items that have a primary use grammatically at the sentence level (i.e., in the ideation plane of discourse) may also be used as discourse markers beyond the sentence level. Such a tendency for languages to raid the grammatical shelf, as it were, in order to accomplish work at the discourse level has been documented for other languages too. McGloin and Konishi (2010, 564), for example, show that the coordinate conjunction *shi* 'and, and so' (coordinative and causal functions within sentence grammar) is now undergoing a shift among younger speakers of Japanese to a sentence-final pragmatic marker, where it no longer coordinates propositions but rather adds a certain emotional (i.e., negative) overtone to a proposition. The fact that *shi* is devoid of an emotional tug when used as a connective within sentence grammar but devoid of its primary coordinating function at the discourse level demonstrates nicely this exploitive nature of languages.[17]

Ojibwe makes a contribution here as well, in that it further expands the pool of candidate markers to include both SECOND-POSITION DISCOURSE MARKERS (supporting claims for the second-position discourse clitic *jį̀ta* in Yagua above) and PREVERBS (which include prefix-like words that act like deictics and that attach to verbs) in support of the claim made for affixes. Such classes are common features in Algonquian languages such as Ojibwe, and their description will be provided in chapter 3.

2.3.3   *TAM (tense-aspect-mood) systems*

Perhaps another relevant dimension of this discussion is the use of tense-aspect forms (i.e., inflectional morphology) in discourse, as discourse-marking devices. Brinton notes that tense-aspect forms have been the subject of study by historical discourse analysts, stating that "[t]ense-aspect morphology, because of its function in conceptualizing and placing event in time, plays a special role in discourse structuring" (2003, 142). What this essentially means is that there is not a particular lexical item that serves as a discourse marker per se, but it is the *shape* of the words themselves that gives global coherence.[18] Therefore, targets for discourse use may be essentially entire verbal inflectional paradigms. In fact, a similar phenomenon has already been identified for the Algonquian language Montagnais, in Cyr (1991), where it has been argued that the traditional Algonquianist designation for the three verb orders in Montagnais as independent, conjunct, and changed conjunct should actually be analyzed as aspectual inflections having discourse functions. While I hesitate to call an entire paradigm a "discourse marker" per se, it is undeniable that inflectional morphology may be utilized for discourse work in the same way that individual linguistic items that have lexical or grammatical uses at the sentence level are enlisted for work above the sentence level. In other words, TAM forms that have specific functions at the sentence level, such as tense, aspect, mood, and temporality, may have more global functions above the sentence level. The identification of such behavior is not new to the literature. The historical present (i.e., the use of the present tense in a past-tense narrative) in medieval texts, for example, has been argued to serve various discourse roles, such as marking foregrounded events, as devices for internal evaluation, denoting main events, introducing central characters, highlighting key descriptive details, framing and staging narratives, marking transitions between episodes, and distinguishing speakers (see Fleischman 1985, 1986 for Old French; Richardson 1991 for Middle English; and Richardson 1995 for Old Norse; see also Brinton 2003, 143). The preterit tense in Totonac (a Mesoamerican language) narratives, while indicating past time and completed action in sentence grammars, serves a discourse function of marking eventlines in narratives. This use of the preterit to mark eventlines in Totonac is further contrasted with the use of other tense aspects (such as the imperfect tense) to mark non-eventline, supportive material (Bishop 1979). Conjunct mode verbs (i.e., verbs that indicate subordinate clauses in sentence grammars) in Kickapoo, an Algonquian language, are used to mark eventlines, acting as independent clauses at the discourse level. This is surprising, since conjunct verbs in Kickapoo are utilized in representing *independent* clauses at the discourse level, a function that such verbs typically do not serve at the sentence level. When conjunct verbs are used in this fashion within discourse, independent verbs primarily mark background, setting, participants, mental or emotional states, topic, or participant prominence (L. Jones and Coleman 1979). Such use of the conjunct verb has puzzled researchers, since while it was known that conjunct verbs may do the work of the independent mode, it was not understood why.[19] Jones and Coleman suggest that this is because the Algonquian literature largely restricts study to isolated sentences. In regard to Kickapoo in particular, they state,

> [I]t would have been impossible to analyze these functions of Kickapoo modes and tenses without a discourse perspective. We believe this is why many of these functions have been heretofore unnoticed in Algonquian languages, at least in the published literature, since much of the published material has been based on the study of isolated sentences, whether isolated due to elicitation technique or due to their extraction from texts. (1979, 91)

Because the heavy use of conjunct verbs in discourse is also a feature of Ojibwe, this will also be discussed in the body of this book. In general, what this means is that while individual lexical items with sentence-level functions may be targeted for work above the sentence level, tense-aspect-mode systems may also be targeted. In the case of TAM forms, it is not the word itself that lends itself for discourse work, but its shape.

2.3.4   Simultaneous textual and interpersonal functions of discourse markers

Recall that both Schiffrin and Brinton recognize the twofold function of discourse markers, in that there are those that contribute to the textual mode of a language and those that contribute to the interpersonal mode of language (Brinton 1996, 38; Schiffrin 2003b, 459). To my knowledge, neither researcher has *explicitly* claimed that a discourse marker could function in both a textual (connective) and an interpersonal (epistemic) function *simultaneously*. By "simultaneous," I do not mean to refer to the multifunctional feature of discourse markers, or the ability of discourse markers to anchor units of talk to various planes of discourse, since both textual and interpersonal discourse markers can be multifunctional. Recall that the Schiffrin example in (9) characterized the discourse marker *but* (a textual marker because it organizes chunks of text) as being "multifunctional" because of its ability to anchor an utterance to four planes of talk, that is, it prefaced an idea unit (a proposition), displayed a participation framework (nonalignment with a prior proposition), realized an action (a rebuttal during an argument), and sought to establish the speaker as a current speaker in an exchange (opened a turn at talk). Schiffrin also showed that the marker *well* (an interpersonal marker because it contributes an attitude toward a proposition) may be multifunctional, since it may "convey the fulfillment of a conversational obligation, for example, an answer to a question [displaying a participation framework], at the same time that it conveys speaker attitude, for example, distance from a proposition [realizing an action]" (Schiffrin 2003b, 459; Schiffrin 1987a, 102–27). In other words, the interpersonal marker *well* also may anchor an utterance to various planes of discourse. The question here then becomes: Can a discourse marker be both textual and interpersonal simultaneously? The answer is apparently yes. For example, Schwenter showed that the Spanish discourse marker *o sea* may serve both a textual and an interpersonal function simultaneously, since it may connect upcoming talk to prior discourse (i.e., in the form of explanations, reformulations, or setting off background information from foregrounded information) while at the same time serving as a command softener, thereby decreasing the illocutionary force of the command "to something more along the lines of advice that should be followed" (1996, 862). This is shown in example (17) with the discourse marker cluster *o sea que*.

(17)   Spanish *o sea que* (Schwenter 1996, 869)[20]

   Y eso lo dice todo el mundo.
   'and that's what everybody (lit. the whole world) says.

o sea que debe ser verdad
[o sea que] it must be true.'

According to Schwenter, *o sea que* in this example "is both connective, in that it specifies how the meaning relation between the two utterances is to be construed, and epistemic, in that it constitutes a subjective speaker comment on the propositional content of the second utterance such that 'I, speaker, believe that this must be true because the whole world says it'" (1996, 869). Schwenter also comments that this is a problem for Fraser, who makes a clear distinction between discourse markers (markers that mark a sequential relation between S2 and S1) and other commentary pragmatic markers (markers that are pragmatic in nature) since such a distinction "ignores instances of DMs that seem to be performing both tasks at the same time" (869).

Koike (1996, 272) makes a similar observation regarding the Spanish discourse marker *ya*, which serves to highlight certain constituents of an utterance in order to contribute an emotional emphasis but also to establish a cohesive link to prior discourse. According to Koike, the emotional emphasis contributed is a feeling of intensity about the proposition and allows a listener who perceives this intensity to become interested and involved in a sequence of events. This function is illustrated in the following example.

(18) Spanish *ya* (Koike 1996, 275–76)

(a) *Y luego en Chiapas . . . en la . . . estabamos en la . . . ¿cómo se llama? En la sierra, ¿sí?*

(b) *Todo era al revés.*

(c) *Los refrescos eran calientes, ¿sí?*

(d) *Las tortillas eran frías.*

(e) *O sea, todo al revés ya.*

(f) *No, llegaba el momento en que ya no podíamos nosotros.*

(a) 'And then in Chiapas . . . in the . . . we were in the . . . what do you call it? In the mountains, yes?

(b) Everything was backwards.

(c) The soft drinks were hot, yes?

(d) The tortillas were cold.

(e)   That is, everything backwards.

(f)   No, the time was coming that we couldn't [take it] any more.'

In this short narrative, the proposition *todo al revés* 'everything was backwards' is repeated twice (both tokens underlined for clarity), first in (18b), and then again in (18e) where it is followed by *ya*. According to Koike, discourse marker *ya* in (18e) serves to highlight the preceding phrase *todo al revés*, giving it an emotional emphasis, while also serving as a cohesive element by making reference to the first occurrence of the same phrase in (18b), *todo era al revés*.

While much of the cross-linguistic literature contains markers that show textual functions or that show interpersonal ones, the previous Spanish examples suggest that some discourse markers may indeed contribute both textual *and* interpersonal functions simultaneously. Though these types of discourse markers appear to be rare (or maybe just unnoticed), our definition of discourse markers must be broad enough to include such markers.

2.4   DEFINING DISCOURSE MARKERS

Based upon these cross-linguistic data then, we can make several observations that might aid in defining discourse markers. First, languages may use available lexical and/or grammatical resources for discourse purposes. In other words, linguistic categories that would lend themselves to discourse work based upon their lexical or grammatical properties would make those categories prime targets for discourse work. So it is not surprising that second-position words, clitics, affixes, and preverbs may serve as possible candidates for discourse work, since many languages make heavy use of these items. Ojibwe is no exception (as we will see). Since English is not a heavily inflected language, nor does it contain second-position words,[21] it would not be likely to contain second-position discourse markers, nor those that occur as clitics or affixes. What we do see in English, however, is the exploitation of existing lexical and grammatical items for discourse work, for example, the use of conjunctions *and, but, or, because*; the use of adverbials *now, then*; and the use of lexicalized phrases *y'know, I mean* (Schiffrin 1987a). We see this behavior in other languages as well. In Israeli Hebrew, *ye* 'and' has a grammatical role as a sentence-level conjunction but may "emerge as a discourse marker" from interaction in conversation (Maschler 1997, 197–98). In Niuean, the lexical item *mitaki* 'good' may have a grammatical role as a modifier or as a predicate, may form more complex words such as the adverb *fakamitaki* 'well, properly', and may occur in a variety of noninitial positions throughout sentences and clauses. As a discourse marker (Massam, Starks, and Ikiua use the term "discourse particle"), *mitaki* 'right' occurs in utterance-initial position and has a discourse function as an affirmation marker, that is, in acknowledgment of information (see Massam, Starks, and Ikiua 2006, 194–95).

Second, while the foregoing markers all have double lives, one as a grammatical or lexical item and another as a discourse marker, the cross-linguistic data also show discourse markers that have no (or very little) referential meaning and have only one function, as interpersonal markers, or as I prefer to call them, MYSTERY PARTICLES (following Longacre 1976). These markers work full-time as discourse markers and are notoriously hard to define. What both types of markers have in common is that they are multifunctional, able to function on different planes of discourse, and they do work above the level of the sentence.

Third, since discourse markers are not limited to the initial position but appear to occur in all positions cross-linguistically, as well as within the morphological environment as affixes, location cannot be a test for identifying linguistic items as discourse markers. Yet, despite this fact, the cross-linguistic data appear to suggest that languages do have predispositions or affinities for certain positions as docking spots for discourse markers. For example, English discourse markers show an affinity for initial position (Schiffrin 1987a). Cantonese discourse markers show an affinity for final position, having been labeled by modern Chinese grammars as "sentence-final particles" (Kwong 1989, 39). Various Danish discourse markers have been analyzed as "positionally restricted to the central field of the sentence" (Davidsen-Nielsen 1996, 299).[22] As we will see, Ojibwe discourse markers show a broader affinity for docking spots, including initial position and second position, as well as positions within the morphological environment in the form of clitics and preverbs.

Fourth, discourse work is not restricted to individual words, affixes, preverbs, or lexicalized phrases, or even mystery particles, but may also be extended to tense-aspect systems. TAM systems, that is, inflectional morphology, may be exploited in order to accomplish work above the sentence level in the same way that individual grammatical or lexical items are exploited for the same reason. As we already have seen, inflectional systems that have a particular grammatical function within sentence grammars may be used to provide overall textual cohesion. This aspect of discourse marking is largely left out of discussions surrounding discourse markers, especially in defining them.[23] The exploitation of inflectional morphology for discourse work in this way has to be included, I argue, if we are to understand the true mechanism behind discourse markers. This perhaps means that we need to broaden the term *discourse marker* to include the use of inflectional morphology.

Fifth, there is no evidence that discourse markers must be syntactically detached from their host clauses, as suggested by Schiffrin's initial characterization. While flexibility of position might be a trait sometimes observed for discourse markers in some less-inflected languages such as Spanish (see Schwenter 1996, 858, for *o sea*) and Italian (see Bazzanella 1990, 633, for *insomma*), and to some extent English (see Schiffrin 1987a, 276, for occurrences of *y'know* in utterance-final position), the cross-linguistic evidence shows that many discourse markers are morphologically bound to their host words as either clitics or affixes. Recall that in Yagua, discourse clitic *jį́įta* occurred in second position. As we will see, Ojibwe has many markers that are confined to second position. Ojibwe also shows one marker occurring as a prefix-like element called a relative preverb (to be discussed in section 3.1.3.1). Given these facts, then, we cannot stipulate syntactic detachability as a test for the identification of discourse markers.

Finally, tonic stress, or the lack of stress, cannot be stipulated either, since many discourse markers do not appear to turn on this distinction. In Schiffrin's data there appeared to be no difference in discourse function between the full form of *because* and its phonologically reduced form *cause*. Moreover, there are no references in the cross-linguistic literature in which tonic stress, or lack thereof, played any significant role in a marker's status as a discourse marker. Such a characterization would seem to exclude discourse markers that do not have a range of prosodic contours, such as the Ojibwe discourse marker *sha* (to be discussed). To my knowledge, this marker has only one prosodic contour (i.e., stressless), but it still has a role within discourse. Whether a particular marker has stress or not appears to be constrained by the language itself, not by constraints originating from discourse processes. Therefore, whether or not a *sus-*

pected marker has tonic stress or not cannot be a viable test for its status as a discourse marker.[24]

Based upon the cross-linguistic behavior of discourse markers, I propose the following definition, updating Schiffrin's prior tentative definition.

(19) An updated definition of discourse markers:

Any linguistic expression, whether it be a word, particle, lexicalized phrase, affix, TAM/inflectional system, or other expression, may serve as a discourse marker, or discourse-marking device, if it operates at both local and global levels of discourse (i.e., bracketing power) and operates on different planes of discourse (i.e., serves some discourse function), contributing to either textual coherence or interpersonal/epistemic meanings, or both simultaneously.

This definition essentially eliminates the first three requirements initially put forth by Schiffrin (1987a) since they are not substantiated by cross-linguistic data, namely that discourse markers be syntactically detached from a sentence, that they occur in initial position, and that they have a range of prosodic contours. Note also that this definition necessarily extends the status of discourse markers (or as I prefer to refer to this process, "discourse marking") to include TAM forms as well, *if* those forms are used for discourse work, for example, in creating textual cohesion. In this way, discourse marking is the *manner* in which words are cast as targets for discourse via the processes of tense, aspect, and mood, rather than the individual linguistic form itself. Therefore, an inflectional paradigm may be exploited for discourse work in much the same way that individual lexical or grammatical items are exploited for the same reason, if that inflectional paradigm has a function that might be exploited, used, or borrowed for discourse work. As the cross-linguistic data show, this is typical discourse marker behavior. Therefore, while unintuitive at first, "word shape" (the use of inflectional systems, or TAM forms) *must* be included within our definition of discourse markers; otherwise we would not be able to account for a large number of languages that make productive use of inflectional forms in order to accomplish a variety of discourse functions. Until now, the literature has largely ignored the use of TAM/inflectional forms within its definitions of discourse markers. My definition includes them.

Put simply, this updated definition says that any linguistic item or TAM form may serve as a discourse marker (or discourse marking device) if it contributes to the textual organization of a narrative or contributes some interpersonal or epistemic meaning in a way that accomplishes some kind of discourse work, whether it be negotiating a turn at talk, realizing some speech act, or establishing some distance from a proposition. The criterion that discourse markers *operate on both local and global levels of discourse* means that discourse markers may link (or bracket) adjacent units of discourse or link units across wider spans of discourse, respectively. Recall that we have already seen this at work for the discourse marker *because* in (8), where it linked adjacent utterances as well as linking an utterance with a whole narrative. What is at the heart of this definition, however, is Schiffrin's observation that discourse markers are multifunctional, a feature of discourse markers that allows them to *operate on different planes of discourse. Multifunctional* here does not mean a dichotomy of monofunctional vs. multifunctional, that is, whether an individual item has one function (e.g., as a hedge) or many (e.g., as a hedge, aspectual marker, and discourse sequencer); rather, it indicates that when the English contrastive marker *but* is used, for example, the speaker may not only be textually creating coherence by contrasting upcoming discourse with prior discourse within the ideational structure ("idea units") but may also be functioning interactively within the action structure to allow the speaker "to make a point in reaction to interruptions, distractions, challenges and disagreements" (Schiffrin 1987a, 177). In other words, a discourse marker does not merely signal some textual or interpersonal function in relation to some propositional content but also simultaneously allows a speaker to express some social, cognitive, interactional, and/or cultural content. Recall that the English discourse marker *but* (as we saw previously) did not just do the mechanical work of contrasting idea units or propositions but also allowed the speaker (Freda) to simultaneously establish her turn at talk (exchange structure), establish her nonalignment with the interlocutor's proposition (participation framework), and provide a rebuttal (action structure).[25] It is this multifunctional feature on different planes of discourse that is the core defining feature of discourse markers, and it is a feature that appears to hold true for discourse markers across languages, whatever their form or position.

Finally, while this definition is broad enough to include any form that a language (or rather its speakers) may designate as a discourse marker, it must be re-iterated here that the actual form or docking spot for discourse markers appears to be largely constrained by the existing grammatical machinery in a given language (i.e., grammar, grammatical categories, lexical inventory). In other words, if a language makes heavy use of affixes, as many of the indigenous languages of the Americas do, then it should be no surprise that some discourse markers in those languages occur as affixes. Conversely, in languages that are not richly inflected, we would not expect to find many, if any, discourse markers that occur as affixes. This is indeed what we find for English. The same is true for potential docking spots for discourse markers. Recall that the Amazonian language Yagua has a discourse marker that occurs as a second-position discourse clitic. Ojibwe, as we will see, has this too. These languages make regular use of second position, and so it is no surprise that second position serves as a potential docking spot for discourse markers. To my knowledge, we find no such markers in English (except for special discourse-related phenomena such as when exemplifying or when contrastive markers are used to highlight the initial element) or in other languages that do not make regular use of second position. My ultimate point here is that speakers of a language *tend* to use the existing machinery available in their language in order to accomplish discourse-related work: not just any machinery, but existing machinery that might *lend* itself to the speaker for work at the discourse level, even if the exiting machinery comes from another language that is accessible to speakers. For example, there is evidence that existing machinery from other languages resulting from language contact can influence both the identity and location of discourse markers. For example, Torres (2006, 616) noted that some Spanish discourse markers have been borrowed into the indigenous speech of both Tojolab'al and Yucatec Maya speakers and now co-occur with indigenous native markers.

(20) Spanish markers borrowed into indigenous speech

(a) Tojolab'al (Torres 2006, 616, quoting Brody 1987, 512)

Entonse ti=wa yajni jaw=ʔi
then then = but now when that = term

'**And** that's how it was.'

(b)   Yucatec Maya (Torres 2006, 616, quoting Solomon 1995, 293)

DESPWÈESÉ	*ká*	*t*	*u*	*tukul*	*t*	*u*	*bino'o[b]*
after-top		then	prog	erg3	think-incomp	prog	erg3	go/incomp-P

kàahah	*chik'intz'ono'ot*
town	Chikindzonot

'**After, then** they were thinking of going to the town of Chikintzonot.'

In these examples, the standard Spanish words *entonces* 'then' and *después* 'after' have both been borrowed into Tojolab'al and Yucatec Maya as markers *entonse* and *despwèese*, respectively, and now co-occur with the native markers *ti* 'then' and *ká* 'then', respectively.

Other types of borrowings occur as well. Maschler, for example, noticed that in Hebrew-German bilingualism "discourse may be separated from its frame of markers so that the discourse happens in one of the two languages and the discourse markers are verbalized in the other" (1997, 203). Also, Zavala (2001) showed that Quechua-Spanish bilinguals have restructured a standard Spanish conjunction, *pues*, as a discourse marker, *pe* or *pes*, in Andean Spanish. What is particularly interesting about Andean Spanish is that not only have the speakers phonologically reduced *pues* to *pe* or *pes* (since Quechua does not permit vowel sequences in its syllabic structures), they have also restructured the position of *pes* from initial position (where Spanish particles borrowed into indigenous languages usually occur) to final position, seemingly based upon Quechua structure (Zavala 2001, 1003–4, quoting Brody 1995, 137). The point here, of course, is that speakers appear to make use of available linguistic machinery either via their own language or by the machinery made available by language-contact situations if the contact language is in frequent use. In the case of Andean Spanish, the identity of the marker *pes* originated from the contact language (standard Spanish) but has been constrained by the indigenous language (Quechua) in both phonological form *and* location.

Ojibwe discourse markers

This discussion of Ojibwe discourse markers will divide them into two major classes: discourse connectives and mystery particles. Discourse connectives in Ojibwe are largely *borrowed* items (my term)—items that have sentence-level uses but that lend themselves to work at the discourse level. They contribute to the overall textual structure of a discourse, functioning to relate prior units of discourse with upcoming discourse. Ojibwe mystery particles, on the other hand, are markers that are largely interpersonal, attitudinal, or epistemic in nature. They are somewhat different from the Ojibwe discourse connectives in that they are not borrowed sentence-level functions that are then used at the discourse level but instead are full-time discourse markers. Ojibwe mystery particles work at both the sentence and discourse levels, all the time. The one common trait that both of these types of discourse markers share is that they do work at a level above the sentence to contribute some discourse effect, either structurally (discourse connective) or pragmatically (mystery particles). The organization of Ojibwe discourse markers into these two categories is largely motivated by the natural division of discourse markers into textual and interpersonal functions, as observed by Schiffrin (2003b, 459) and Brinton (1996, 38). All discourse markers in this book will be further divided into those that occur in initial position, those that occur in second position, and those that occur as a relative root.

3.1   DISCOURSE CONNECTIVES

3.1.1   *Initial position*

The following discourse markers fit most of the criteria for English discourse markers described by Schiffrin, in that they all occur in initial position, may have tonic stress, show syntactic detachability from their containing clauses (except for *mii dash*, which shows loose detachability), and have both primary functions in the ideational plane of discourse (in sentence grammars) and secondary functions in other planes of discourse (above the sentence level). In other words, like some of the English discourse markers such as *and, but,* and *because,* for example, these discourse markers (except for *onzaam*) have functions that reflect their grammatical or lexical use in sentence grammars. Their sentence-level functions are essentially *exploited* to perform work above the sentence level. While this is the predominant pattern, *onzaam* 'because' does not show this tendency, or at the very least, it is not transparent how its discourse function is related to its sentence-level meaning, 'overly, too much', if at all. This is not problematic, however, since it has been observed that some functions of discourse markers do not entirely reflect their functions within sentence grammars (see Grimes 1975, 4; Schiffrin 1987a, 320; Schourup 1985, 123). Nevertheless, all of these discourse markers bracket linguistic units in some way on both local and global levels, relating prior text to upcoming text in ways that achieve textual coherence. In other words, they act as the "discourse glue" that holds or binds a discourse together. The type of coherence created is largely dependent upon the discourse marker in use. The major discourse connectives observed in the data are discussed in the following sections.

3.1.1.1   *inashke*

In sentence grammar, the interjection command particle *inashke* 'look!' is an attention getter, similar to the function of the Japanese interjection word *hora* 'look!, see!, listen!' (Nakao 1995, 93). It also has various truncated forms, such as *nashke, shke, ke, inake, ina,* or just *na*.[1] Its function is actually twofold in that it not only attracts attention (much like the English *hey!* would do) but attracts attention to something or someone as a way of pointing something or someone out. Like its Japanese counterpart, the linguistic form *inashke* is not based upon a "seeing" root per se and is never involved in the formation of words indicating *sight, seeing,* or *looking.* It is purely an attention-getting word and may optionally occur with words that denote seeing or hearing. This usage is demonstrated in (21), glossed as AT ("attention getter") for convenience.

(21)   Attention-getter *nashke*

(a)   *Nashke   maakigiyaan.*

       AT   I am healing over

       'Look where I'm healing over!'

(b) *Nashke bizindan.*
     AT   listen

     'Listen!'

(c) *Nashke!*

     AT

     'Look!, See!, Listen!'

As a discourse marker, this basic attention-getting function of *inashke* is also seen above the sentence level, where it is used as a discourse highlighter, highlighting salient information. When used as such, it has a function similar to the English discourse marker *you see*, but again, while the English counterpart is based upon an actual "seeing" word, the Ojibwe marker *nashke* is not. It is, therefore, not its lexical meaning but its grammatical function as an attention getter that is borrowed for discourse work.[2] In its general discourse function as a discourse highlighter, *inashke* brackets and marks upcoming talk as being more salient, allowing speakers to mark special insights or knowledge that might provide the listener with perspective, to draw out distinctions, or to mark the exposition of examples or confirming speaker disposition. This highlighting function shows that *inashke* is both forward- and backward-looking since it sets off (or brackets) upcoming text in order to mark it as salient in relation to prior text. These functions are discussed below.

An example of *inashke* marking insights occurred in a narrative about traditional healers. Prior to the *inashke* utterance in the following example, the speaker first relates the method by which traditional healers were given knowledge of medicines and how to diagnose illnesses, that is, via spiritual means. The speaker then reveals what they were able to do with that knowledge, an utterance preceded by *shke* (glossed as DM for "discourse marker").[3]

(22) *inashke* marking insights (Clark 2003b, 54, audio)

(a) *Ongow   wiin   mewinzha-go gekenimagig   nenaandawi'iwejig,*
     these   contrast   long ago   the ones I knew healers

     manidoon   ogii-miinigowaan   onji-gikendamowaad   mashkiki
     spirits   they gave it to them from whence they know medicine

miinawaa	ezhiwebizinid		anow	owiij-anishinaabewaan
and	what's wrong with them		them	their fellow Indians

awiiya	nanaandomigowaad.
someone	when s/he asks them for help

(b) | **Shke** | mewinzha, | dibaajimowaad | ongow | gaa-nanaandawi'iwejig, |
|---|---|---|---|---|
| DM | long ago | they tell | these | who healed people |

mii	miinawaa-go	gaa-zhi-mikamowaad	biinjayi'ii	awegonen	etenig
DP	and	then found	inside it	what	put

imaa	owiiyawing	wa'aw	ayaakozid,	awegonen	o'ow
there	in his/her body	this	sick person	what	this

gaa-aakozhiishkaagod.
what made him/her sick

(a) 'As for the healers long ago that I know of, the spirits gave them their knowledge of medicine and to know what was wrong with their fellow Indians when someone asked them for help.

(b) **You see**, a long time ago, these that healed people would diagnose, and found inside the sick person's body what was ailing them.'

The information highlighted by *shke* in this utterance is special knowledge, knowledge that might not be well-known these days about traditional healers. The speaker first explains where traditional healers received their knowledge and then follows that statement up with an insight, that is, what the traditional healers used to do with their attained knowledge. The use of *shke* to highlight upcoming text in (22b) allows the speaker to set that information off as significant from prior text in (22a). This use also occurs in the next few lines of this story, where the speaker highlights their healing instruments, that is, bones. Because the use of bones to heal people is somewhat of a lost art and largely an unknown fact these days among the younger generation (and non-Indians), the use of *shke* here allows the speaker to give special attention to this fact.

(23) *inashke* marking insights (Clark 2003b, 54, audio)

(a) | Mii | dash | i'iw | imaa, | nashke | mii | noongom | inigaaziyang |
|---|---|---|---|---|---|---|---|
| and | then | that | there | DM | DP | today | we're pitiful |

> *gaawiin awiiya ayaasiiwag geyaabi aapiji ongow*
> not someone there is no one anymore hardly these
>
> *ge-nanaandawi'inangig.*
> those who could heal us

(b) **Shke** *wiinawaa ongow, mewinzha gaa-nanaandawi'iwejig*
DM they these long ago those that healed people

miinawaa anow odookanimiwaan gii-aabaji'aawaad nawaa
and those their bones they used them and

awegonen gaa-miinindwaa ji-aabajitoowaad.
what what was given to them for them to use

(a) 'See, that's why we're so pitiful these days, there aren't very many people anymore who could heal us.

(b) **You see**, these who healed people a long time ago, would use their bones and whatever they were given to use.'

Inashke may also highlight upcoming text in order to draw out distinctions. In the following example, *inashke* is used to show such a distinction between the use of the Ojibwe and English languages.

(24) *inashke* (Clark 2003a, 50, audio)

(a) *Gaawiin ige gidaa-gashkitoosiimin weweni ji-ikidoyang i'iw*
not also we wouldn't be able to carefully for us to say that

ge-ikidoyangiban.
what we would say

(b) **Shke** *ojibwemoyang gigikendaamin waa-ikidoyang.*
DM when we speak Ojibwe we know what we want to say

(a) 'We also would not be able to say correctly what we would say.

(b) **You see**, when we speak Ojibwe, we know what we want to say.'

The distinction being drawn here is the one between the use of the English language and the Ojibwe language by a bilingual speaker. In short, an Ojibwe speaker could not be exactly sure of what she or he is saying when using English but would know were she or he to use Ojibwe. The use of *shke* in (24b) allows the speaker to draw special attention to the use of Ojibwe so as to make the distinction more salient in relation to prior text.

Sometimes *inashke* may precede the exposition of examples, having roughly the force of the English expression *for example*. In such cases, upcoming text highlighted by *inashke* usually represents a real-life example of a description given in prior text. This example-giving function is given in (25).

(25)   *inashke* in providing examples (Clark 2003b, 55, audio)

(a)   *Mii   dash   bebakaan   weweni   ogii-kikendaanaawaa   awegonen*
       then   and   each different carefully   they knew it   what

      o'ow   enaabadak   o-mashkiki.
      this   how utilized this medicine

(b)   **Shke,**   *wa'aw   nookomisiban   mii-ko   gaa-paa-izhi-mamood*
      see   this   my grandmother   used to   would pick

      o-mashkiki   gekendaagwadinig   ge-inikaagod   a'aw   anishinaabe,
      this medicine   known to be   to affect him/her   that   Indian

      gii-agoodood   endaad,   gii-paasang,   gii-na'inang.
      hanged it up   her house   dried it   put it up

(c)   **Nashke**   *ingoding   miinawaa,   ogii-pi-odisigoon   awiiya,*
      see   pretty soon   and   she/he approached her   someone

      "wa'aw   nenaandawi'iwed   indig,   gidayaan   i-mashkiki   giiwenh
      this   healer   tells me   you have   the medicine   apparently

      ge-minokaagoyaan."
      that would be good for me

(a)   'And so they each knew different utilizations of medicine.

(b)   You see, my grandmother used to pick medicine known to affect people, and would hang it in her house, dry it, and put it away.

(c)   [**Nashke**] Pretty soon, someone came to her, "This healer told me you apparently have the medicine that could help me."'

The function of *inashke* in (25) is to point out examples of a process, event, or tradition. A description is given and then followed by illustrating examples. Prior to the example in (25a), for example, the speaker was describing how each village had their own particular knowledge of different medicines known to heal people, and traditional healers would send people to particular villages where there were people who had the appropriate medicine. It is after this description that the speaker gives the example of his grandmother and the example of someone visiting her. Both utterances are prefaced by *inashke*. This example-giving function of *inashke* can be seen in the following example as well, where the speaker gives a description about Ojibwe clans and then proceeds to give an example of that description.

(26) *inashke* in providing examples (Kegg 1993, 142)

(a) *Mii ingiw anishinaabeg, mii giiwenh ezhi-inawendiwaad*
DP those Indians that apparently how they are related

akeyaa ezhi-odoodemindiwaad.
way when they have the same totem

(b) **Nashke** *aʼaw waabizheshi, iniw waabizheshiwan gaawiin*
see that marten that marten not

odaa-wiidigemaasiin.
she/he couldn't marry him/her

(a) 'Those Indians were related to each other in a way when they had the same totem.[4]

(b) A marten, **you see**, couldn't marry another marten.'

In (26), the speaker first describes the tradition that persons having the same clan did not marry each other because they were related by clan. This description is then followed up with an illustration, that is, that a marten clan member could not marry another marten clan member. In this way, *inashke* allows the speaker to provide an example of how the general taboo against marrying a member of your own clan might be violated.

Sometimes speakers may use *inashke* to make clarifications or explanations as part of its highlighting function. One example of this is illustrated in the following excerpt, in which the speaker clarifies his own contribution to the language loss of the younger generation.

(27)   *inashke* to make clarifications (Clark 2003c, 58–59, audio)

(a)   *Gaye niin igo   imaa   indaa-anaamindiz   igo   dibishkoo*
       also   I   EMPH   there I should blame myself EMPH   same as

       epiitiziwaad   ongow   niij-anishinaabeg   epiitiziyaan   gaa-izhaajig
       age   these   my fellow Indians   the age I am   who went

       imaa   gikinoo'amaadiiwigamigong.
       there to school

(b)   **Nashke** *azhigwa   eni-apiitiziyaan,   gaye   niin*
       see   now   as I come of age   also   I

       gii-maajii-noodendamaan   o-dibishkoo   gaye   niin   gii-kikenimagwaa
       I started feeling flirtatious same as   also   me   when I knew them

       ongow   ikwezensag   ayaawaad   ikwezensiwiwaad   gii-gikenimagwaa.
       these   girls   there are   are girls   when I knew them

(c)   *Mii   imaa   gii-wiikwajitooyaan   gaye   niin   wii-shaaganaashiimoyaan.*
       that there I tried   also   me   to speak English

(a)   'I too should blame myself the same as the others that are of my age who
       went to school.

(b)   **You see**, after I came of age, I too started feeling flirtatious when I noticed
       that the girls were girls.

(c)   That's when I too tried to speak English.'

In (27a), after stating that he and his generation are to blame for the loss of
Ojibwe language use, he immediately gives the reason in (27b), accenting it with
nashke. In short, he explains that his contribution to the current predicament
originated (at least in part) from his personal desire to talk to girls at school.
Since they did not speak Ojibwe, he had to speak English. Used in this way,
inashke marks this clarification.

   In arguments between two people, *inashke* may be used to point out something that was perhaps obvious to the speaker but not to listeners, having
roughly the force of the English *see!* (with rising intonation). In these argu-
mentative situations, *inashke* may appear as *ina*, for example, [ɪnʌ], [ɪna], with
rhetorical lengthening on both vowels accompanied by stress on the initial

vowel [i:na:]. The following example provided by Mille Benjamin illustrates this usage.

(28) *ina*

> **Ina,** *gidaano-inin.*
> see   I tried telling you
>
> 'See, I told you.'

In monologic narratives where there is only one speaker, this function can be seen also. This is shown in the following example when the speaker points out a result of not having any traditional healers anymore (from the example above).

(29) *inashke* (Clark 2003b, 54, audio)

(a)   *Shke mewinzha, dibaajimowaad ongow gaa-nanaandawi'iwejig, mii*
     see   long ago   they tell   these   the healers   DP

     miinawaa-go gaa-zhi-mikamowaad biinjayi'ii awegonen etenig imaa
     and   they found it   inside it   what   be put   there

     owiiyawing wa'aw ayaakozid, awegonen o'ow gaa-aakozhiishkaagod.
     in his body   this   who is sick   what   this   what made him/her sick

(b)   *Mii dash i'iw imaa,* **nashke** *mii noongom inigaaziyang*
     DP   and   that   there   see   DP   today   we are pitiful

     gaawiin awiiya ayaasiiwag geyaabi aapiji ongow
     not   someone   they don't exist   anymore   extremely   these

     ge-nanaandawi'inangig.
     who could heal us

(a)   'You see, a long time ago, these that healed people would diagnose, and found inside the sick person's body what was ailing them.

(b)   **See**, that's why we're so pitiful these days, there aren't very many people anymore who could heal us.'

In both examples, *inashke* functions to point out something that has the effect of strengthening the point of view of the speaker. In (28), the speaker uses *ina* to point out a predicted event. In (29b), the speaker uses *nashke* to point out that because there are so few traditional healers these days, Indians are adversely affected in modern times. In both cases, this "pointing out" or highlighting function of *inashke* has the effect of confirming a preexisting belief or condition put forth by the speaker, a belief or condition that perhaps was not previously obvious or appreciated by interlocutors (that is, those listening).

While the previous examples show that *inashke* may have various functions in discourse—that is, prefacing descriptions of special insights as a way to provide perspective, drawing out distinctions, presenting examples, and confirming speaker disposition—these realizations are only manifestations of the underlying function of *inashke* as a discourse highlighter, which originates from its sentence-level function. Above the sentence level, *inashke* allows the speaker to highlight upcoming text in order to mark it as salient in relation to prior text.

3.1.1.2   *miinawaa*

In the dictionary, *miinawaa* is defined as meaning 'and, also, again' (Nichols and Nyholm 1995, 89). Its primary role in sentence grammars is as a coordinating conjunction, but it may also have minor functions as an adverb or as an adjective. As a coordinating conjunction, *miinawaa* may coordinate various constituents as long as they are the same category, and it usually occurs in between the coordinated clauses. This is shown in (30), where *miinawaa* is shown to coordinate noun phrases, adjective phrases, and verb phrases.

(30)   *miinawaa* as a coordinating conjunction

(a)   (Kegg 1993, 66–67)

Wegwaagi[5]	*iniw*	*aya'aan*	*mashkodesiminan*	***miinawaa***
look	that	whatchamacallem	beans	and

gookooshan	*imaa*	*ezhi-dagozonid.*
pork	there	cooking with something

'Why look, there were beans **and** pork cooking in there.'

(b)   (Anderson 1999)

Naawigiizisookwe	*gii-onaanigozi,*	***miinawaa***	*gii-kizhewaadizi.*
Naawigiizisookwe	she was happy	and	she was kind

'Naawigiizisookwe was happy and kind.'

(c)   (Kegg 1993, 154–55)

Mii	*eta*	*go*	*gaa-izhichiged,*	*apane*	*gii-izhaad*	*iwidi*
DP	only	EMPH	what he did	always	he went	over there

Gabekanaansing	*bibooninig,*	*agoodood*	***miinawaa***	*wanii'iged.*
Portage Lake	in the winter	that he snares	and	that he traps

'That's all he did, always going there to Portage Lake in the winter, snaring **and** trapping.'

In (30a) *miinawaa* coordinates two noun phrases: *mashkodesiminan* 'beans' and *gookooshan* 'pork'. In (30b), it coordinates two verb phrases (independent clauses): *gii-onaanigozi* 'she was happy' and *gii-kizhewaadizi* 'she was kind'. In (30c), it coordinates two subordinate verb phrases (subordinate clauses): *agoodood* 'that he snares' and *wanii'iged* 'that he traps'.[6]

As an adverb, *miinawaa* has a meaning equivalent to the English *again*, signaling the reoccurrence of an event. As an adjective it has an additive meaning, having roughly the meaning of the English *another.* These meanings are shown in the following example.

(31)   *miinawaa*

(a)   adverbial (Kegg 1993, 106–7)

"*Gego*	***miinawaa***	*ingoji*	*daa-izhaasiin,*[7]
don't	again	somewhere	she/he should not go

Naawakamigookwe,"	*ikido.*
Naawakamigookwe	she says

'"Don't let Naawakamigookwe go anywhere **again**," she said.'

(b)   adjectival (Clark 1998a, 8, audio)

Mii	*imaa*	*naaniibawiyaan*	*gomaapii*	*go*	***miinawaa***	*bezhig*
DP	there	I'm standing around	awhile	EMPH	another	one

mindimooyenh	*zaagewe.*
old lady	she/he appears

'I stood there awhile and **another** old lady appeared.'

Above the sentence level, *miinawaa* has a function that largely mirrors its sentence grammar usage as a coordinator, but it works on a more global level in order to coordinate idea units. It acts as a discourse coordinator, coordinating similar discourse units. As Schiffrin showed for the English discourse marker *and*, "the presence of *and* signals the speaker's identification of an upcoming unit which is coordinate in structure to some prior unit" (1987a, 141). This is certainly also true for Ojibwe. In other words, when *miinawaa* occurs, it is coordinating upcoming discourse units with some prior discourse unit. This is shown in the following example. Note that I have formatted the sentences containing *miinawaa* to make its discourse structure more visible.

(32)   *miinawaa* (from Kegg 1993, 108–9)

(a)   Gaawiin   awiiya   iwidi   daa-daasiin   imaa
       not   someone over   there should not live   there

       wanako-neyaashi.
       end of the point

(b)   Gii-taawag   iko   iwidi   anishinaabeg,   ingodogamig.
       they lived   used to   over there   Indians   one household

(c)   Bezhig   iwidi   inini   gii-taa,   gaa-izhi-nibod.
       one   over there   man   he lived there   then he died

(d)   Mii   **miinawaa**   gaa-izhi-adaawangewaad   oshk'-aya'aag,   mii   i'iw
       DP   and   they then rented   young couple   DP   that

       waakaa'igan,
       house

(e)   **miinawaa**   iniw   oniijaanisan
                                             and   that   his/her children

                                             imaa   gaa-izhi-nibonid.
                                             there   then died

(f)   **Miinawaa**   imaa   aabiding   akiwenzii   gii-adaawanged   miinawaa
       and   there   one time   old man   he rented   and

       mindimooyenh.
       old lady

(g)   Mii   **miinawaa**   a'aw   akiwenzii
                                                DP   and   that   old man

                                                gaa-izhi-nibod.
                                                then died

(a)   'Nobody will live there on the end of that point.

(b)   There used to be some Indians living there, one household.

(c)   **One man lived there,**   **and then he died.**

(d)   **And** then a young couple rented that house

(e)   **and** one of their children died there.

(f)   **And** once again an old man and old woman rented it.

(g)   Then **again** the old man died . . .'

In this example there are three sets of discourse units, here in the form of set-up propositions and their consequent propositions, which are: (1) someone rents the house, and (2) they consequently die. Strikingly, each occurrence of *miinawaa* in this example coordinates a similar prior discourse unit. For example, coordinated with the set-up proposition *one man lived there* in (32c) are the set-up propositions *and then a young couple rented that house* in (32d) and *and once again an old man and old woman rented it* in (32f). Coordinated with the consequent proposition *and then he died* in (32c) are the consequent propositions *and one of their children died there* in (32e) and *then again the old man died* in (32g). With the coordinated structures extracted, the structure of each coordination would look like the following.

(33)   Coordinated discourse units

(a)   Discourse unit #1: set-up proposition—*someone rents the house*

   One man lived there
   miinawaa *then a young couple rented that house*
   miinawaa *once again an old man and old woman rented it*

(b)   Discourse unit #2: consequent proposition—*they consequently die*

> *then he died*
> **miinawaa** *one of their children died there*
> **miinawaa** *the old man died*

What is striking about this example is that it also contains a sentence-level usage of *miinawaa* in (32f) where it coordinates two noun phrases, *old man* and *old woman*, that is, *akiwenzii* … **miinawaa** *mindimooyenh* 'an old man … **and** old woman'. What this ultimately shows is that *miinawaa*, like the English discourse marker *and*, is multifunctional (i.e., functioning on more than one plane of discourse), since it may work at the sentence level coordinating two nouns but also may operate at both local levels (i.e., adjacent units) and global levels (i.e., across wider spans of discourse) of discourse in order to create textual coherence.

While *miinawaa* may act as a discourse coordinator much like its English counterpart *and*, there are differences. For example, Schiffrin (1987a, 138–41) has shown that the English marker *and* may work locally, globally, or at both levels. In other words, *and* may link events associated with individual discourse topics on a local level, and it may also link discourse topics. This structure would look like the following, where *and* coordinates the two topics, TOPIC 1 and TOPIC 2, and also coordinates the local events associated with each of those topics.

(34) English discourse marker *and* at both local and global levels

TOPIC 1	(global)
and EVENT	(local)
and EVENT …	(local)
and TOPIC 2	(global)
and EVENT	(local)
and EVENT …	(local)

This structure is exemplified by an example given in Schiffrin 1987a that shows *and* working on both local and global levels within the same discourse. For convenience, the topics are underlined and the event structures indented. All occurrences of *and* are in bold type.

(35) (Schiffrin 1987a, 140)

[Do either of your daughter in laws work?]

a.   No but they did.

b.   Both my daughters in laws worked.

c.   Uh: <u>my older daughter</u> in law worked for four years while my son was in school.

d.   **And** she didn't become uh pregnant until he graduated.

e.   **And** uh: she feels that once her children are in school, she'd like to go back.

f.   **And** <u>my younger daughter</u> in law, uh: they got married when she was eighteen.

g.   **And** she uh: was just starting Beaver.

h.   She took up that pre nursery school?

i.   For two years?

j.   Y'know that get set program?

[continues with discussion of school program]

In (35b), the phrase *both my daughters in laws* establishes the speaker's daughters-in-law as the two discourse topics. Each discourse topic (i.e., global level) is then expanded into event structures (i.e. local units), such as events within general support and within specific support (Schiffrin 1987a, 137). Lines (35c–e) describe the experiences of the older daughter, and (35f–j) describe the experiences of the younger. For example, the first topic, *my older daughter* (underlined), is expanded into two event structures: (1) *she didn't become uh pregnant until he graduated* and (2) *uh: she feels that once her children are in school, she'd like to go back*, both of which are prefaced by *and*. The second discourse topic, *my younger daughter* (also underlined), is expanded into two event structures as well: (1) *they got married when she was eighteen* and (2) *And she uh: was just starting Beaver*. What this ultimately shows is that *and* in English is able to link discourse topics as well as linking their associated event structures. A major pattern in Ojibwe, however, shows that *miinawaa* usually links only the discourse topics, leaving event structures associated with those individual topics to be marked with asyndetic connection "zero" (i.e., asyndetic, meaning the juxtaposition of clauses or sentences without the use of conjunctions).[8] This can be demonstrated with the following example.

(36) *miinawaa* (Kegg 1993, 152–53)

(a) | *Mii* | *dash* | *ayi'ii* | | *misko-waabowayaan* | *iko—* |
|---|---|---|---|---|---|
| DP | then | whatchamacallit | | red blanket | used to |

gii-izhi-wiindewan	*mewinzha*	*gichi-waabowayaanan—*	*mii*	*i'iw*
it was called thus	long ago	big blankets	it is	that

egwazhed.
what he covered up with

(b) | **Miinawaa** | *gaawiin* | *wiikaa* | *gii-kiichiwakwaanesiin.* |
|---|---|---|---|
| and | not | ever | he did not take his hat off |

(c) *Gii-waabizhagindibe.*
he was bald

(d) | *Mewinzha* | *giiwenh* | *gii-aakozi.* |
|---|---|---|
| long ago | apparently | he was sick |

(e) | *Akina* | *dash* | *ogii-wanitoonan* | *iniw* | *wiinizisan.* |
|---|---|---|---|---|
| all | but | he lost them | those | his hairs |

(f) | *Oonh,* | *gichi-aya'aawi* | *a'aw* | *akiwenzii.* |
|---|---|---|---|
| Oh | he is very old | that | old man |

(a) 'And a *misko-waabowayaan* 'red blanket'—that's what they called those big blankets long ago—that's what he wore.

(b) [**miinawaa**] He never took off his hat.

(c) He was bald.

(d) It was said that he had been sick long ago.

(e) He lost all his hair.

(f) Oh, that old man was ancient.'

In (36), there are two topics (which are semantically related to the overall topic of the *old man*): (1) the blanket the old man wore, and (2) the old man never took off his hat. Only the second topic, however, is expanded into event structures in (36c–f) that amount to background information, that is, *he was bald, it was said that he had been sick long ago, he lost all his hair,* and *oh, that old man was ancient.* This has the following structure:

(37)   *miinawaa* at both local and global levels

TOPIC 1	(global)
miinawaa TOPIC 2	(global)
EVENT	(local)
EVENT . . .	(local)

While the two topics are coordinated by *miinawaa*, the event structures associated with the second proposition are not. Rather, it is asyndetic connection
"zero" (i.e., no use of coordinating conjunction *miinawaa* 'and') that links the
event structures associated with topic 2. There appears to be no requirement,
however, that discourse topics themselves be linked by *miinawaa* in Ojibwe,
since topics may be found that are not marked by *miinawaa*. Schiffrin (1987a,
139) showed this for marker *and* as well, when she found that the transition from
the first discourse topic to the second may be linked by *so*, rather than *and*. She
also showed that *and* may share environments with other markers as well, even
the contrastive marker *but*. Discourse topics may also be transitioned by other
markers in Ojibwe, such as *nashke* or *mii*, or by asyndetic connection "zero" (i.e.,
by no connector at all).

Based upon these examples alone, it appears that Ojibwe makes use of asyndetic connections much more productively than does English.[9] This perhaps explains why *miinawaa* does not appear in narratives with the frequency that *and*
appears in English. For example, Schiffrin (1987a, 128) noted that 1,002 clause-
sized idea units in her corpus were prefaced by *and*, compared to 440 by *but*, 206
by *so*, and only 53 by *or*. A quick scan of the Ojibwe narratives examined for this
book show no such frequency for *miinawaa*—not even close. In fact, *miinawaa*
appears relatively infrequently compared to other sentence-initial markers such
as *nashke*, marker complexes based upon *mii*, or even asyndetic connection
"zero." This ultimately speaks to the general optionality of discourse markers as
noted by Schiffrin (1987a), which appears to be the case with *miinawaa*.

3.1.1.3   *onzaam*

In the dictionary, *onzaam* is listed as meaning 'too much, excessively, extremely'
(Nichols and Nyholm 1995, 109), for example, **onzaam** *gisinaa* 'it's **too** cold'.
This is, in fact, its use within sentence grammars, which is well known. Its dis-

course function, however, displays a relation of causality between units of discourse, having the force of the English *because*. The following shows this usage of *onzaam* (or *zaam*).

(38)   *onzaam* (Staples 2007)

> Apane-sa   wiin-go   ogii-ayaan   aw   gwiiwizens
> always   him/her   she/he had it   that boy
>
> ge-miijid,   **zaam**   odedeyan   geget   gii-wawiingezi
> what she/he is going to eat   because   his father   truly   was skillful
>
> gii-kiiwased   naa   gaye   gii-wewebinaabiid.
> hunted   and   also   fished
>
> 'But the boy always had something to eat, **because** his dad was especially good at hunting and fishing.'

In (38), there are two propositions: (1) *the boy always had something to eat*, and (2) *his dad was especially good at hunting and fishing*. The comma after the first clause indicates a significant pause, showing that *onzaam* occurs within the intonational contour of the following clause. The use of *onzaam* to accent (i.e., to occur with) the second proposition allows the interpretation that the second proposition is the *cause* of the first proposition, that is, P1 *because* P2. What is also important about this example is that *onzaam* bears little resemblance to its lexical meaning of *too much, excessively, extremely*, since there is no degree distinction being made in this example by the use of *onzaam*. In other words, the meaning conveyed here is **because** *his father was skillful*, not that the boy's father was *too skillful*. The fact that it does not denote extreme degree (at least for Mille Lacs speakers) is shown by the following example provided by Marge Anderson.

(39)   *onzaam*

(a)   Aanish   ge-onji-anoonag   bezhig   indinawemaaganag   da-naadid   o'ow?
      why   should I have   one   my relatives   to get it   this

(b)   Gidaa-miizh igo   **onzaam**   geyaabi   gibaakaakosijige.
      you should give it to me   because   still   you are open

(a)   'Why should I have one of my relatives get this?

(b)   You should just give it to me **since** you're still open.'

In (39), *onzaam* precedes the proposition *you're still open*. Since stores are either open or closed, a degree distinction cannot be indicated by *onzaam* here. In other words, a store cannot be *too open*, or *extremely open*, it is just *open*. This appears to suggest that *onzaam*, in its discourse role, has become fully lexicalized at Mille Lacs as a marker that denotes *causation*, rather than as a marker of *degree*. Other dialects are reputed to have this usage as well, although the variety of Ojibwe spoken at Red Lake (another Minnesota dialect) appears not to have undergone a complete lexicalization, since *onzaam* appears only to be used wherever extreme degree is involved (John D. Nichols, personal communication).

The use of *onzaam*, however, is not the only way to express causality in Ojibwe. Causality may be expressed by using a variety of linguistic devices, such as asyndetic arrangement of clauses (pragmatically inferred) or grammatical elements, that is, the use of relative root *onji-* 'because'. The use of *onzaam* as a causality marker, then, appears to be optional, since other linguistic devices may be used to accomplish the same work. This is shown by the following examples.

(40) Causality without *onzaam*

(a)   (Mille Lacs sessions)

Gidaa-miizh igo   *geyaabi*   *gibaakaakosijige.*
you should give it to me   still   you are open

'You should just give it to me **since** you're still open.'

(b)   (Kegg 1993, 134–35)

Miish   *ezhi-mookawaakiiyaan*   *wii-pimishkaayaan.*
and then   I cried   I want to go ride in a boat

'I started crying **because** I wanted to go paddling.'

(c)   (Eagle 1998, 18, audio)

Wa'aw gimiinin *asemaa* *gaawiin* *o'ow* *ji-maanenimigoyan*
this I give you tobacco not this so you won't make you feel bad

*gid**oonji**-baapi'isinoon.*
because I wasn't laughing at you

'Here's some tobacco so you won't feel bad **because** I wasn't laughing at you.'
(lit. 'Here's some tobacco as I wasn't laughing at you to make you feel bad.')

(d)   (Kegg 1993, 114–15)

Mii	gaa-**onji**-gosag,	"Ingitigaan"	gii-izhid.
DP	why I was scared of him	my garden	he told me

'I was really scared of him **because** he said "Ingitigaan 'my garden'" to me.'

In (40a, b), there is no one word that means 'because'; rather, it is the arrangement of clauses and context that allows a causal relationship. In other words, causality is pragmatically inferred. For both examples in (40c, d), it is the use of the relative root *onji-* that allows a causation interpretation. The fact that *onzaam* is nonobligatory is not surprising, since discourse markers are commonly said to be "non-obligatory utterance-initial items that function in relation to ongoing talk and text" (Schiffrin 2003a, 57). The fact that other linguistic devices may do the work that *onzaam* does is not surprising, since, as Schiffrin (1987a, 57–59) argues for English, discourse work may be accomplished by other linguistic devices, such as lexical repetition, reiteration, thematic continuity on the local levels (clause to clause), metalinguistic phrases, and syntactic parallels. Here it is asyndetic and grammatical devices that do the work that *onzaam* may optionally perform as a discourse marker.

3.1.1.4   *dibishkoo*

In the dictionary, *dibishkoo* is listed as meaning 'just like, even, equal, direct' (Nichols and Nyholm 1995, 45). At the sentence level, those meanings are indeed in effect. The following are typical examples of *dibishkoo*.

(41) *dibishkoo*

(a)   (Kegg 1993, 14)

Mii	ezhi-desa'oniked,	**dibishkoo**	go	nibaagan.
DP	and so makes a platform	just like	EMPH	a bed

'She made a platform **just like** a bed.'

(b) (Mille Lacs sessions)

    Gaawiin   *na*   *mii*   *iw*   *dibishkoo . . . ?*
    not   INTERR   DP   that   same as

    'Isn't that the same as . . . ?'

(c) (Kegg 1993, 60–61)

    Dibishkoo,   *bakwezhigaansan*   *miinawaa*   *ziinzibaakwadoons*
    just like   cookies   and   candy

    indashamig   *a'aw*   *adaawewininiikwe; . . .*
    she fed me   that   lady storekeeper

    'The storekeeper fed me things **like** cookies and candy . . .'

In discourse, *dibishkoo* has a function similar to a reformulation marker, with roughly the force of the English *in other words*. In this function, *dibishkoo* reformulates prior discourse in upcoming text in order to either make prior discourse more clear or allow the speaker to elaborate on a general point. Within sentence grammars, *dibishkoo* is more or less a linguistic equals sign, equating one object with another, for example, *mii aw dibishkoo ma'iingan* 'He is just like a wolf'. At the discourse level, however, *dibishkoo* brackets larger discourse units, that is, sentences, in order to allow speakers to *flesh out* prior discourse in the attempt to make that prior discourse clearer. This is shown by the following examples.

(42) *dibishkoo*

(a) (Clark 1998a, 8, audio)

    (i) *Mii*   *wapii*   *nabaj*   *idi*   *gaa-maajaayaan,*   *opime-ayi'ii*
        DP   when   probably   over there   after I left   on the side of it

       gii-izhaayaan.
       when I went

    (ii) **Dibishkoo**-*go*   *ingii-paa-nanda-bami'idiz.*
        just like   I was going around looking for ways to support myself

    (i) 'That's the time probably when I left there, when I went somewhere else.

    (ii) **In other words**, I was going around looking for ways to support myself.'

(b)　(Kegg 1993, 152–53)

Mii	*miinawaa*	*gigizheb*	*goshkozigwen,*	*mii*	*miinawaa*	*bi-maajaad,*
DP	again	morning	must wake up	DP	again	left here

izhaad	*iwidi*	*Gabekanaansing,*	**dibishkoo**	*sa*	*go*
to go	over there	place name	just like	DM	EMPH

washki-giiwe.
she/he comes back

'And in the morning when he woke up, he left here to go there to Portage Lake, **just like** a round trip.'

The use of *dibishkoo* in both examples in (42) shows that the speakers are reformulating prior discourse in order to make it more clear or meaningful. For example, in (42a) the speaker implies that he left the reservation by the use of the expression *opime-ayi'ii gii-izhaayaan* '(lit.) when I went to the side of it'. By the use of *dibishkoo*, the speaker then makes clear what he meant by this implicit statement, that is, that he was going around looking for ways to support himself. This same sort of reformulation can be seen in (42b). There, the speaker describes an old man's journeys throughout the course of a day. This description is then reformulated with the phrase **dibishkoo** *sa go washki-giiwe* '**just like** a round trip.' What is particularly interesting about this example is that there is another word specifically meaning 'round trip': *biskaabii*. The question here is why didn't the speaker just use the word *biskaabii* rather than *washki-giiwe*, which literally means 'turns and goes home'? The answer, I suggest, is that the use of *dibishkoo* in discourse is to reformulate in order to clarify. The use of *dibishkoo* allows the speaker to describe exactly what is going on or further clarify, rather than just naming the old man's day journeys.

So, while *dibishkoo* could be thought of as an equals sign within sentence grammars, for example, NP *is* **just like** NP, this core function is also active at the discourse level. At the discourse level, however, its function is not to show equivalence per se, but to allow the speaker to clarify or flesh out prior discourse in order to make that prior discourse more clear. In this way, *dibishkoo* textually brackets upcoming discourse in order to reformulate prior discourse.

3.1.1.5   *mii dash*

The lone particle *mii*, on which *mii dash* is based, is a very prolific particle in Ojibwe, as it has a wide variety of uses both at the sentence level and within discourse. In an earlier work (Fairbanks 2008), I showed that *mii* has three major functions: as a deictic particle (i.e., having a pointing function), as an aspectual marker, and as veridical marker. As a deictic particle, *mii* may stand in for physical referents (such as people or things) or time frames, or it may act as a modifier by providing further focusing power to the item it is modifying.

(43)   Deictic function of *mii*

(a)   *mii* as a pronoun

    Mii   *gaa-ikidoyan.*
    DP   what you said

    '**That** is what you said.'

(b)   *mii* as a temporal deictic (Clark 2003b, 56–57, audio)

    (i) *Wiin*   *odibendaan*   *i'iw*   *epiitagindaasod*   *i'iw*
       him/her   she/he owns it   that   how much it costs   that

       gikinoo'amoonang   *aaniin*   *enaapineyang.*
       teaching us   what   how we are sick

    (ii) **Mii**   *izhinizha'onang*   *oodi*   *mashkikiiwigamigong*
       DP   when they send us   over there   to the drug store

       ji-izhaayang   *mii*   *gii-ozhibii'ang*   *imaa*   *mazina'igan*   *awegonen*
       for us to go   DP   that he wrote it   there   paper   what

       dino   *mashkiki*   *ge-miinigooyang.*
       kind   medicine   that we'll be given

    (i) 'It's they who own it, how much they charge for giving us a diagnosis.

    (ii) **That** is **when** they send us to the drug store with a prescription that the doctor wrote out for the appropriate medicine.'

(c)   *mii* as a determiner

(i) **A'aw** (=) *Jaaj.*
    that one   George

    '**That one** (focused) is George.'

(ii) **Mii**   *a'aw*   (=)   *Jaaj.*
    DET   that one   George

    'That **very** one is George.'

In (43a, b), *mii* stands in for a physical object and a temporal time frame, respectively. For example, in (43a), *mii* stands in for the noun phrase *what you said*. In (43b.ii), *mii* stands in for the time frame associated with the phrase *how much they charge for giving us a diagnosis*. Both tokens of *mii* make anaphoric reference to a prior referent. The only difference between these two occurrences of *mii* is that in (43a) the complement of *mii* is a nominalized verb, that is, *gaa-ikidoyan* 'what you said', and in (43b.ii) the complement of *mii* is a plain conjunct verb, that is, *izhinizha'onang* 'that she/he sends us.' In the nominal predicate construction in (43c.ii), however, *mii* does not stand in for anything, but rather, it acts like a determiner, in that it modifies another element. Its function as a modifier is to *further focus* the demonstrative *a'aw* 'that one', which is already in a syntactically focused position.[10] The use of *mii* in this way allows speakers to spatially locate objects (especially when pointing to them so as to leave no doubt about their selection). This demonstrative vs. determiner function is similar to the use of demonstratives in English (though English has no other specifier that adds the focusing power that *mii* does in Ojibwe), since they too may stand alone (as pronouns) or act as modifiers (determiners) of other elements, such as in the following English examples involving the English demonstrative *that*: (1) **that** is red, and (2) **that car** is red. In the first example, *that* is a pronoun (i.e., standing in for a noun), but in the second example, *that* modifies the noun *car.* Such is the case with *mii* in (43c). When it appears by itself, it stands in for objects (as a pronoun), but with the additional ability to stand in for time frames. When it functions as a determiner (or specifier), as in **mii** *a'aw Jaaj* above, *mii* functions to further focus the demonstrative pronoun *a'aw* 'that one', getting a more focused meaning: 'that **very** one.'

As an aspectual marker, *mii* marks what I have termed IMMEDIACY ASPECT. Immediacy aspect expresses the "immediate phasal change of a temporal event or condition, typically showing either the immediate completion of an event, or its immediate inception" (Fairbanks 2008, 198). Many times, expressions containing aspectual *mii* are translated by speakers using the English temporal adverb *now*.

(44) Aspectual use of *mii* (adapted from Fairbanks 2008, 198)

(a) *Iskigamide.*
boil down/INDEP
'It's boiling down.'

(b) *Mii iskigamideg.* (completive)
ASP boil down.0/CONJ
'It's boiled down.'

(c) *Giwiisin.*
2.eat/INDEP
'You are eating.'

(d) **Mii** *wiisiniyan.* (inceptive)
ASP eat.2/CONJ
'**Now** you're finally eating.'

The aspectual use of *mii* can also be seen with the use of the past-tense marker *gii-*. The expression without *mii* represents actions that occurred sometime in the past, but the expression with *mii* represents that the action has just occurred.

(45) Aspectual use of *mii* (Fairbanks 2008, 199)

(a) *Ingii-wanendaan.*
1.PAST.forget/INDEP
'I forgot it (sometime in the past).'

(b) *Mii gii-wanendamaan.*
ASP PAST.forget.1/CONJ
'I forgot it (just now).'

As a veridical marker, *mii* has an epistemic function and marks that the "speaker has no doubt about the verity of a statement or proposition being proposed by its containing clause(s), resulting in roughly the English glosses: *it is fact, it will happen, there is no doubt that, it's a sure thing, for good, really*, etc." (Fairbanks 2008, 206–8). I consider this function to be a discourse function, as discussed in detail in section 3.2.1.1. Therefore, a quick example should suffice for now.

(46) Veridical marker

(a) *Gaawiin nigikendanziin.*
not I don't know
'I don't know.'

(b) **Mii** *gaawiin nigikendanziin.*
VER not I don't know
'I have no idea.'

In (46), there are two negative sentences, but it is the occurrence of *mii* with the negative sentence that projects the attitude that the speaker has no doubt about the proposition *I don't know.*

From these data, we can see that *mii* has a variety of sentence-level functions, but it is the deictic feature of *mii* that is borrowed for work at the discourse level within the discourse complex *mii dash* (or *miish*). Discourse complex (or cluster) *mii dash* consists of two components, *mii* and *idash*. The second element, *idash*, is a discourse marker itself and will be discussed in detail in section 3.1.2.1. In short, *idash* is a type of topic marker (the term is used loosely here).[11] It allows speakers to move on to new topics, breaking with prior discourse. Thus, while having separate individual functions, *mii* and *idash* function as a unit as a DIS-COURSE SEQUENCER. This discourse complex has become such a common occurrence in Ojibwe discourse that it appears to show signs of lexicalization (though not complete), since *mii dash* shows a loose syntactic connection to its containing clauses. In other words, while *mii* at the sentence level shows a very strict syntactic requirement for conjunct verbs, for example, aspectual use of *mii* where *mii* must occur with plain conjuncts, *mii dash* may occur with both conjunct *and* independent-order verbs.[12] As a discourse complex then, *mii dash* has the overall function within discourse to advance narratives, having roughly the force of the English *and then* or *and so*. A typical usage is given in the following example.

(**47**)   Discourse sequencer (Benjamin 2006)

(a)   *Gegoo   wawaanimigooyaang,   mii   imaa   ezhaayaang   ingiw*
      thing   when we get stumped   DP   when   we go   those

      chi-aya'aag   gagwejimangidwaa.
      elders   we ask them

(b)   ***Mii   dash*** *weweni   ezhi-wiindamawiyangidwaa   mii   o-keyaa*
      DP   DM   carefully   then they tell us   DP   this way

      omaa   giinawind   ezhitwaayang.
      here   we   our way of life

(a)   'Whenever we need to know something, that's when we go to the elders and ask them.

(b)   **And then** they carefully tell us the way we do things here.'

In this example, *mii dash* has the function of advancing the narrative to the next event, action, or detail. In this sense, *mii dash* is able to temporally relate prior talk with upcoming talk by showing the natural progression of events, that is, going to the elders *and then* being instructed. This backward-looking and forward-looking feature of *mii dash* is characteristic of its underlying deictic (or pointing) function. In this example, the temporal deictic feature of *mii* is quite transparent, since the events are temporally based. There are cases, however, where *mii dash* brackets details or commentary rather than temporally based events. This is shown in the following example, where the speaker explains that a long time ago each community had knowledge about different types of medicines and that the knowledge of those medicines was a collective knowledge.

(48) *mii dash* (Clark 2003b, 55, audio)

(a)   *Gaawiin   ongow   anishinaabe,   ganabaj   awiiya   kina   gegoo*
    not   these   Indian   probably   someone   all   things

    mashkiki   odaa-bi-gikendanziin.
    medicine   she/he would not come to know it

(b)   *Eniwek,   eniwek   ge-gikendaasopan   kina*
    quite   quite   she/he would have to be   knowledgeable

    ji-ganawendang   o'ow   mashkiki,   awegonen   ge-minokaagod
    to keep it   this   medicine   what   what is good for him/her

    a'aw   anishinaabe,   gegoo   inaapined.
    that   Indian   thing   when she/he gets sick

(c)   **Mii   dash**   *bebakaan   weweni   o-gii-kikendaanaawaa*
    DP   DM   each different   carefully   3-PAST-know it.3P/INDEP

    awegonen   o'ow,   enaabadak   o-mashkiki.
    what   this   how utilized   this medicine

(a)   'No one person would know everything about medicine.

(b)   One would have to be pretty knowledgeable to keep all the medicine that's good for people when they got sick with something.

(c)   **And so** they each knew different utilizations of medicine.'

Examining this example, we find that *mii dash* occurs with independent-order verb *ogii-kikendaanaawaa* 'they knew it' (contrary to sentence-level behavior) and advances the narrative by providing additional commentary, not by providing the next temporal event.[13] Though the clauses are not temporally related, they are sequentially aligned with *mii dash*.

What these data really show is that *mii dash* is a cluster that occurs in initial position. While *mii* has specific sentence-level functions, it is borrowed for work above the sentence level within the discourse cluster *mii dash* in order to sequentially link chunks of discourse. These chunks of discourse may be either temporal events or nontemporal events, such as commentary. Also, the fact that *mii dash* may also occur with both conjunct and independent-order verbs (showing a loose syntactic attachment to its containing clauses, or perhaps none) further supports the claim that *mii dash* is indeed a discourse marker in its own right. Like other discourse connectives, it largely derives its discourse-sequencing feature from sentence-level phenomena—in this case, from the underlying deictic feature of the deictic particle *mii*.

3.1.2   Second position

Ojibwe is a language that makes heavy use of second-position particles—particles that typically occur only in the second position of an utterance. For example, in the formation of common interrogative expressions in Ojibwe, the interrogative particle *ina*, or its clitic form *-na*, must occur as the second element of its containing sentence or clause, for example, *geyaabi* **ina** *gibakade* 'Are you still hungry?' Given this fact, it is no surprise that a significant number of Ojibwe discourse markers, such as *idash* or the second-position mystery particles to be discussed later, would also find a home in second position. Theories about discourse markers, therefore, must inevitably include second position as a potential docking spot for discourse markers. While location itself cannot be a formal criterion for defining discourse markers, a discussion delimited by location (as I have done here) shows that languages in general, including Ojibwe, may utilize the existing machinery or infrastructure (e.g., the common use of second-position words or clitics) already inherent within the language itself for discourse work. For Ojibwe, one of these existing mechanisms is the second position.

3.1.2.1   *idash* as a contrastive marker

While the foregoing markers largely satisfy Schiffrin's initial characterization that discourse markers occur in initial position, there are those that do not. One such marker is *idash*. In my earlier work, *idash* was formally labeled as a SECOND-POSITION DISCOURSE MARKER, which sometimes may occur as a SECOND-POSITION DISCOURSE CLITIC (Fairbanks 2008, 187). As this label indicates, *idash* must occur in the second position of a clause or sentence. But like many discourse connectives, it has functions in sentence grammar as well as within discourse above the sentence level. In sentence grammar, *idash* has a very restricted use within interrogative sentences as an intensifier, allowing speakers to ask for exact information, clarification, or elaboration. This function is illustrated in the following.

(49)   *idash* in sentence grammar

(a)   *Wegonen?*   (b)   *Wegonen*   **dash?**
      what   what   exactly

      'What?'   'What does that mean (exactly)?'
                               'What (are you looking for)?'

(c)   *Awenen?*   (d)   *Awenen*   **dash?**
      who   who   exactly

      'Who?'   'Who is it exactly?' (out of a group of people)

Note that in (49a, c) where the examples appear without *idash*, only the bare meaning of the interrogative particle is indicated. In (49b, d), however, the use of *idash* has an intensifying function. The expression in (49b) has differing glosses depending on the context, but the use of *idash* in these expressions has the same effect, that of clarification or of eliciting exact meaning. On one occasion, Marge Anderson was told that there was something wrong with her hotel room. In response, she used the expression in (49b) to get elaboration. Further inquiry revealed that the room was reputed to be haunted. Another example of this is in (49d), where *idash* allows the speaker to inquire for more specific information. This intensifying use of *idash* in interrogative sentences such as these appears to be quite common.

In discourse, *idash* functions as a contrastive marker. As such, *idash* allows the speaker to contrast upcoming talk with prior talk, having the force of the English *but*.

(50)   Contrastive *idash*

(a)   (Mille Lacs Sessions)

Wenda-nibwaakaa	*inenindizo,*	*bagwanawizi*	***dash.***
she/he is really smart	she/he thinks of him/herself	she/he is dumb	but

'He thinks he's smart, **but** he's dumb.'

(b)   (Clark 2003a, 50, audio)

(i) | *Shke* | *ojibwemoyang,* | *gigikendaamin* | *waa-ikidoyang.* |
|---|---|---|---|
| see | we speak Ojibwe | we know | what we want to say |

(ii) | *Zhaaganaashiimoyang* | ***idash,*** | *gaawiin* | *kina* | *gigikendanziimin* | *i'iw* |
|---|---|---|---|---|---|
| we speak English | but | not | all | we do not know | that |

zhaaganaashiimowin.
English language

(i) 'See, when we speak Ojibwe, we know what we want to say.

(ii) **But** when we speak English, we don't know all of the English language.'

The contrastive marker *idash* not only allows upcoming talk to be contrasted with prior talk but also is able to show this contrastive relationship from second position, much like *but* is able to do from initial position in English. In (50a), for example, the proposition of the second independent clause, *he's dumb*, is being contrasted with the prior clause, *he thinks he's smart*. In (50b.ii), the subordinate clause *when we speak English* is contrasted with the prior subordinate clause *when we speak Ojibwe* in (50b.i). Note, however, that because *idash* must occur in second position, it is not syntactically detached from its containing clause like its English counterpart *but*. This supports the idea that discourse markers need *not* be detached from their surrounding clauses in order to show a discourse relationship, and it further confirms that languages indeed use preexisting machinery in the language to accomplish discourse effects. The use of the second-position word *idash*, I argue, is an example of this.

While the previous examples have shown that *idash* may contrast single clauses on a local level, the data show that *idash* may contrast larger units of discourse on a more global level as well. In such cases, *idash* does not appear, at least on the surface, to be selecting a contrastive relationship with prior clauses. A case in point is the following example from a narrative in which the speaker is talking about the return of the crow, which is the first bird to return before the spring.

(51) *idash* ([Clark?] 2006, 13)[14]

(a) *Gii-minwendam   Anishinaabe   azhigwa   nwaandawaad*
      she/he was glad   Indian   now   when she/he heard

 bineshiinyan   dagoshininid   gii-kikendang   azhigwa   ji-aayaabawaanig
 birds   arriving   they knew   now   getting warmer

 azhigwa   gabe-biboon   giikajid.
 now   all winter   being cold

(b) *Gii-ikidowag   iko,   "hey giwaabanishimin."*
      they said   customarily   hey we are going to make it

(c) *Geget **idash** ogii-manaaji'aawaan   iniw   bineshiinyan,*
      truly   DM   they respected him/her   that   bird

 gii-inendamoog   mii   ongow   baadoonangig   ziigwan.
 they thought of them as   DP   these   the ones who bring us   spring

(d) *Mii **dash** igaye,   gaawiin   ogii-nooji'aasiwaawaan   baanimaa*
      DP   DM   also   not   they did not hunt him/her   until

 gakina   gii-paashkaawe'owaad   wewaawanojig.
 all   that they had hatched their eggs   those that have eggs

(a) 'The Indians were happy when they heard the birds arriving because they knew that's when it starts getting warmer after a cold winter.

(b) They used to say, "Hey, we're gonna make it."

(c) **And** they really respected the birds. That's how they thought of these ones that bring us spring.

(d) **And** also, they didn't hunt them until all the birds had hatched their eggs.'

On the surface, *idash* in (51c) does not appear to be showing a contrastive relationship, in that it does not show a contrast between the propositions of its containing sentence with that of the preceding sentences. In other words, the proposition *they really respected the birds* in (51c) is not in semantic contrast with *The Indians were happy when they heard the birds arriving* in (51a), nor the proposition *They used to say, "Hey, we're gonna make it."* in (51b). The convention of translating these *idash*'s as 'and' only further complicates what is really going on here. Closer examination of this narrative reveals, however, that while the propositions themselves are not being contrasted, topic flow is. Another way of saying this is that *idash* allows a break with prior talk in order to transition to a new topic, a topic shift. This has an additive effect of marking transitions from topic to topic. In English, as Schiffrin has shown (as we already saw), these global transitions are marked by *and*, but in Ojibwe, transitions from global topics (which are dissimilar or unrelated) are marked by *idash*, leaving *miinawaa* to coordinate similar details (coordinated content) within these global topics.

For example, in (51), there are three discourse topics: (1) Indians were happy when the birds came back, (2) Indians really respected the birds, and (3) they never hunted them until they had hatched their eggs. There is really no logical semantic nor temporal link between the transition from the first topic to the second topic or from the second topic to the third topic. Also, these topics do not contain any inherent contrasting content that would lend itself to a contrastive relationship, as we saw for the examples in (50). Here *idash* does not facilitate a propositional contrast, but instead it facilitates a contrast in discourse action, that is, transition. In other words, *idash* signals a break from further elaboration within a given topic in order to transition to a new one. Therefore the contrast is realized with the introduction of new topics.

It is this contrastive action — that is, breaking with prior content — that allows for smooth transitions into what may be new and unrelated content within a narrative. As a result, the use of *idash* has an additive effect, since it helps to organize topics and events within the development of a story. The following example illustrates this additive effect. It shows how *idash* is used by a narrator to provide information about three different participants in a story: a brave, his wife, and the curtain of their wigwam. In this story, some Ojibwes went out to search for their enemies, the Dakotas. This excerpt includes an explanation of the seating arrangement of an Ojibwe brave and his wife within their lodge, as well as an explanation as to the kind of door they had on that lodge. A Dakota brave then enters their lodge, and the Ojibwe brave, being startled and frightened, jumps over the fire in the lodge and falls down. The Ojibwe brave's wife, showing bravery, then picks up an axe and clubs the Dakota over the head.

(52) *idash* (Nichols 1995, 54–55, story told by Jim Littlewolf)[15]

(a) Gii-miigaadim   ingwana   imaa,   gaa-tazhi-miigaading
there was a battle   turns out   there   where the battle was

gii-kabeshiwaad.
they were camping

(b) Mii   imaa   gii-miigaadiwiingen   imaa   dazhi-gabeshiwaad.
DP   there   there must have been a battle   there   where they camp

(c) Wiiwan-**sh**   odayaawaan;
and his wife   he had her

(d) mii   imaa   wenji-wiidabimaad   ishkwaandeming,   mii   a'aw   ogichidaa,
DP   there   why he sits with her   at the door   DP   that   brave

(e) wiin   igo   niigaanizi   gaye   miigaadiwind   wiin   igo
he   EMPH   he leads   also   when there is a battle   him   EMPH

iwidi   niigaan,   ani-miigaazod.
over there   in front   as he goes into battle

(f) Wa'aw   **idash**   ogichidaa,   mii   imaa   namadabiwaad
this   DM   brave   DP   there   that they are sitting

ishkwaandeming   miinawaa iniw wiiwan.
at the door   and that his wife

(g) Gibiiga'igaade   **dash**   i'iw   ayi'ii   ishkwaandem   wiigiwaam.
be curtained   DM   that   whatchamacallit   door   lodge

(a) 'It turns out that there was a battle there, they were camping where the battle was.

(b) There must have been a battle there where they were camping.

(c) He has a wife;

(d) he's sitting next to her at the doorway, that brave.

(e)   He leads the battle, he is at the front going into battle.

(f)   This is that brave, sitting at the doorway with his wife.

(g)   There is a curtain on the door of the lodge.'

After a brief background statement in (52a, b) about a battle having taken place where they were camping, the narrator uses *idash* to introduce three topics (here, new participants or characters within the story), all accented by *idash*: that the brave had a wife in (52c), the brave's position by the door in (52f), and the curtained door of the lodge in (52g). It is the contrastive feature of *idash* that allows the narrator to jump from participant to participant, in essence, breaking from prior discourse (details of a particular participant) in order to move on to other pertinent details or participants in the story. It is not propositional content itself that finds itself in contrast but the narrator's discourse action of participant description that does.

In the stories examined for this book, a pattern emerges. Basically, a topic is introduced that is not accented by *idash*. Thereafter, all transitions to new topics are accented by *idash*. It is the accumulation of these topics that serves in the development of stories. Once a topic is introduced by *idash*, however, the subtopics or support structures attached to that particular topic usually do not contain any further occurrences of *idash*. Events attached to particular topics are usually connected asyndetically, and coordinated structures, should they occur, are usually coordinated by *miinawaa*. This pattern usually occurs until the end of a narrative. This pattern has the structure in (53) and is illustrated with the example in (54):

(53)   *idash*[16]

Topic 1
    SUBTOPICS (background, events, support, elaboration)
Topic 2 **idash** . . .
    SUBTOPICS (background, events, support, elaboration)
Topic 3 **idash** . . .
    SUBTOPICS (background, events, support, elaboration) . . .

(54)   *idash* (Kegg 1993, 152–53)

TOPIC 1

(a) | *Bezhig* | *igo* | *akiwenzii* | *ingii-wiij'-ayaawaanaan.* |
      | one | EMPH | old man | we stayed with |

BACKGROUND

(b)   *Ogii-odawemaawinan*   *a'aw*   *mindimooyenh.*
      she had him as a sibling   that   old lady

BACKGROUND

(c)   *Aazhawakiwenzhiinh*   *gii-izhinikaazo.*
      Aazhawakiwenzhiinh   he was named so

TOPIC 2   BACKGROUND

(d) | *Miish* | *iko* | *waasa,* | *ingii-taamin* | *Gabekanaansing* |
      | DM | used to | far | we lived there | At the End of the Trail |

      gii-izhi-wiinde.
      it was named so

TOPIC 3   EVENT

(e) | *Miish* | *a'aw* | *akiwenzii* | *gigizheb* | *onishkaad,* | *babiichiid,* |
      | DM | that | old man | morning | he gets up | he puts his shoes on |

      aniibiish   *gashkibidood,*   *ziinzibaakwad*
      tea   he ties up   sugar

      miinawaa   *bangii*   *bakwezhiganan,*
      and   a little   bread

      ezhi-bimoondang.
      and packs it on his back

(a)   'We had a certain old man staying with us.

(b)   He was the old lady's brother.

(c)   His name was Aazhawakiwenzhiinh.

(d)   We used to live far away at Portage Lake which was called Gabekanaansing "At the End of the Trail".

(e)   The old man got up in the morning, put his moccasins on, tied up some tea, sugar, and a little bread, and packed it on his back.'

The first three lines, (54a–c), bring up the first topic, the old man; (54d) introduces the second topic, that the speaker and the old man used to live at Portage Lake; and (54e) introduces the third topic, the old man's daily travels. Note that the event structures associated with these topics are not linked by *idash*, nor by *miinawaa* (except clause internally, where there is coordination), but by asyndetic connection. Note also that while the first topic is not accented by *idash*, the last two topics, in (54d, e), are. The general pattern exhibited in this excerpt prevails through the whole story and serves as a major pattern for stories in general.

3.1.2.1.1 *Digressions*

There is further evidence for this contrasting feature of *idash* within discourse in the form of discourse digressions or discourse asides, marking discourse that is not relevant to the flow of the narrative. Discourse marked by *idash* in these cases usually allows the speaker to give some quick background detail in order to contextualize immediate upcoming talk. Note how *idash* only breaks the flow of prior discourse in order to perform this function. This is shown in the following examples.

(55) *idash* in digressions (Kegg 1993, 104–5)

(a) *Ingoding   igo   aabanaabiyaan   gaa-biijibatood*
pretty soon   EMPH   I look back   who was running toward me

enda-gichi-ginoozi   a'aw   inini.
he is very tall   that   man

(b) *Imbiminizha'og,   gichi-enigok   maajiibatooyaan.*
he's chasing me   real hard   I started running

(c) *Ziibiins   imaa   bimitigweyaa,   mitig   imaa   aazhawaakoshing,*
creek   there   it flows by   log   there   lying across

mitigoog   igo   niizh.
logs   EMPH   two

(d) *Gaawiin-sh   igo   aapiji   dimiisinoon   i'iw   ziibiins,*
but not   EMPH   very   not deep   that   creek

aazhawigaaziibatooyaan   miinawaa   ezhi-aabanaabamag.
I wade across running   and   then I look back at him

(e) *Enda-gichi-mindido.*
     he is quite big

(f) *Mii   go   ezhi-aazhawigwaashkwanid   imaa   ziibiinsing,*
     DP   EMPH   then he jumps across   there   at the creek

     gichi-enigok   bimibatooyaan.
     real hard   I run

(a) 'Then I turned around to look and there was a real tall man running toward me.

(b) He was following me, so I started running just hard.

(c) There was a creek there with a log, two logs, lying across it.

(d) That creek wasn't very deep, and I waded right across and looked back at him again.

(e) He was really big.

(f) He jumped right across at the creek, and I ran real hard.'

Here, *idash* in (55d), which occurs as clitic *-sh* on the negator particle *gaawiin*, does not introduce a new topic on a global level but only quickly breaks the flow of prior talk (a description of being chased by a tall man) in order to provide a brief background detail (the creek wasn't very deep) for upcoming talk (that she was able to wade through). This usage is seen again later on in the story, when the speaker breaks the flow of prior discourse in order to provide background for upcoming discourse.

(56) *idash* in digressions (Kegg 1993, 104–7)

(a) *Ingoding   igo   omamaan   iniw   odoopwaaganan—*
     pretty soon   EMPH   he takes him/her   that   his/her pipe

     ginwaakoziwan—   onashkina'aad.
     she/he is long   he fills him/her

(b) *Mii   imaa   nanaamadabid   a'aw   animosh.*
     DP   there   sitting around   that   dog

(c) *Zagwaswaad,   eshkwaa-zagwaswaad,   ingoding*
     he smokes him/her   after he finishes smoking him/her   pretty soon

	igo	eni-izhi-zaaga'ang	a'aw	animosh.
	EMPH	she/he goes out	that	dog

(d) *Ingii-owiiyawen'enyinan* **dash** *a'aw akiwenzii.*
    I am namesake to him   but   that   old man

(e) *"Niiyawen'enh,"   indig,   "gaawiin   animoshiwisiin   a'aw   omaa*
    my namesake   he tells me   not   not a dog   that   here

    ba-biindiged,"   ikido.
    who came in   he says

(f) *"Mii   imaa   iniw   ozidan,   bakaan   izhi-naagwadiniwan,"*
    DP   there those his/her feet different   how they look

    indig.
    he tells me

(g) *Oo,   yay,   gichi-zegiziyaan.*
    oh   my   I am really scared

(a) 'After a while he took his pipe — it was long — and filled it.

(b) That dog was sitting there.

(c) He smoked and when got through smoking, the dog went out.

(d) I was namesake to that old man.

(e) "My namesake," he said to me, "that wasn't a dog that came in here," he said.

(f) "His feet were different," he told me.

(g) Oh, my, was I scared.'

In this story, a dog that was chasing the speaker came into her house. An old man who stayed with her family filled a pipe and smoked it, and the dog subsequently left. The old man then tells the speaker that it was not a dog at all, because its feet were different looking. In the middle of describing this event, in (56d) the speaker breaks the flow of this description in order to provide a quick unrelated comment, accented by *idash*, that she is the namesake to the old man. While the comment is unrelated to the flow of the story and the eventline of the prior sentence, the use of *idash* appears to allow the speaker to contextualize the following sentence, in which the old man calls the speaker *my namesake*.

Sometimes these digressions do not break with prior discourse in order to provide background information or contextualization for upcoming discourse, as we have seen in previous examples. Rather, the discourse marked by *idash* in such examples appears only to represent *elaborations* of prior discourse. While still representing a break with prior discourse, the use of *idash* in these situations only does so in order to allow speakers to provide a brief detail regarding previous discourse. This is shown in the following excerpt from a story in which an old man goes to get medicine at a lake. After he sings some spiritual songs, someone emerges from the water to provide the old man with medicine.

(57)   *idash* in digressions (Kegg 1993, 156–57)

(a)   *Bezhig   giiwenh   a'aw   akiwenzii   ezhi-maajaad,   naadid   mashkiki.*
       one   apparently   that   old man   then he leaves   he gets   medicine

(b)   *Miish   giiwenh   iwidi   jiigibiig   ezhi-namadabid*
       and then   apparently   over there   on the shore   then he sits

       giiwenh,   ezhi-nagamod   manidoo-nagamonan,   ingoji-sh   igo
       apparently   then he sings   spiritual songs   about   EMPH

       niiwin,   niiwin   nagamonan,   iniw   manidoo-nagamonan.
       four   four   songs   those   spiritual songs

(c)   *Mii   giiwenh   ezhi-maajijiwang   i'iw   zaaga'igaans.*
       DP   apparently   then it starts to whirl   that   little lake

(d)   *Miish   giiwenh   ingoding,   ingoding   igo,   mii   imaa*
       and then   apparently   pretty soon   pretty soon   EMPH   DP   there

       awiiya   ezhi-mookiid.
       someone   then he emerges

(a)   'One old man went to get medicine.

(b)   He sat right on the lakeshore and sang spiritual songs there, **about four of them.**

(c)   That lake started to whirl.

(d)   Then somebody came up from the water.'

The lines in (57a–d) describe a sequence: an old man leaves to gather medicine at the lake, he sits on the shore and sings some spiritual songs, the lake begins to whirl, and finally a being emerges from the water, which eventually provides the old man with medicine. In (57b), however, the speaker uses *idash* (occurring here as clitic *-sh*) to break from the general eventline in order to provide an elaboration (in bold type) to the preceding clause *sang spiritual songs there*. In short, this break from the eventline allows the speaker to specify the number of songs that the old man sang.

In sum, it is these breaks in flow that show the contrastive feature of *idash* in discourse. It is not the individual propositions that are contrasted; instead, it allows for a contrast in discourse action.

3.1.2.1.2 *Backgrounding and foregrounding*

While *idash* may break the flow of prior discourse in order to introduce a new topic or create a digression, *idash* may also be used to show a contrast between backgrounded and foregrounded content. This sort of contrasting function usually occurs on a more local level, usually within subtopics rather than in major transitions from topic to topic. Many times these contrasts are part of larger discourse units, that is, in the formation of major background themes.

(58) background vs. foreground (Kegg 1993, 152–53)

(a) *Mii* **dash** *ayi'ii*   *misko-waabowayaan* *iko—*
DP   but   whatchamacallit   red blanket   used to

   gii-izhi-wiindewan *mewinzha* *gichi-waabowayaanan—* *mii* *i'iw*
   it was called thus   long ago   big blankets   DP   that

   egwazhed.
   what he wore

(b) *Miinawaa* *gaawiin* *wiikaa* *gii-kiichiwakwaanesiin.*
and   not   ever   he did not take his hat off
   BACKGROUND

(c) *Gii-waabizhagindibe.*
he was bald
   BACKGROUND

(d) *Mewinzha* *giiwenh* *gii-aakozi.*
long ago   apparently he was sick

FOREGROUND

(e) *Akina* **dash** *ogii-wanitoonan iniw wiinizisan.*
   all   DM   he lost them   those his hairs

(f) *Oonh, gichi-aya'aawi a'aw akiwenzii.*
   Oh   he is very old that old man

(a) 'And a *misko-waabowayaan* 'red blanket'—that's what they called those big blankets long ago—that's what he wore.

(b) He never took off his hat.

(c) He was bald.   **background**

(d) It was said that he had been sick long ago.   **background**

(e) He [**dash**] lost all his hair.   **foreground**

(f) Oh, that old man was ancient.'

In (58), there are two tokens of *idash*, in (58a) and (58e). The first token, in (58a), introduces the global topic of what the old man wore, that is, a red blanket and a hat that he never took off. The second token of *idash*, in (58e), occurs within support of this major topic as a device to contrast local backgrounded content, that is, events that lead to his hair loss, with local foregrounded content, that is, that he lost all his hair. In short, the background information in (58c) and (58d) contextualizes the foregrounded information in (58e), and it is *idash* that links these two discourse actions.

This sort of contrast between local backgrounded and local foregrounded content can also be seen in a story where an Indian man is taken to court for fighting. Before this man is introduced in this story, however, the speaker provides this global background episode.

(59) *idash* (Clark 1998a, 8, audio)

(a) *Mewinzha-***sh** *igo idi,   jibwaa-nisidotamowaad aapiji ingiw*
   long ago   EMPH over there before they understood very   those

   anishinaabeg i'iw chimookomaanimowin, gii-ayaawag idi
   Indians   that English language   there were those over there

gaawiin	*igo*	*gegoo*	*ogii-kagwayakotanziinaawaa*		*gegoo*		
not	EMPH	thing	they didn't hear it right		thing		

inindwaa.
when they are spoken to

(b) *Miish*   *ige*   *apane,*   *mii-go*   *iw*   *wapii,*   *ganabaj*   *gemaa-ge*
      and then   also   always   DP   that   time   probably   maybe

      1937,   *1938,*   *geget,*   *gii-minikweshkiwag*   *aanind*   *ingiw*   *anishinaabeg,*
      1937   1938   truly   they drank a lot   some   those   Indians

      gii-kiiwashkwebiiwaad.
      they got drunk

(c) *Aaningodinong-sh*   *gii-tebibinaawag*   *miigaadiwaad,*
      sometimes   they were caught   they are fighting

      gaa-zhi-gibaakwa'ondwaa,   *i'iw*   *miigaazong*   *miinawaa-go*   *awiiya*
      and then they were locked up   that   fighting   and   someone

      bapakitewaawaad.
      they beat him/her up

(a) '**And** a long time ago over there, before those Indians understood English very well, they were those who sometimes didn't hear things correctly when they were told something.

(b) **And** all the time at that time, maybe 1937 or 1938, some Indians were big drinkers and would get drunk.

(c) **And** sometimes, they would get caught fighting each other and they would get locked up for fighting and beating someone up.'

There are three tokens of *idash* in this background episode, glossed with the English *and*. The first two tokens introduce major topics in the development of the general background of the story, that is, that Indians sometimes misheard what was being spoken to them in English and that some Indians used to drink a lot and get drunk; the third token of *idash* marks a local contrast between the foregrounded content in (59c), that is, that sometimes they were thrown in jail for fighting and beating someone up, with the backgrounded content in (59b). The content in (59b) is analyzed here as backgrounded (locally), since it contextualizes upcoming discourse in (59c). In this sense, the content in (59b) is dependent upon the content in (59c), since (59c) is the important piece of information for understanding the rest of the story, not (59b).

3.1.2.1.3 idash *in adjacency pairs*

In the interactive plane of discourse, the contrastive feature of *idash* can also be seen within adjacency pairs. Adjacency pairs (following Schiffrin 1987a, 84) are situations where there is a query and a response, such as in the following exchange.

(60) *idash* within an adjacency pair

Q: *Aaniin   ezhi-ayaayan?*
how   how are you

'How are you?'

R: *Nimino-ayaa.   Giin   **dash?***
I am good   you   and

'I'm fine. **And** you?'

In such situations within English discourse and in translating such situations from Ojibwe to English, the use of *and* is a common convention. We have seen this previously, where many examples involving *idash* were translated using the English coordinator *and* rather than with the English contrastive marker *but*. As we have seen, however, the use of the English coordinator *and* to translate *idash* is only a translating convention, and not a true representation of the function of *idash*. After all, Ojibwe contains a discourse coordinator as well, *miinawaa*, but its use within adjacency pairs such as the one in (60) would be ungrammatical. Also, the preceding discussion showed that Ojibwe does not make use of the coordinator *miinawaa* in building texts via the accumulation of topics. Rather, it uses the contrastive marker *idash* to do this work, the work that *and* does in English. So it is no surprise that Ojibwe would use *idash* within adjacency pairs such as the one in (60). In short, the use of *idash* in (60) allows the interlocutor to break the flow of discourse centered around him- or herself in order to make the same query to the originator of the question.

3.1.3   *Preverbs*

3.1.3.1   Relative preverb *izhi*

Ojibwe has one additional element that I analyze as a discourse marker, although its primary grammatical function is as a RELATIVE ROOT or RELATIVE
PREVERB (Valentine 2001, 160, 421–23; see also Nichols 1980, 141–46, who calls
them RELATIVE PREFIXES when not occurring as roots inside words). This element is *izhi* 'thus, thither, how, in what manner'. In the Algonquian literature,
relative roots (and by extension, relative preverbs) are defined as elements that
"specify various relations between a verb and some element, which may serve to
indicate the predicate's source, reason, manner, location, quantity, degree, or extent" (Valentine 2001, 421; see also Nichols 1980, 141).[17] They may appear either
as roots inside words or as compounded prefixal elements called "preverbs."[18]
This is shown for *izhi* in the following examples.

(61)   Relative element *izhi*

(a)   Relative root *iN-* (Clark 1998a, 8, audio)

... odinaan	giiwenh	mii	iw	gaa-**i**nitang
he tells him	apparently	DP	that	how he heard it

'. . . he tells him **how** he heard it.'

(b)   Relative preverb izhi- (Mille Lacs sessions)

Aanawi-go	minobii'igaadeni	mazina'igan,	gaawiin	dash
even though	it is written good	resume	not	but

izhi-nibwaakaasiin.
she/he is not that smart

'Even though he's got a good resume, he's not **as** smart as he says he is.'

Relative roots exhibit a rather interesting syntactical feature that is worth mentioning here, since it will prove to be relevant later on when the use of plain conjunct verbs within discourse is discussed. In certain environments, when relative
roots (relative preverbs as well) are present within the verb itself or within the
verbal complex of verbs inflected in the conjunct, the mere presence of the relative root or preverb appears to invoke the use of initial change, either on the verb

itself or on the verbal complex as a whole.[19] This tendency was also noticed by Valentine for Odaawaa, a dialect of Ojibwe (see Valentine 2001, 960, where he notes, in regard to verbs within *mii-* clauses, "If the verb contains a relative root, it usually shows changed conjunct"). The following example shows this process.

(62) Relative roots invoke initial change

(a)   *Gego*   *anaamimishiken*   *wiininoyan.*
     don't   don't blame me   be fat.2/CONJ

     'Don't blame me that you are fat.'

(b)   *Gego*   *anaamimishiken*   *ekaamoyan.*
     don't   don't blame me   IC.be so fat.2/CONJ

     'Don't blame me for how fat you are.'

In this example, two words relating to *fatness* are used, along with the same carrier sentence *don't blame me that*: *wiinino* 'she/he is fat' and *ikaamo* 'be so fat'. While not so transparent on the surface, the morphological structure of *ikaamo* is made up of the relative root *iN* 'in a certain manner' and *-gaamo* 'fat'. Within the same syntactical environment, it is *ikaamo* that undergoes initial change to *ekaamoyan*, not *wiinino* (which contains no relative root). At this point, it is unclear to me why initial change would be triggered by the mere presence of a relative root. This process applies to relative preverbs as well (to be discussed more in section 4.2).

While *izhi* has a primary function as a relative root within verbs, or as relative preverbs within verbal complexes, it has a secondary function in discourse as a discourse connective. Nichols recognized this usage as well, saying that in narrative discourse, *izhi* "links clauses or sentences sequentially" (Nichols 1980, 144). Though he did not characterize *izhi* as a discourse marker per se, *izhi* shows all the signs of a discourse marker: able to link prior text with upcoming text, adding textual coherence, having a function within sentence grammar as well as being borrowed for discourse work above the sentence level, and so on. As a discourse connective, it carries the meaning roughly equivalent to the English *and then, and so* (see also Nichols 1980, 144, who first noted this), showing that it is *izhi*'s indexical function (that is, its power of associating outside content to the verb to which it is attached) as a relative prefix that is being exploited for discourse work. The following example is a typical usage. Note that when using *izhi*, no other discourse-structuring device is needed in order to advance the narrative, although *miish* (a discourse marker complex, the abbreviated form of *mii dash*) may optionally occur before a clause containing *izhi*. Note that I gloss *izhi* as RP ("relative prefix").

(63) Relative preverb *izhi* as discourse marker

(a)   (Eagle 1998, 18, audio)

Gaa-izhi-wiindamawid   nimaamaa,   "Ambe wiib!"
IC.PAST-RP-ask.3>1   my mother   come on hurry

'**And then** my mom told me, "Hurry!"'

(b)   (Nichols 1980, 144, transliterated, original gloss)

Miish   *gaa-izhi-gagwejimag   wa'aw   mindimooyenh   "aandi..."*
and thus   IC-thus-that I ask her   this   old lady   where

'**And** I asked the old lady. "Where ..."'

In these examples *izhi* does not function as a relative root in the way that it does at the sentence level (where it may indicate manner or direction) but functions rather to advance a narrative to the next event, linking prior and upcoming text. What it retains, however, within discourse is its indexical use. At the sentence level, *izhi* indexes (or relates) an outside word to its containing verb in order to indicate manner or direction. It is this indexical power that is being borrowed for work at the discourse level in order to cohere larger discourse units on a more global scale.

In sum, what all these discourse connectives have in common is that they all have sentence-level functions that are in turn exploited for work at the discourse level. Those elements that have core lexical or grammatical functions within sentence grammars find themselves as targets of discourse, since they easily lend themselves for work on more global levels. Recall that this was the case, for example, for the coordinating conjunction *and* in English. At the sentence level it coordinates similar linguistic categories, but at the discourse level it coordinates similar units of discourse. Recall that this was the case for the Ojibwe coordinator *miinawaa* as well.

As Schiffrin (1987a) also noted, however, some English discourse markers, such as *oh* and *well*, have very little or no meaning. For these types of discourse markers, their meaning can be defined only by their use within discourse. This is why such markers are notoriously hard to define individually. They are dependent upon the context in which they are being used for their meaning to become clear. In this sense, because their use is not based upon an underlying sentence-level use, lexical or grammatical, they are what I call full-time discourse markers. In other words, while discourse connectives may occur alongside their sentence-level uses, discourse markers that have little or no meaning are always on the job. And as we will see, their job within Ojibwe is to project attitude. The next section will explore a number of these type of markers in Ojibwe.

3.2   MYSTERY PARTICLES

The discourse particles to be described in the following sections are discourse markers that are notoriously hard to characterize; they are similar to some of the discourse markers described by Schiffrin (1987a) for English, such as *oh* and *well*. The major difference between these markers and those described in prior sections is that these particles carry no, or very little, lexical content. As a result, they are very difficult to characterize (if at all) as individual words. For example, English speakers would be hard-pressed to explain the meaning of *oh* and *well* with any degree of confidence. The same is true for these Ojibwe particles. In the old missionary dictionary compiled by Frederic Baraga, for example, the difficulty in defining these types of particles is evident from his statement in regard to the particle *gosha*, where he is forced to explain its pragmatic use within discourse rather than to provide a simple lexical meaning: "This word cannot be given in English. It signifies that a repetition is made, or that something which is told, is known" (Baraga 1992, 142). Even in a pedagogical reference grammar written by a native speaker of Ojibwe from the Lac Seul community in Canada, mystery particles *gosha*, *goda*, and *naa* are listed only as "filler word[s]" (Ningewance 2004, 254, 315). Like the markers *oh* and *well*, these Ojibwe discourse particles can only be characterized based upon their function in discourse.

Therefore, in order to describe these largely undefinable particles, I will use the term MYSTERY PARTICLE. This term was first coined by Longacre (1976) in his description of such particles in some indigenous languages of Central and

South America. In describing the following Ojibwe particles, I follow Longacre in the formal use of the term *mystery particle*, not because they are mysterious to their users, who have an unconscious knowledge of their use, but because they "defy analysis even at a relatively advanced stage of research" (Longacre 1976, 468). The reality is that they are difficult to define, even for their users. Because of this difficulty, all glosses for mystery particles will carry the abbreviated label of "DM" (discourse marker), rather than a quick and dirty English gloss. While pauses may occasionally accompany these markers, many times they do not. Significant pauses, if any, will be marked with a comma. Three types of mystery particles will be discussed in the sections to come. Those that occur in initial position will be discussed in section 3.2.1, those that occur in second position will be discussed in section 3.2.2, and second-position clusters will be discussed in section 3.2.2.7.1.

3.2.1   Initial position

3.2.1.1   *mii* as a veridical marker
The particle *mii* has three major functions in Ojibwe: as a deictic particle, as an aspectual marker, and as a veridical marker (Fairbanks 2008). In Fairbanks 2008, I characterized *mii* primarily as to function, not category. In terms of discourse, *mii* is certainly a discourse marker, though it has both textual and epistemic functions in discourse. In fact, it shows the multifunctional behavior typical of discourse markers cross-linguistically. It has specific uses at the sentence level but also additional uses at the discourse level. These functions were discussed in detail in my earlier work, and so only a concise exposition will be given here. In that work, one of the functions of *mii* was as a veridical marker. Veridical markers, according to Payne, express "an increased intensity of the truth of the proposition, something like the adverbial use of *really* in English" (1997, 254). In other words, the use of *mii* as a veridical marker in Ojibwe reveals the attitude of the speaker toward his or her proposition, indicating that the proposition is a sure thing, viewed as fact, that there is no doubt about the verity of the proposition, or that a serious statement is being made. Possible translations include *it is fact, it will happen, there is no doubt that, it's a sure thing, for good,* and *really.* For example, negative declarative sentences occurring with *mii* show an increased degree of speaker verity toward the proposition. I have heard the elders use *mii* in this way on numerous occasions, especially when they got

stumped about a question that was presented to them. Typical uses of *mii* in this manner are given in the following.

(64) Negative declarative sentences with *mii*

(a) *Gaawiin   nigikendanziin.*
     not   I don't know

     'I don't know.'

(b) **Mii**-sa   *gaawiin   nigikendanziin.*
     VER-DM   not   I don't know

     'I **really** don't know.' (after much thought)
     'I have **no idea**.' (after much thought)

In the negative sentences in (64), *mii* strengthens the verity of the proposition, indicating *really* or *no idea*, as opposed to a bare negative proposition *I don't know*. As we will see, *sa*, a mystery particle itself, does not contribute this meaning; rather, it contributes the feeling of finality, that is, *after much thought, finally giving up*. As an example of this, one of the elders, Millie Benjamin, uttered the sentence containing *mii* in (64b) after having spent some time and effort trying to figure out an answer to one of my questions. This usage is also found in a story by Jim Clark, when he was speaking about the difference between traditional medicine people and modern doctors. In short, when Indians got ill a long time ago, they were sent to a specialist, much like people today are sent to specialists for specific illnesses. In referring to a specialist, he uses the mystery particle *mii*.

(65) Veridical *mii* (Clark 2003b, 55, audio)

Mii   iniw   gaa-izhinizhawaad   iwidi,   awedi   mii   gekendang
DM   that   sent him/her   one over   there   VER   who knows it

i'iw   mashkiki   ge-minokaagoyan.
that   medicine   that could heal you

'They then sent him over there, to **a specialist** who could heal you.'

In (65), to describe a *specialist*, the mystery particle *mii* and the nominalized verb *gekendang* 'she/he who knows it' are used, not a word meaning 'specialist'.

In his explanation of traditional doctors, Clark explains that in those days different villages had people who knew different medicines. When people got ill, they were sent to those people who possessed knowledge of the appropriate medicine for their particular illness. It is the use of *mii* that allows the speaker to describe those traditional doctors who possessed expert knowledge of their particular medicines.

In a statement about cultural taboos or cultural beliefs, *mii* is utilized to show that the speaker is certain that certain events will happen as a result of a broken taboo. The use of *mii* in these constructions shows the speaker's attitude of surety. This is illustrated with the following examples.

(66) *mii* in taboos (from Benjamin, n.d.)[20]

(a) *Giishpin mindaweyan, **miigo**   gezhiwawaabishkiganzhiiyan.*
    if   you pout   VER.EMPH you will have white spots on fingernails

    'If you like to Mindawe [pout], you will have telltale "white spots" on your fingernails!'

(b) *Giishpin zazaagiziyan, **miigo**   gezhizipogwayaweyan.*
    if   you are stingy VER.EMPH you will have a crater in the back of your neck

    'If you are Zazaagiz [stingy], you will have a crater in the back of your neck!'

The second clause of each statement in (66) is accented by mystery particle *mii*. *Mii*, in turn, is accented by the emphatic clitic *go*, and the presence of *mii* triggers the use of conjunct-order inflection on the verbal complexes (i.e., *mii*-clauses). Notice too that independent-order inflection is not used here; for example, *giga-wawaabishkiganzhii* 'you will have telltale white spots on your fingernails', would not entail the use of *mii*. What this essentially means is that speakers have two morphological options in representing these future events, *mii*- clauses or independent clauses. The question here is, why use *mii*- clauses when independent clauses such as *giga-wawaabishkiganzhii* would accomplish the same function? The answer lies in the function of mystery particle *mii*. As argued in my earlier work on *mii* (Fairbanks 2008, 200), *mii*- clauses are stronger statements. They are stronger in the sense that *mii* conveys the speaker's attitude of certainty toward his or her proposition, that is, they have an epistemic function. In other words, the use of *mii* in these statements signals that speakers see their propositions as sure things and that there is no doubt that such events will happen. Independent clauses, on the other hand, would only convey bare propositional content, having no such epistemic effect, for example, *giga-wawaabishkiganzhii* 'you will have telltale white spots on your fingernails', *giga-zipogwayawe* 'you will have a crater in the back of your neck'.

As part of its veridical function, the epistemic use of *mii* can be seen in related functions as well. These include the use of *mii* within emotionally charged statements, or in ribbing (i.e., teasing). This is illustrated in utterances by Marge Anderson in (67a) and Elfreda Sam in (67b).

(67)

(a)   Emotionally charged statements

    Mii-go   *bijiinag*   *gii-pi-naanind.*
    VER-EMPH just now came and got her

    'They finally came and got her!' (after several days)

(b)   Ribbing

    Mii   *na*   *gii-tagoshinowaad*   *bineshiinsag?*
    VER   INTER they arrived   little birds

    'Did little birds come?'

Marge made the statement in (67a) when she learned that a murdered tribal member was finally found after having been left dead in her backyard for several days. In representing the proposition *they finally came and got her*, again, speakers have two morphological choices, the use of a *mii-* clause or independent morphology, for example, *gii-pi-naanaa* 'they came and got her'. When I later queried Marge about the use of *mii* in this statement against the same example without *mii*, she stated that the *mii-* clause captures the seriousness of the situation, while it would not express the same seriousness were *mii* not used. The statement in (67b) was a ribbing that I received from Elfreda. She was teasing me about my messy handwriting on my folder, because it looked like a lot of little birds came and made a bunch of little tracks all over it. Again, the speaker has other options in representing this teasing proposition without the use of *mii*, such as, *Gii-tagoshinoog ina bineshiinsag?*, but it is ultimately a *mii*-clause that was chosen for my ribbing. I have heard this ribbing use of *mii* on various occasions.

What is ultimately significant here is that *mii* serves as a discourse stressor in much the same way that English uses intonation contours to mark the same function within English discourse. As noted in Fairbanks (2008), *mii* does not make use of intonation contours within discourse as English does. English speakers make use of intonational contours to increase the illocutionary force of narratives, while Ojibwe speakers use *mii* for this same function. When used in this way, *mii* may make the utterances that it occurs with more serious. This can be seen in the following excerpt from a letter written by a native speaker (Na-gan-i-gwun-eb 'Leading-Feather-Sitting') to Reverend Gilfillan in 1893. While reading the following excerpt, readers might find it helpful to ask themselves why *mii* is being used in (68b, c).

(68)   *mii* in serious statements[21] (Na-gan-i-gwun-eb 1893)

(a)   *Niijii*   *bangii*   *giwiindamoon.*
       my friend   a little   I tell it to you

(b)   **Mii**-*sa*   *agaawaa*   *gii-dagwishinaan.*
       that-is   hardly   that I arrived

(c)   **Mii**-*gegaa*   *gii-pi-niboyaan.*
       so-almost   that I died coming

(d)   *Aapiji*   *ningii-pi-aakoz*   *nayaanzh*   *biinish*   *noongom.*
       extremely   I was sick coming   even   till   now

(e)   *Gegaa*   *zhayigwa*   *negadamaan*   *o'ow*   *aki.*
       almost   already   I leaving   this   earth

(f)   *Endogwen*   *geyaabi*   *midaasogon*   *ge-bimaadiziyaan.*
       it is doubtful   yet   ten days   that I will be living

(a)   'My comrade, a little I tell you.

(b)   [**Mii**-sa] I barely made it here.

(c)   [**Mii**] I almost died.

(d)   I'm really sick even until today.

(e)　It's almost time for me to leave this earth.

(f)　It is doubtful that I have ten days left to live.'

In (68), there are two tokens of *mii* within *mii-* clauses, and the question immediately becomes, why? If *mii* is understood to be a discourse sequencer here, then the use of *mii-* clauses here is odd, since it is unclear what temporal events *mii* would be linking. The deictic function of *mii* (that is, its pointing function) does not appear to be indicated here either. Furthermore, the use of *mii-* clauses to begin letters in this fashion is inconsistent with the writing patterns of other letters from native speakers to Reverend Gilfillan. If we take into account the context of this letter, however, it becomes immediately clear why the speaker uses *mii-* clauses in (68b, c). The speaker uses *mii* as a discourse stressor (or as a veridical marker) as result of the severity of the context in which it is said. In other words, *mii* marks the speaker's statements *I barely made it here* and *I almost died* as being serious and dire. The speaker is conveying to Reverend Gilfillan the seriousness of his statements, which were indeed very serious.

3.2.1.2　*mii* as a command softener

Mii may have a softening effect as well when used with imperatives. When used in this manner, *mii* usually co-occurs with the preverbal unit *izhi* and has the effect of decreasing the force of imperatives to the point that they are really not imperatives any longer, but suggestions. This may be seen in the following example from one of my meetings with the elders. I was eyeing a bowl of delicious wild rice with cut-up wieners in it. I had already had a few bowls but still wanted more. One of the elders, Maggie Kegg, caught me looking at the bowl and said to me the following utterance accented by *mii* and preverb (or relative root) *izhi*.

(69)　*mii* as an imperative softener

> **Mii-go**　　　**izhi-gidaanawen.**
> DM-EMPH　　RR-eat it up
>
> 'Go ahead and eat it up.'
> 'It's okay if you eat it up.'
> 'Just eat it up.'

On examination, a few things are noticeable. First, *mii* is not functioning as a deictic particle, as an aspectual marker, or as a discourse sequencer. Rather, its function here is purely to soften the "blow" of the imperative *gidaanowen* 'eat it up!' so that it is less direct to interlocutors. Second, the preverbal unit *izhi*, whose function in other contexts is as a relative root or as a discourse sequencer itself, has no referent outside the imperative construction on which to perform a sequencing function. The use of *mii* and *izhi* in this way is, therefore, characterized here as idiomatic. The elders also reported that the use of the emphatic clitic *-go* in these types of constructions is optional, showing that forms such as *mii izhi-gidaanawen* are also grammatical.

3.2.1.3 *awenh, inenh*

Mystery particle *awenh* is used to deny prior propositions, always occurs in initial position, and is usually followed by a pause (marked in examples by a comma). It may occur alone as well. An example of this lone usage occurred when one of the elders was complaining about the state of the language and made the comment that there weren't any more speakers left. To this, another elder interjected with a resounding *Awenh!* 'Nuh uh!' An example of *awenh* within texts is given in (70).

(70) Denying particle *awenh*

(a) (Mille Lacs sessions)

Awenh!
DM
'Nuh uh!'

(b) (Clark 1998a, 8, audio)

Awenh,	*gaawiin-sa*	*niin*	*wiikaa*	*zhiiwitaagan*	*gemaa-ge*	*iw*
nuh uh	not-DM	I	ever	salt	or-also	that

waasamoomakakoons	*ige*	*ingimoodisiin.*
battery	also	I didn't steal

'Nuh huh, I never stole any salt or battery.'

Interestingly, the elders explained that *awenh* is the word that males use and *inenh* is the women's version. In actual practice, however, women also use *awenh*. The person who made the resounding interjection in (70a) was Elfreda, and one of the other female elders also admitted that even though she knows that *awenh* is primarily used by males, she uses it too.

3.2.1.4 *aaniish*

Mystery particle *aaniish* has varying forms. Most often it occurs as the cluster *aaniish naa*, with minor occurrences of a phonologically reduced form, *aanish naa*, or lone particle *aanish*. The use of *naa* appears to increase the illocutionary force of *aaniish* (for more on *naa*, see section 3.2.2.7). Also, when queried, speakers inflate the reduced form *aanish* back to *aaniish*. Therefore, I will collectively refer to all variants as just *aaniish*. The major function of *aaniish* is to mark justifications or qualifications of actions, behaviors, or conditions, having the force of the English *well, after all*, or the phrase *what do you expect?* A typical situation in which *aaniish* might be used is where there is some misalignment of expectations or assumptions, on the part of either the speaker or some other person in relation to someone or something, and the speaker feels a need to provide some statement that would explain, qualify, justify, or reconcile that misalignment. Examples of this usage are shown with all three variants in the following examples.

(71) Justifying function of *aaniish*

(a) (Kegg 1993, 106)

"Aaniish   naa   indanokiimin   gaye   dapaabiyaan,"   ikido.
DM   DM   we are working   also   that I look out   she says

'"**Well**, it was because we were working, and I looked out," she said.'

(b) (Kegg 1993, 136)

Aanish   naa   mashkawizii   a'aw   biindaakwaan   iidog,
DM   DM   be strong   that   snuff   must be

biindaakweng . . .
taking a pinch of snuff

'[**After all**] How strong that snuff must be taken in a pinch.'

(c)   (Clark 1998b, 54–56, audio)

(i)   ***Aanish***   *ingagwejimigoog.*
       DM   they ask me

(ii)   *Mii   gaa-izhi-wiindamawagwaa,   "Mii-go izhi-boonitoog,"   ingii-inaag.*
       DP   and so I told them   leave it alone   I told them

(i)   '**Well**, they asked me.

(ii)   That's when I told them, "Leave it alone," I told them.'

In (71a), a woman had stated that the "drunks" were keeping her up all night, and
when it had become calm, she looked out of her window early in the morning
and saw a mysterious tall figure walking around at someone's house. It is then
that she uses *aaniish naa* to accent the statement *it was because we were working* in (71a), where she appears to justify why she was looking out of her window.
In short, she was checking on the drunks but saw the mysterious figure instead.
Prior to making the statement in (71b), Maude Kegg related that as a little girl
she once got seriously ill from taking a pinch of snuff tobacco and putting it in
her mouth (apparently to imitate the adults). She started throwing up and was
nearly convulsing. She used *aanish naa* to accent her utterance in (71b), which
represents a justification for her sudden illness. In (71c), Jim Clark was asked by
a man to explain how one might mix the Indian religion with the white man's
religion in order to practice both. Rather than providing them with the answer
they want, he tells them that they should not mix the two and to leave it alone.
Because his answer is contrary to expectation, he qualifies his statement *they
asked me* with *aanish* in order to convey the attitude *they asked me for my opinion and I gave it to them even though they didn't like it*. In all of these examples,
there is some misalignment of expectation that the speaker must address. In
(71a), a reader of the story might misunderstand why the woman was looking
out of her window early in the morning; in (71b), Kegg did not expect snuff
tobacco to be so potent; and in (71c), the man asking about combining religions
was presumably expecting an answer that was in line with his expectations, but
he ultimately did not get one. For such misalignments, the various speakers in
these examples provided statements that sought either to correct the respective
misalignment or to justify it.

Sometimes *aaniish* allows the speaker to provide extra-topical information or extra-topical background information through a qualification of some action or behavior. This is shown in the following example, where Maude Kegg uses *aanish naa* to qualify her own hard work.

(72) Using *aaniish* to provide extra-topical background information (Kegg 1993, 60–61)

(a) Gii-agaasaani   azhigwa   ogitigaan   gaa-o-bashkwashkibidood.
    it was small   now   her garden   that she weeded

(b) **Aanish**   **naa**   niwiidookawaa gaye niin bangii go   imaa;
    DM   DM   I help her   also   me   a little EMPH there

    azhigwa onaagoshig gaye gaa-izhi-giizhiitaad, imaa adaawewigamigong
    now   evening   also   and so she finished   there   at the store

    biindiged, dibaajimod, dibaajimoyaang gii-kiizhiikamaang gitigaan.
    enters   tells of   we tell of   we finished it   garden

(a) 'The garden she went to weed was small.

(b) **Well**, I helped her a little there, and then when it was getting to be evening she finished, went into the store, and said that we had finished the garden.'

In (72), the use of *aanish naa* appears to help Maude qualify her own contribution to her grandmother's weeding.[22] In other words, by using *aanish naa*, Maude appears to be saying, *Lest you think I didn't help my grandmother, you're wrong, because I did.* The evidence for this comes from (72a), where Maude explicitly states that it was her grandmother who went to weed the garden, apparently forgetting to include her own (the speaker's) contribution. As a remedy, she uses *aanish naa* in (72b) to qualify her statement of her own hard work, albeit a small contribution.

Sometimes *aaniish* marks some resolve or determination to do something after a good reason or motivation to do so has presented itself. Many times the resolution is the natural choice among other possibilities. This is illustrated in the following example.

(73)   *aaniish* marking resolve

(a)   (Kegg 1993, 110–11)

    (i)   "*Miinawaa   giizhikaandag   agoozh   imaa   endaayan.*"
        and   cedar bough   hang him/her   there   your house

    (ii)   ***Aaniish   naa   mii*** *azhigwa   gaa-izhi-asag   a'aw   giizhikaandag*
         DM   DM   DP   when   and so I put   that   cedar bough

        imaa   ishkwaandeming.
        there   at the door

    (i)   '"And hang a cedar bough there where you live."

    (ii)   **Well**, then I put a cedar bough there at the door.'

(b)   (Clark 1998c, 20, audio)

    (i)   *Giwaabandaanaawaadog   ko   awiiya   zhishigagowed.*
        you all must see   customarily   someone   vomits

    (ii)   *Mii   sa   go   gaa-izhinawag   i'iw   enaanzod*
        DP   DM   EMPH   how I perceived him/her   that   how she/he is colored

        a'aw   bebezhigooganzhii.
        that   horse

    (iii)   ***Aanish*** *mii   sa   iidog   Zhishigagowaan   inga-izhinikaanaa.*
         DM   DP   DM   DUB   Puke   I'll call him/her

    (i)   'You must've all seen when someone throws up.

    (ii)   That's how he looked to me in his color.

    (iii)   **Well**, I'm going to name him Puke.'

In (73a), the speaker was advised by her cousin to hang a cedar bough at her house in order to keep an evil being from coming around. Not wanting to risk it, she resolves to hang up the cedar bough. Her resolve is marked by *aaniish naa* in (73a.ii). In (73b), the speaker was given a new horse, and because the horse had spots on it that resembled vomit (i.e., it was an appaloosa), he decided to call his new horse Puke. He prefaces his statement of resolve in (73b.iii) with *aaniish*. In both cases, the speakers have choices: the expected choice, or the unexpected one. In (73a), for example, the speaker has two choices: hang the bough, or don't.

Since it is in the speaker's best interest to hang the bough, she does so. In (74b), the speaker may call his horse anything he wants but opts to call the horse as he perceives it, as looking like puke.

The common thread through all of these examples is the constant presence of competing expectations, a potential for misalignment of those expectations, and the pressure to reconcile those expectations. Many times, misaligned expectations or assumptions can have negative consequences for the speaker, who runs the risk of looking lazy or foolish or whose actions or motivations might be misunderstood by interlocutors. As a remedy for this, a speaker may use *aaniish* to provide justifications, qualifications, or explanations that would align interlocutor expectations and assumptions with those of the speaker.

3.2.2   Second-position mystery particles

The mystery particles in the following sections all occur in the second position of a sentence or clause. The second-position markers to be discussed in the following sections are *isa, sha, gosha, bina,* and *naa.* Many of these mystery particles also occur within a number of discourse marker clusters. The clusters to be discussed are *sa go, sha go naa, gosha naa, sha naa, da naa, bina naa,* and *sa naa.* Also, because it has been the practice for other researchers to analyze such clusters as occurring in one position rather than in multiple positions, I will follow that practice here (see Brody 1989; Davidsen-Nielsen 1996; Torres 2006). For example, the cluster in bold type in the expression *gaawiin **sha go naa** indeapiitizisiin* 'I'm not that old' will be analyzed in this book as collectively occurring in second position, not in second, third, and fourth positions, respectively. Also, since the semantics of the individual markers involved in clustering largely remain transparent, that is, a product of its parts, I will first characterize each marker individually and then discuss its use within clusters rather than providing one huge section on all of the clusters.

3.2.2.1   *isa*

Mystery particle *isa* (which sometimes occurs as clitic *-sa*) is a general marker of CONCLUSIVITY or FINALITY. In other words, *isa* signals that some event, utterance, or narrative has come to an end. This core function has differing manifestations within discourse, such as marking narrative closings, relinquishments (signaling that the speaker's efforts have ceased), conclusory gist statements

(statements that get to the point after the speaker has provided some fuzzy details) and resulting action (actions that occur as a result of some event or events) and strengthening the speaker's position or disposition (abating the position or disposition of others in prior discourse). One other minor function of *isa* is as a placeholder, allowing speaker pause within discourse.

3.2.2.1.1 isa *as a marker of closings*

One of the most common uses of *isa* is to mark the end of a story or narrative, marking conclusivity on the action plane of discourse. It has roughly the meaning or attitude of the English *it is finally time*. It is on the action plane of discourse because the speaker uses *isa* to signal that an end to his or her discourse has arrived. These closings typically involve the use of demonstrative pronoun *i'iw* 'that' and quantitative particle *minik* 'amount' along with the deictic particle *mii* in the formation of *mii*- clauses (regarding *mii*- clauses, see Fairbanks 2008; Valentine 2001, 963–73; Rhodes 1998, 286–94). The following expressions are typical endings for the stories told by Maude Kegg (1993).

(74) Narrative closings

(a) *Mii* **sa** *go* *i'iw.*
    DP DM EMPH that

    'That's it.'

(b) *Mii* **sa** *go* *minik.*
    DP DM EMPH amount

    'That's all.'

In Maude's collection of stories (a total of forty-one stories), closings that employed the use of *isa* or *sa* were by far the most common. Less common were closing statements without *isa*. In the absence of *isa*, it was the propositional content that bore much of the burden of signaling the end to the story. As with the conclusory closings involving *isa* previously, the conclusory expressions without *isa* also employed the use of *mii*- clauses. In Maude's stories (Kegg 1993), there were only three such occurrences. These closing expressions are given in the following example.

(75) Closing *mii-* phrases without *isa*

(a)   *Mii*   *i'iw.*

       DP   it

       'That's it' (lit. 'that is it', but idiomatically to end a discourse)

(b)   *Mii*   *eta*   *go*   *imaa*   *minik*   *gezikwendamaan.*

       DP   only   EMPH there   amount what I remember

       'And that's all I remember of that.'

(c)   *Miish* *eta* *imaa* *minik*   *gekendamaan.*

       and   that   only   there amount what I remember

       'That's all I remember.'

While explicit propositional content may form the basis of a closing, mystery particle *isa* shows that it may carry much of the burden that a purely propositional expression may have. With the exception of the idiomatic expression in (75a), the amount of burden carried by *isa* is evident, for without it (at least for these examples), more propositional content appears in order to do the work of concluding or giving up the floor.

3.2.2.1.2 isa *as a marker of relinquishment*

While *isa* marks narrative closures on an action plane of discourse, it has another function within the interactional plane of discourse, marking a general attitude of speaker relinquishment. This function is interactional because *isa* may be used to signal that a speaker has relinquished his or her time to provide an answer to a question or has given up. For example, anytime questions arose that required a lot of discussion and contemplation on the part of the elders and that did not eventually end with an answer, the use of *isa* was commonly heard in their expressions of relinquishment. In such cases, there is a question put forward, a period of contemplation on the part of the addressee, and then a relinquishing expression accented by *isa* that releases the addressee from the responsibility of providing an answer; that is, *isa* shows that the speaker has relinquished his or her effort and has, in effect, given up in trying to either recall or figure out the answer. I have heard the following phrases from the elders on numerous occasions.

(76)   General attitude of relinquishment

(a)   *Mii-**sa***   *go*   *namanj.*
      VER-DM.CL   EMPH   don't know

      'I have no idea.'

(b)   *Mii-**sa***   *gaawiin*   *nigikendanziin.*
      VER-DM.CL   not   I don't know

      'I really don't know.'

This is also shown in the following email interaction with a Mille Lacs Ojibwe speaker. The speaker was asked how he would translate a certain English expression into Ojibwe, to which he stated the following, accenting his response with *isa*:

(77)   *isa* in relinquishment expressions (David Aubid, email communication, 2008)

(a)   *Iw*   *dash*   *gaa-gagwejimiyan.*
      that   and   what you asked me

(b)   *Amanj*   **isa**   *iidog.*
      don't know   DM   DUB

(a)   'And what you asked me about.

(b)   I [**isa**] don't know.'

The propositional content of the expression *amanj iidog* in (77b) itself means *I don't know*. Mystery particle *isa* projects a relinquishment from providing a definitive answer. This is evident because, after he made that comment, he then offered up seven possibilities, one of which he was quite unsure of. The marker *isa* signals to listeners (or email readers) that, after some thought, he has relinquished his responsibility to provide a definitive answer.

3.2.2.1.3   isa *as a marker of conclusory gists*

Within monologic narratives, *isa* has a related function in marking conclusory GISTS, where it has a meaning similar to that of the discourse markers *at any rate* or *anyways* in English. What I mean by *gist* is that the speaker's precursory descriptions culminate in a main point. The exact details of those precursory descriptions, however, are not important, and they are, in a sense, *relinquished* in order to get to the point. In such cases, the speaker offers up a set of general descriptions (which may be guesses or a subgroup of events) of some process, event, or even utterances by other people, after which the speaker provides a gist sentence or expression, accented by *isa*, which gets to the eventual main point. This usage is quite consistent in Maude Kegg's stories, and the following example is typical. It comes from a story about Maude as a little girl seeing a steamboat from a lakeshore. Before seeing this boat, however, she describes the circumstances that allowed her to see it.

(78) *isa* (Kegg 1993, 26–27)

(a) | *Mii* | *eta* | *go* | *imaa* | *gikendamaan* | *namadabiyaan* | *jiigibiig.* |
|---|---|---|---|---|---|---|
| DP | only | EMPH | there | I know | I am sitting | on the shore |

(b) | *Maagizhaa* | *gaye* | *gaa-wewebanaabiiwaagwen,* | *maagizhaa* | *gaye* |
|---|---|---|---|---|
| maybe | also | they must have been fishing | maybe | also |

gaa-ishkwaa-iskigamizigewaagwen.
they must have finished boiling sap

(c) | *Gii-paakibii'an* | **sa** | *wiin* | *igo.* |
|---|---|---|---|
| lake was open | DM | for sure | EMPH |

(d) | *Namadabiyaan* | *ganawaabandamaan* | *gichi-jiimaan* | *bimibidemagak* |
|---|---|---|---|
| I am sitting | I am watching it | big boat | going by |

naawagaam.
middle of lake

(a) 'All I remember is sitting on the shore.
(b) Maybe they were fishing or had just finished boiling sap.
(c) The lake was open **anyway**.
(d) I was sitting there watching a big boat go across the middle of the lake.'

In this story we find Maude sitting on a shore. In (78b), she tries to recall the possible reasons why she was sitting on that shore, such as that they were either fishing or had finished boiling sap. In (78c), using clitic -*sa*, she gets to her point, that is, that the lake was open *anyway*. This point allows her to provide the circumstances that led to the eventual sighting of the big boat in (78d). Note that the exact details in (78b) are really not material to her gist statement in (78c). The use of the hedge word *maagizhaa* 'maybe' and dubitative inflection on the verbs in (78b), that is, *-gwen*, suggests that she is unsure of the exact reasons why she was on that beach. The point that she was making in the end was that the lake was open, and it was this expression that was accented by *-sa*.

Sometimes these gist expressions are summations of prior guesswork. In such cases there are precursory descriptions of events or objects that represent only a subgroup of those events or objects, and then a follow-up expression, accented by *isa*, that sums up those descriptions. The following example illustrates this usage of *isa*.

(79) *isa* (Kegg 1993, 44–45)

Akina	*gegoo*	*omaajiidoonaawaan*		*iniw*	*akikoon,*	*bakwezhigan,*
all	thing	they take him/her along		that	kettles	flour

akina	**sa**	*gegoo*	*waa-aabajitoowaad*	*wii-wiisiniwaad.*
all	DM	thing	what they want to use	when they want to eat

'We took everything along, kettles, flour, everything [**sa**] they wanted to have to eat.'

In this example, *kettles* and *flour* represent a subgroup of items that they would bring along. Again, the exact items are not important. Rather, the point being made here is that they would bring what they wanted to eat, that is, *akina* **sa** *gegoo waa-aabajitoowaad wii-wiisiniwaad* 'everything they wanted to have to eat', and it is this point, or the gist expression, that is accented with *isa*.

3.2.2.1.4 isa *as a marker of resultant action*

Sometimes *isa* marks RESULTANT ACTION, or a RESULTANT CONDITION. There are two essential elements surrounding the use of *isa* in these types of constructions: the event (or events), and an event (accented by *isa*) emanating from that event (or events). In other words, an event (or a series of events) occurs, and as a result of that event (or events), some action or condition, or a logical next step, occurs as a natural consequence of that action. What this means

is the existence of the resultant action is dependent upon the prior event. This
does not mean, however, that there is necessarily a cause-and-effect relationship
(though one may exist) between the event and its resultant event. It only means
that the resultant action or condition somehow emanates from the initial event,
either because it is a logical consequence of that action or because it is *a* next
possible logical step following that event. In short, the first event (or events) acts
as a setup for what eventually happens. This is shown in the following example,
where a mallard duck is killed.

(80) *isa* (Kegg 1993, 58–59)

(a) *Zhiishiib   imaa   gii-paa-ayaa,   ininishib;   mamaad   iniw*
    duck   there   was around there   mallard   takes him/her   that

    asiniin,   gaa-izhi-bakite'waad.
    rock   and so she hit him/her

(b) *Mii   sa   gaa-izhi-niiwana'waad.*
    DP   DM   and so she killed him/her

(a) 'There was a duck there, a mallard, and she picked up a stone and hit it.

(b) She [**sa**] killed it.'

In (80a), a series of events occurs: a mallard duck is spotted on a lake, a rock
is picked up and thrown at it, and it is hit. These events lead to the demise
of the mallard duck, which is captured with resultant phrase, *mii sa gaa-izhi-
niiwana'waad* 'she killed it' in (80b), accented by clitic *-sa*. While this series represents a cause-and-effect relationship, this is not a necessary requirement. The
following example, in which a grandmother volunteers herself and her granddaughter, Maude Kegg, to go weed a garden for someone, shows this. The following morning, they pack a lunch and leave for the garden.

(81) *isa* (Kegg 1993, 58–59)

(a) *Mii   dash   a'aw   nookomis,   "Niin   igo*
    DP   DM   that   my grandmother   I   EMPH

    inga-o-bashkwashkibijige indaanis,"   odinaan   iniw   ikwewan.
    I will go and weed my daughter   she tells her   that   woman

(b)   *"Naawakamigookwe   inga-wiijiiwaa,"*   *ikido.*
      Naawakamigookwe   I go with her   she says

(c)   *Mii*   **sa**   *azhigwa*   *gegizhebaawagadinig*   *aapiji*   *gaa-izhi-nawapwaaniked,*
      DP   DM   now   in the morning   early   and so she made a lunch

      maagizhaa   *gaye*   *bakwezhiganan*   *gaa-maajiinaagwen*
      maybe   also   bread   what she must have took along

      miinawaa   *akikoonsan—maagizhaa*   *gaye*   *waa-aniibiishikegwen*
      and   little pail   probably   also   what she wants to make tea with

      imaa,   *gaa-onji-maajiinaad*   *iniw*   *akikoonsan,*   *akikoon,*   *akikoonsan*
      there   why she took it along   that   little pail   pail   a little pail

      igo—   *gaa-izhi-maajaayaang.*
      EMPH   and so we left

(a)   "'I'll go and weed her garden, my daughter," my grandmother told the woman.

(b)   "I'll go with Naawakamigookwe," she said.

(c)   Real [**sa**] early in the morning, she made a lunch, maybe she took bread along
      and a little pail—I guess she took along the little pail because she wanted to
      make tea in it—and then we left.'

The initial event in (81a–b) is the grandmother's volunteering for the weeding.
The resultant event in (81c) is them preparing a lunch the following morning
and leaving for the garden. This resultant event is accented by clitic *-sa*. The
initial volunteering is not the cause of their departure for the garden but is the
reason for it. The departure represents a natural consequence emanating from
their initial act of volunteering, and it is this event that is marked by *-sa*.

3.2.2.1.5   isa *as a position strengthener*

Mystery particle *isa* is also used in situations where there is an incongruence between competing propositions, perspectives, dispositions, or expectations. Many
times, this is an obvious incongruence, and the use of *isa* in such cases allows
the speaker to project an attitude that his or her perspective (or propositional
content put forth by the speaker) trumps, challenges, or corrects any challeng-
ing perspectives, positions, or dispositions, and that his or her position should be
the prevailing one, and obviously so. This function has the effect of ultimately

strengthening the speaker's position. This is shown by the following example, where an Ojibwe man is standing before a judge to be charged with assault and battery. He misinterprets the judge's indictment, however, and offers a defense against that misinterpreted indictment. His defense is accented by *isa* (in this case, clitic *-sa*).

(82)   Position strengthening feature of *isa* (Clark 1998a, 8, audio)

(a) | *Miish* | *ige* | *wiindamaagod* | *odigoon* | | *iniw* | *dibaakonigewininiwan,* |
      |---------|-------|----------------|----------|--|--------|------------------------|
      | and then | also | he tells him | he says to him | | that | judge |

"You	*are*	*charged*	*to*	*the*	*salt*	*and*	*battery,"*	*inaa*	*giiwenh.*
you	are	charged	to	the	salt	and	battery	he is told	apparently

(b) | *Ganawaabamaad* | *iniw* | *dibaakonigewininiwan,* | *"Awenh,* | *gaawiin-sa* |
      |-----------------|--------|------------------------|----------|-------------|
      | looking at him | that | judge | | nuh uh   not-DM |

niin	*wiikaa*	*zhiiwitaagan*	*gemaa-ge*	*iw*	*waasamoomakakoons*	*ige*
I	ever	salt	or also	that	battery	also

ingimoodisiin,"	*odinaan*	*giiwenh*	*mii*	*iw*	*gaa-initang.*
I did not steal it	he tells him	apparently	DP	that	the way he heard it

(a)   'And also the judge apparently tells him, "You are charged to the salt and battery."

(b)   Looking at the judge, he tells him apparently how he heard it, "Nuh uh, I [sa] never stole any salt or battery."'

Not having a good command of the English language, the Ojibwe man misinterprets the judge's indictment of *assault* and *battery* as being an indictment of stealing some *salt* and a *battery*. In (82b), the Ojibwe man accents his denial *nuh uh, I never stole any salt or battery* with *isa* (in this case, clitic *-sa*). While the propositional content of his denial forms the basis of his defense, mystery particle *isa* allows him to make his case against a charge that he views as ridiculous. In other words, *isa* appears to allow him to express an attitude such as, *I would never do such a silly thing, how dare you think that I would do such a thing.* Functionally speaking, *isa* allows the Ojibwe man to establish his position as the prevailing view, albeit under false pretenses.

Another example of this usage appears in the following example, in which a little girl, Maude Kegg, was taking beads away from the adults. Instead of taking beads from them, she was urged to go around to all the wigwams to beg for beads. Here, while there is no charge of guilt or a defense against that charge, there is indeed a competition of dispositions: those of the adults and that of the child.

(83) *isa* (Kegg 1993, 92–93)

(a)   "*Naawakamigook,*"   *ikido*   *bezhig*   *a'aw*   *ninoshenh,*   "*aaniin*   *nanda*
       Naawakamigook   she says   one   that   my aunt   why   DM

       babaa-zaagidon[23]   *imaa*   *iniw*   *wiigiwaaman!*"
       go around begging   there   those   wigwams

(b)   *Ingikinoo'amaag-sh*   *ge-ikidoyaan.*
       she taught me   what I will say

(c)   "*Giga-miinigoo*   *manidoominensag.*
       you will be given   beads

(d)   *Mii*   *mewinzha*   *gaa-izhichigeng.*"
       DP   long ago   what was done

(e)   *Inzhaagwenim*   **isa**.
       I am hesitant   DM

(f)   *Ingagiibaadiz.*
       I am foolish

(g)   *Indagaashiinh.*
       I am small

(h)   *Nimisawenimaag*   *gaye*   *ingiw*   *manidoominensag,*   *gaa-izhi-agwazhe'id*
       I want them   also   those   beads   so she covered me

       moshwens.
       shawl

(a)   "'Naawakamigook," said one of my aunts, "why don't you go around and beg there at the wigwams?"

(b)   She taught me what to say.

(c)   "You'll be given beads.

(d) This is what they used to do long ago."

(e) I was hesitant **isa**.

(f) I was foolish.

(g) I was small.

(h) But I wanted the beads badly, so she covered me with a shawl.'

Here, Naawakamigookwe (Maude Kegg as a little girl), is urged to beg for beads and is even told what to say at the entrance of the wigwams. Reflecting upon this at the telling of this story, she reveals in (83e) that she was hesitant at the time and accents this statement with *isa*. In (83f–g), she even goes on to give justification for her hesitation, that is, that she was *foolish* and *small*. Underlying this, there are two dispositions at play in this story: that of the girl's aunts, who want her (a little girl) to go around to all the wigwams to beg for beads, and the little girl's hesitancy due to her childish nature and size. While the propositional content in (83e–g) forms the basis of her disposition, the use of *isa* allows her obvious difference in perspective, that is, that a little girl would have the fortitude to go around begging for beads. It allows her to show that her disposition is contrary to their disposition, reinforcing her disposition against that of her aunts. In short, *isa* allows the speaker to project the attitude, *I obviously could not do such a thing, contrary to what they think.*

The proposition-challenging feature of *isa* can be seen in the following exchange, found in a story in the Nett Lake dialect, which is related to the Mille Lacs dialect. In this story, two brothers who are still in their mother's womb are fighting over who will be the first to be born. One says that he will be, and the other challenges him with a remark accented by *isa*.

(84) *isa* (W. Jones 1917, 4–5)

(a) *O'ow   idash   madwe-ikidowan:*   "*Niin   ninga-zaziikiz.*"
    this   but   the other is heard saying   I   I will be the eldest

(b) "*Gaawiin,*" *madwe-ikido*   *bezhig* *biinish* *igo*   *ikido*   *aw*
    not   he is heard saying one   even   EMPH   he says   that

    bezhig: "*Gaawiin   gidaa-zaziikizisii.*
    one   not   you could not be the eldest

(c)   *Niin   **isa**   ninga-zaziikiz."*
       I   DM   I will be the eldest

(a)   'This was what one was heard to say: "I wish to be the first brought forth."

(b)   "No," one was heard saying, even did one say, "you cannot be the first-born.

(c)   I am [**isa**] the one to be the eldest."'

Sometimes *isa* is involved in propositional contrasts in such a manner that the propositional standing of the proposition containing *isa* is strengthened in relation to prior propositions. As in (84), a speaker may exert his or her dominance over another by the use of *isa*, but speakers may also increase the illocutionary force of a proposition by the use of *isa*. This can be seen in the following example, where two ways of handling knowledge are being contrasted.

(85)   *isa* (Clark 1998b, 56, audio)

(a)   *A'aw   dash   Chi-mookomaan   kina   gegoo   wiin   gekendang*
       that   but   white people   all   thing   him/her   what he knows

       mazina'iganing   ogii-ozhitoon,   mazina'iganing   ogii-ozhibii'aan.
       in a book   she/he makes it   in a book   she/he writes it

(b)   *Miish   igo   akina   awiiya   noongom   ge-nisidotanzig*
       and then EMPH   all   someone   today   she/he would not understand it

       aanawi-go   odaa-agindaan.
       even though   he could read it

(c)   *Gaawiin-sh   gegoo   wiin   imaa   odaa-ondinanziin*
       not   thing   him/her there   she/he would not get it from there

       mazina'iganing   ji-agindang   noongom.
       in a book   if she/he reads it   today

(d)   *Aano-gikendaasod,   gaawiin   odaa-gashkitoosiin   ji-gikendang*
       even though she/he is smart   not   she/he would be able   to know it

       i'iw   enamanji'od   a'aw   Anishinaabe.
       that   what he means   that   Indian

(e)   *Imaa   **isa**   wiin   i-gaa-ina'oonind,   ke   gaawiin*
       there   DM   him/her   the thoughts she/he was given see   not

> *wiin*   *ingoji*   *okanawisinzinini* *ogii-ozhibii'anziin*
> him/her somewhere it is not written   she/he does not write it
>
> *i-gaa-pi-ina'oonind.*
> the thoughts that she/he was given

(a)   'But as for white people, they put everything they know into a book.

(b)   And no one today would understand it even though they could read it.

(c)   They wouldn't get anything out of it if they read it today.

(d)   Even though they are knowledgeable about it, Indians wouldn't be able to know the true meaning of it.

(e)   With [isa] the knowledge that he was given, you see, their knowledge wasn't written anywhere.'

In this story, the speaker was asked whether it would be possible to combine the Indian religion and the white man's religion into one. This query ultimately led the speaker to contrast the ways in which white people and Indian people handle their knowledge. While there is a contrast being made between these propositions, this contrast is largely a pragmatic one due to the contrasting content inherent in the propositions themselves. The use of *isa*, therefore, is not marking contrast in the way that, say, *idash* does; instead it is used to strengthen the illocutionary force of the Indian way of handling knowledge. It allows the speaker to exert and validate the Indian way of handling knowledge. In other words, the nuance that *isa* allows to be displayed might be equivalent to the following: *They have their way and we have our own. Let them do it their way, and we'll do it our way, which is a perfectly legitimate way of doing it.*

3.2.2.1.6 isa *as a placeholder*

Some minor uses of *sa* appear to be as CONTINUERS, or as placeholders, a function similar to that of the marker *uh* in English.[24] Used in this way, *sa* functions to maintain the floor for the speaker, allowing the speaker to continue his or her story in preparation for upcoming talk. Many times (but not always), pauses or very slight pauses occur after *sa* and do not exhibit sentence-final intonation. That these usages are narrative continuers is evinced by the high frequency of their use in stories that are being made up on the spot, as opposed to narratives based upon real-life events, in which details are not being fabricated as the story goes on. For example, most of the stories I have collected for this book average zero to five occurrences of *sa* per story. In one story that was completely made up on the spot, there were a total of eleven occurrences of *sa*. Also, in the Gilfillan letters (from the 1800s), Reverend Gilfillan usually glossed *sa* as 'rest voice'. While this is not its only function (and this gloss may have been used overproductively), it is a function that speakers are consciously aware of. A few examples of this usage should suffice. Commas in these examples represent significant pauses in the narrative by Jim Clark.

(86) (Clark 2003a, 52, audio)

Mii	*imaa*	*onzaam*	*enigok-ko*		*owiikwajitoonaawaa*	*iw,*
DP	there	overly	try hard — customarily		they try	that

i'iw-sa,	*anooj*	*idi*	*keyaa*	*wiin*	*enaabaji'aawaad*	*anow*
that-DM	various	there	way	him/her	how they utilize	this

asemaan . . .
tobacco

'That's when they try too hard, **that uh**, in the various ways they are utilizing tobacco . . .'

(87) (Clark 2003a, 50, audio)

Endogwen	*igo*	*gikendamogwen*	*awegonen*	*nendodang*
it is doubtful	EMPH	that he knows	what	what he's asking for

o'ow-sa,	*enwed*	*gaa-ina'oonind*		*wiin*	*wayaabishkiiwed*
this-DM	language	that was given to him		him	white person

ge-wiin	*ji-inwed.*
also — him	to speak

'I don't know if he knows what he's asking for with **this uh**, language that was given to the White Man to speak.'

For this speaker, *sa* rarely showed up except in spots such as these, where there was some hesitation or pause before continuing on.

3.2.2.1.7 sa go

Mystery particle *isa* sometimes occurs with the emphatic marker *igo* to form
the cluster *sa go*, which has the major function of allowing speakers to make
interjections that are somehow connected to something that has just been mentioned within the discourse, or as a result of some event. Interjected content may
be conclusory gist statements, elaboration, or just extra information, whether it
be relevant or irrelevant. It is almost as if the speaker, once a topic or event has
been brought up, remembers something significant about that topic or event
and interjects it into the discourse. It is important to note that these so-called
RESULTANT INTERJECTIONS typically occur as a *result* or consequence of some
aforementioned topic or event. Utterances with the cluster *sa go* typically do not
occur as the initial statement. The use of *sa go* in making resultant interjections
can be seen in the following example, where the speaker makes an interjection
that is not relevant to the story at hand but is relevant to a topic just mentioned,
that is, playing on the shore.

(88)   *sa go* (Kegg 1993, 116–17)

(a)   *Mii   imaa   jiibaakwewaad   ingiw   ikwewag,*
      DP   there   they are cooking   those   women

      wii-sagaswe'iwewaad,   *izhiwidoowaad   imaa   niimi'idiiwigamigong.*
      when they want to have a feast   they bring it   there   to the dance lodge

(b)   *Babaa-dazhiitaayaan*   *jiigibiig   imaa   neyaashing,   giigoozensag*
      I am playing around there   shore   there   at the point   minnows

      imbabaa-debibinaag.
      I am going around catching them

(c)   *Anooj   **sa   go**   imaa   asiniinsan   imaa.*
      various   DM   DM   there   little rocks   there

(d)   *Baanimaa   go   imaa   inaabiyaan   agidaaki*
      suddenly   EMPH   there   I look there   on top of the hill

      gaa-namadabid,   mii   a'aw   Gichi-jaagigaabaw   gii-inaa.
      he who was sitting   DP   that   Gichi-jaagigaabaw   he was called

(e)   *Oo,   yay,   gichi-zegiziyaan.*
      oh   goodness   I am really scared

(a)   'The women cooked there for the feast and took it to the dance lodge.

(b)   I was playing around on the shore at the point catching minnows.

(c)   There were [**sa go**] all sorts of stones there.

(d)   Suddenly I looked up and there was Gichi-jaagigaabaw as he was called sitting on top of the hill.

(e)   Oh, goodness, I was very scared.'

In this excerpt, the speaker (the little girl) was playing around on the shore when she noticed an old man who really scared her sitting on top of the hill. The overall story is really about how the little girl stole fry bread in order to feed an old man who was always taunting her by saying things such as *I'm gonna eat you* and *I'm gonna marry you when you grow up*. In her description of what she was doing when she noticed the old man sitting on the hill, she interjects the fact that there were all sorts of stones on the shore. Now, these stones make no further appearance in the story, showing that their mention is purely an interjection. Though the stones are irrelevant to the story as a whole, they are relevant to her prior mention of her playing on the shore, catching minnows.

Another, similar use shows up in the next excerpt, from a story about the making of a *bootaagan*, a device used to dehusk wild rice. The speaker explains how they took care of the *bootaagan* to make sure it never got wet and that they would cover it with a birch bark roll when it rained. Notice that her interjection about covering the *bootaagan* at night is accented with *sa go*.

(89) *sa go* (Kegg 1993, 128–29)

Mii	*ezhi-wenda-ganawenimangid*		*igo*	*weweni*	*gaye*
DP	then we really take care of him/her		EMPH	carefully	also

ji-nisaabaawesig		*ezhi-badagwana'wangid,*	*maagizhaa*
so that she/he does not get wet		then we cover him/her	maybe

gaye	*wiigwaasabakway*	*imaa*	*gimiwang,*	*niibaa-dibik*	*sa*	*go*
also	birch bark roll	there	when it rains	at night	DM	DM

gaye	*aabaji'aasiwangid.*
also	when we do not use him/her

'We took care of it properly so it didn't get wet, covering it, perhaps with a birch bark roll, when it rained or at night [**sa go**] when we weren't using it.'

Though the English translation does not capture the function of *sa go* very well (due to the broad translations), it appears that the speaker was very deliberate about mentioning the fact that they used to cover the *bootaagan* when it rained (to prevent it from getting wet) but then apparently remembered that they also covered the *bootaagan* at night when they were not using it. This point is interjected and accented by *sa go*. The fact that the final utterance, accented by *sa go*, is offset by a comma suggests that the speaker was indeed making an interjection here, that is, a resultant interjection.

One final example of the use of *sa go* occurred after I asked a question that apparently stumped one of the elders, Marge Anderson. After a long silence ensued, she interjected the following utterance, accenting it with *sa go*.

(90) *sa go* (Mille Lacs session)

Mii	*sa*	*go*	*wawaanimigooyaan.*	(after having been stumped)
DP	DM	DM	that I am stumped	

'They stumped me.'

What all these examples show is that the core meaning of *isa* (or its clitic form, *sa*) in marking finality or resultant content is still largely transparent within the cluster *sa go*. Though the cluster has an additional function in marking interjected content, it is content that occurs as a direct result of prior discourse. Recall also that *sa go* made its appearance in the closing of narratives as well.

There are cases of *sa go*, however, where it functions as a continuer, similar to the use of the lone particle *isa* as a placeholder (as previously described). This usage appears to be purely stylistic and quite individualized. For example, one speaker at Mille Lacs was well known for accenting his public discourses with a generous use of *sa go* as a way of continuing his narrative, or as a way to allow himself time to think of what to say next. I have observed this stylistic use of *sa go* only by him. At any rate, *isa* is a very prolific particle and still has uses that remain unexplored. It is clear, though, that its many functions within discourse largely stem from its core function of marking finality.

3.2.2.2   *gosha*

Mystery particle *gosha* has traditionally been characterized as an emphatic particle or an emphatic particle that heightens assertiveness (Nichols and Nyholm 1995, 61; Rhodes 1985, 176). While it is true that *gosha* may add an assertive flavor to utterances, for example, *Kaa gsha wiin* 'No, and that's final' (Rhodes 1985, 176), I submit here that this assertiveness is only one of the nuances emanating from *gosha*'s core function as a marker of ACTUALITY. Its use typically allows speakers to reveal the true state of reality (imagined or real) either to themselves or to other interlocutors. *Gosha* usually arises where there is a conflicting view of reality on the part of interlocutors. In resolving this conflict, the use of *gosha* has the result of *setting the record straight*, as it were. Given this characterization, it is easy to see why *gosha* (or *gsha* in Eastern Ojibwe) might have an assertive nuance, especially in a situation where two competing worldviews are at play. For example, a spoiled child might want candy, but responsible parents who know better might assert their authority over their child by refusing to buy candy for their child. The use of *gosha* in a statement such as *kaa ghsa wiin* reveals to the child the actual state of things, that is, that candy is not good for him or her and that Mom or Dad is not going to buy it. The point being made here, of course, is that *gosha* is assertive in this case only because of the context in which the utterance is said and because of *gosha*'s core function as a marker of actuality, not because *gosha* encodes assertiveness. This is supported by the data, where the subtle play of context and the use of *gosha* to mark actuality results in other nuances, many of which are obviously not assertive. For example, in the following story the use of *gosha* reveals that what was initially thought to be a serious situation really was not, resulting in a feeling of relief. Here a little girl, Maude Kegg, had stolen and later had eaten some fine, broken wild rice that flew out from a winnowing basket. Later that night she became bloated from eating the rice and started throwing up. Her grandmother got really scared, as there was no Indian doctor around. In the end, her grandmother figured out that she was just bloated, accenting her statement with *gosha*.

(91) *gosha* (Kegg 1993, 132–33)

> *"Oonh, yay yay, baasinigo **gosha** wa'aw," ikido.*
> oh goodness she/he is bloated DM this she/he says
>
> *Mii gaa-izhi-ishkwaa-zegizid.*
> DP so she stopped being scared
>
> "'Oh, goodness gracious, she's just bloated [**gosha**]," she said, and so she wasn't scared anymore.'

Here, Maude's grandmother, not knowing initially what is wrong with her granddaughter, is really frightened by her granddaughter's condition. It is only after finding out that it is because her granddaughter is bloated from eating winnowed wild rice, and not something more serious, that her grandmother is relieved. By accenting *baasinigo* 'she is bloated' with *gosha*, she is revealing the true state of Maude's condition and that it was not as serious as initially thought. We can tell this from the following utterance about the grandmother: *mii gaa-izhi-ishkwaa-zegizid* 'and so she wasn't scared anymore'. Presumably, Maude's grandmother would not have ceased to be afraid had it been a serious condition.

Another situation occurred when Maude was being followed home by a big, mysterious dog. Upon arriving home, she screamed, and the ladies at her house heard her and ran to her to see what was wrong. Finding out that it was just a dog (which normally scares little kids), they make a statement to that fact, accenting it with the second-position mystery particle cluster *gosha naa*.

(92) *gosha* (Kegg 1993, 104–5)

(a) *Mii go imaa aabanaabiyaan, geyaabi ko biminizha'od.*
  DP EMPH there I look back still as usual following me

(b) *Gichi-aayaazhikweyaan, bimibatooyaan gichi-enigok.*
  I cry really loud I run really hard

(c) *Mii gaa-izhi-noondawiwaad ingiw ikwewag, biijiba'idiwaad.*
  DP and they heard me those women running to me

(d) *"Aaniin," indig.*
  what's wrong she/he tells me

(e) *"Awiiya   imbiminizha'og,"*   *indinaag.*
    someone   she/he is following me   I tell them

(f) *"Animosh* **gosha naa** *a'aw,"* *ikidowag.*
    dog   DM   DM   this   they say

(g) *"Dibi   naa   wenjibaagwen,"*   *ikidowag.*
    I wonder   DM   where she/he comes from   they say

(a) 'I looked back there and he was still following.

(b) I screamed real loud and ran just hard.

(c) The ladies heard me and came running.

(d) "What's the matter?" she said to me.

(e) "Somebody is following me," I told them.

(f) "Goodness, it's a dog [**gosha naa**]," they said.

(g) "I wonder where he came from," they said.'

Once the women find out that it is just a dog following her, they reveal this fact by the statement in (92f), *goodness, it's a dog [***gosha naa***]*. While the published translation appears to suggest extreme excitement, the elder Lillian Rice suggested that the feeling here is one of relief. While it is true, however, that the little girl was very frightened by the big dog that followed her home, one of the women present did not appear to share Maude's fear. This is evinced by the fact that the statement in (92g) does not show a high intensity of excitement. The conflict, in reality, was that Maude thought she was in grave danger, and the adult women with considerably more life experience knew that she actually was not. So while the use of *gosha* in this example appears to signal relief, this is only a result of the use of *gosha* to mark actuality.

Another example showing this feeling of relief by the use of *gosha* is provided in (93). At one of our meetings, an elder showed up with some other visitors. When offered food by another elder, the visiting elder said the following utterance, accented with *gosha*.

(93) *gosha*

(a) *Imbaa-nanda-wiisin*   ***gosha.***
     I am looking around to eat   DM
     'I'm looking for someplace to eat [**gosha**].'

When I queried Marge about the statement in (93), she explained that what was implied here with *gosha* was that the visiting elder was *actually* hungry but was overly shy about helping herself to the potluck, possibly because she had not brought anything herself. The feeling that *gosha* helps to create in this response is probably best represented by the English phrase *Actually, I WAS hungry, and I'm glad you asked. Gosha,* therefore, functioned in this example to reveal the woman's true disposition, but only after the speaker was relieved to find out that it was okay to eat. The conflicting points of view, of course, were that the elder thought it would have been rude to take part in the potluck, and the viewpoint of everyone else at the potluck was that it was completely okay.

The emotional token of *relief* is not always indicated by the use of *gosha,* however. Sometimes the speaker is simply revealing his or her own disconnect from reality. In the following example, Maggie Kegg thought it the polite thing to offer more tea to someone but was met with a resounding *no.*

(94) *gosha*

(a) Speaker A: *Geyaabi   na   aniibiish awiiya?*
                 still   INTERR   tea   someone

(b) Speaker B: *uhm uhm*
                 no . . . .

(c) Speaker C: *Indaano-gii-kagwejimaa* ***gosha,*** *"no!"* *indigoog.* (laughing)
                 I tried to ask her   DM   no   they tell me

(a) Speaker A: 'Anyone want more tea?

(b) Speaker B: uhm uhm (=no)

(c) Speaker C: I tried to ask her [**gosha**], they told me "no!"' (laughing)

Speaker A asks if anyone wants more tea, Speaker B responds with *uhm uhm* (=no), and Maggie immediately interjects with the comment that she already tried to ask those present if they wanted more tea, but they adamantly refused her offer. Though lighthearted in nature, this example shows the use of *gosha* as resolving conflicting views of reality. In short, Speaker C thought it completely okay to offer tea to someone (which is socially acceptable and expected), but to her surprise was met with vehement opposition.

The core function of *gosha* appears to be helping speakers reveal the truth of a situation, a truth known or recognized by the speaker but somehow not to interlocutors. This can be shown in the following humorous story, in which a grandmother and granddaughter visit a friend who spoke a dialect of Ojibwe in which pants were considered to be of animate gender, contrary to their own dialect, in which pants were considered inanimate. Upon hearing an exchange about a pair of pants, the little girl makes a remark about the pants being alive. Her grandmother responds to her comment, accenting her response with *gosha*.

(95) *gosha* (Nichols 1988, 6–7)[25]

(a) *Ikwezens   miinawaa   ookomisan   izhaawaad   adaawewigamigong.*
     little girl   and   her grandmother   they go there   to the store

(b) *Mii   dash   gaani-izhi-noogishkaawaad   imaa   owiijigamishkawaaganiwaan.*
     DP   DM   and then stopped off   there   their neighbors

(c) *Ikwezens   ookomisan   ezhi-gagwejimaad,   "Aaniin   ezhichigeyan?"*
     little girl   her grandmother   and asks him/her   what   are you doing

(d) *"Ingiboode'igwaazon   indagonaa."*
     my pants   I am hanging him/her up

(e) *Eni-maajaawaad   gomaapii   gii-ikido   ikwezens,   "Bimaadiziwidogenan*
     as they leave   later on   she/he says   little girl   she/he must be alive

     iniw   ogiboode'igwaazonan."
     that   her pants

(f) *"Gaawiin,   mii   **gosha**   omaa   ezhi-giizhwewaad   ongow   Anishinaabeg."*
     no   DP   DM   here   how they speak   these   Indians

(a) 'A girl and her grandmother were going to the store.

(b) On the way, they stopped off at a neighbor's house.

(c) The girl's grandmother asked the neighbor, "What are you doing?"

(d)   "I'm hanging up my pants."

(e)   Some time later, after they had left there, the girl says, "Could it be that those pants of hers are alive?"

(f)   "No, that's [**gosha**] just the way that these Indians speak around here."'

Within the context of this story, the grandmother is not assertively deriding her granddaughter for her faulty logic, but merely revealing the fact that the dialect spoken by her friend refers to pants (grammatically speaking) in the same way that it refers to people. In English, the revealing of such information is usually accomplished by the use of the word *just* accompanied by a special intonation contour that marks such revealed information, that is, rising intonation over *that's* and *speak* within the phrase **that's just the way that these Indians speak around here**. As already noted, Ojibwe does not use intonation contours in the way that English does. This becomes quickly evident when listening to an Ojibwe narrative. Intonation contours within narratives typically remain relatively flat throughout the whole discourse, while English discourse shows a rich use of stress and intonation contours in order to produce a number of nuances. Given these facts, it is not surprising that Ojibwe would use discourse markers, such as *gosha* in this case, in order to reveal to a little girl the actual state of things.

In short, *gosha* makes its appearances in situations where speakers want to make a revelation that is somehow significant or relevant to the situation at hand. The information that speakers reveal usually makes the situation more clear to interlocutors or in some way reveals the interlocutor's skewed view of reality. Another way of saying this is that *gosha* allows speakers to provide or interject the *reality* of a situation (as seen through the eyes of the speaker), a reality that the speaker perceives as not being visible to interlocutors. Many times, this revelation of reality has a relieving effect if the information that *gosha* is accenting is found out to be contextually benign in nature when it was once thought to be malignant. As we have seen, the opposite could be true too. It is not that *gosha* encodes the meaning of assertiveness or relief but that the subtle play of context and the core function of *gosha* does.

3.2.2.3   *sha*

Mystery particle *sha* is presumably a contraction of *gosha*, but because *sha* appears to have a slightly different distribution and usage than *gosha*, I chose to talk about *sha* separately. For example, while discourse marker cluster *sha go* is attested in the data, cluster *gosha go* (which would be the inflated form of *sha go*) is not. Other nuances that appear in the data for *sha* that do not appear for *gosha* also point to a slight divergence in the usage and function of *sha* as opposed to *gosha*. So while *sha* appears to share *gosha*'s core function as a marker of actuality, it has other nuances, such as a self-pity-invoking function that I have not been able to observe with the use of *gosha*. Based upon this evidence, it is possible that *sha* originated as a contraction of *gosha* but has since become its own discourse marker operating in more narrow contexts.

A major function of *sha* in the data has been as a particle that speakers use to set people straight (a feature we saw with *gosha*). In this function, *sha* may (but does not always) have a lightly derisive feel to it (either as a serious proposition or in jest), since speakers commonly use *sha* to *get after* interlocutors (i.e., give them hell) in order to show them the reality of a situation or the illogicalness of their behavior. While it could be argued that the feeling of derision is a product of the context in which *sha* is being used, my observation is that *sha* appears to occur in higher frequency than *gosha* within these derisive contexts. Its core function can be seen, nonetheless, in the following example, when Millie Benjamin was asking me whether I gave an explanation to a woman from the BBC (British Broadcasting Company) about how Ojibwes view dreams culturally. I had initially misunderstood her to be asking whether someone else had, and she quickly corrected me using *sha*.

(96)   *sha*

> *Giin*   **sha**   (after being confused as to whom she was referring to)
> you   DM
> 'No, you!'

In this instance, I, the interlocutor, was in a state of confusion, as I kept giving Millie the wrong explanation due to my misunderstanding of whom we were talking about. After a few unsuccessful attempts at getting an appropriate response, Millie finally corrected me with the expression in (96), accompanied by a hint of impatience and derision since I should have known whom she was talking about.

Sometimes the interlocutor does not need correcting per se but needs an answer to something that has bewildered him or her. The use of *sha* marks that the information revealed to interlocutors is either surprising, not obvious, unsuspected, or unexpected. The response, accented by *sha*, has the effect of eliminating the interlocutor's bewilderment. For example, in the following interaction, I had brought a picture (at the request of an acquaintance) of an old Ojibwe woman who had long since passed away. An acquaintance who had given me the picture had asked me if I would show the picture to the elders to see if they could identify her. Marge, not knowing that I had brought the picture, asked Millie at the table how *she* got the picture. The response to this question was accented by *sha*.

(97)   *sha*

(a)   Marge: *Well, how'd you get that?*
(b)   Millie: *Awanigaabaw* **sha** *obiidoon.*

(a)   Marge: 'Well, how'd you get that?
(b)   Millie: Awanigaabaw [sha] has brought it.'

Not captured in (97a) is Marge's intonation that accompanied her query. Her query (in English) exhibited a heightened level of bewilderment, almost like saying, *Well, how **in the world** did you get that?* That she was in a state of bewilderment or amazement is supported by the fact that the presentation of the photo of the old woman who had long since passed away was quite out of context and random for the purposes of our meeting. It was in this state that Marge made the query as to how Millie obtained the photo, to which Millie responds, accenting her response with *sha*: *Awanigaabaw* **sha** *obiidoon* 'Awanigaabaw [sha] has brought it'. The use of *sha* here appears to do two things. First, it counterbalances the heightened emotional state present in Marge's query. Second, *sha* supports the surprising or unexpected revelation that Awanigaabaw, that is, me, who did not even know the old woman, nor would I be expected to have her picture, had brought it. The use of *sha* in this example also allows Millie to correct Marge's assumption (or perceived assumption) that Millie brought the photo. So, in effect, Millie's response is like saying, *It was Awanigaabaw, not me, who has brought it.*

Also, when speakers use *sha* to refer to themselves, they are, in effect, censuring themselves as a way of eliciting pity. As an example of this, one native speaker used *sha* in regard to her own inadvertent behavior, as a way to admit her mistake, censure herself, and elicit pity from those present. In the following interaction between the elders, Dorothy Sam, ruins a surprise birthday gift by inadvertently telling the person for whom the gift was intended about the surprise. Once she realizes her faux pas, she uses *sha* to accent her own statement that she had *spilt the beans* and to elicit pity.

(98)   *sha*

(a)   Marge: *Oda-waabandaan   Pameda?*
             is she gonna see it   Pameda   (someone's name)

(b)   Millie: *Baanimaa   apii   um   michaatooyaan,   niwii-agoodawaa*
             later   on   um   when I make it big   I want to give her a gift

             dash   um   mii   azhigwa   gegaa   da-dibishkaad.
             but   um   DP   time   almost   to be her birthday

(c)   Marge: *Dikinaagan   na?*
             cradle board   INTERR

(d)   Dorothy: *I   just   got   through   calling   her,   ingii-wiindamawaa.*
               I   just   got   through   calling   her   I told her

(e)   Millie: *Nooo!*
             no

(f)   Dorothy: *Yeah   I did.   Told.*   (Everyone laughs.)
               yes   I did   told

(g)   Millie: *Chi-odoon.*
             she/he has a big mouth

(h)   Dorothy: *I   had   no   idea,   oh!   Nichi-odoon.*   (Laughing continues.)
               I   had   no   idea   oh   I have a big mouth

(i)   Dorothy: *Ingii-wiindamawaa   **sha**.*
               I told her   DM

(a)   'Is Pameda gonna see it?

(b)   Later on when I make it big, I want to give it to her as a present. It's almost her birthday.

(c)   Is it a cradle board?

(d)   I just got through calling her, I told her.

(e)   Nooo!

(f)   Yeah I did. Told.

(g)   She has a big mouth.

(h)   I had no idea! I have a big mouth.

(i)   I spilt the beans [**sha**]!'

In (98d), Dorothy, not yet knowing her inadvertent error, reveals to the group that she had just called the very person that Millie wanted to give a cradle board to and told her of Millie's plan to give the cradle board away as a birthday gift. In (98e), the emotional state increases as the sentiment of Millie turns to disbelief, evident by her response to the news: *nooo!*. In (98h), Dorothy realizes her error, and then in (98i) makes the statement that she spilt the beans, accenting her statement with *sha*. The use of *sha* in this example has the feeling of self-reproach and self-pity. In short, the speaker is *getting after* herself for messing up the surprise.

As part of the general chastising feature of *sha*, there are occasions when speakers will use *sha* in order to reveal and confront interlocutors with their (the interlocutor's) faulty logic evinced by their (the interlocutor's) actions or utterances. In other words, speakers may use *sha* to throw interlocutors' faulty logic in their own face as a way of showing them where they have gone wrong. What the speaker is revealing with *sha* is the truth, or reality (as they see it), of a situation, which they view as not apparent to interlocutors. In these situations, *sha* usually (but not always) occurs within a second-position cluster involving the emphatic marker *igo* (usually occurring as *go*) and occasionally with the mystery particle *naa* (to be discussed in section 3.2.2.7). This function is shown by the following interaction between the elders. Once a month at our meetings, the tradition was to have a potluck. At one of these potlucks, Jim noticed that there was fry bread, but no peanut butter. It was at this point that he mentioned that he was allergic to peanut butter, but his very next step was to call home to see if someone could bring some peanut butter to the meeting. After he got off the phone, Marge queried him about the apparent contradiction, accenting her censure with *sha* and emphatic marker *igo* (appearing here as contracted form *go*).

(99) *sha go*

(a) Speaker A: *(Hangs up from asking someone to bring peanut butter.)*

(b) Speaker B:
Mii	*na*	***sha***	***go***	*booch*	*nandwewendaman?*
DP	INTER	DM	EMPH	anyways	that you are asking for it

'Are you [**sha go**] asking for it anyways?!'

In (99), Marge queries Jim as to why he would be asking for peanut butter when he just stated that he was allergic to it. Marge, recognizing the illogicality or unreasonableness of Jim's actions, uses the second-position mystery particle cluster *sha go* to confront him about this, albeit in a teasing manner. In a way, Marge is *getting after* Jim while also showing Jim his illogical action.

This censuring feature can be seen in the following examples as well, where an elder reveals and reproaches an assumption by interlocutors that he is really old. The response to this assumption is accented by the second-position mystery particle cluster *sha go naa*.

(100) *sha*

Gaawiin	***sha***	***go***	***naa***	*inde-apiitizisiin.*
not	DM	DM	DM	I am not old enough

'I'm not [**sha go naa**] that old!' (lit. I am not old enough.)

Here, *sha* reveals the unreasonableness of the interlocutor's assumption, *go* is emphatic, and *naa* adds emphasis. The combination allows the speaker to refute the interlocutor's faulty logic, this time, a wrong assumption about the age of the elder.

In short, *sha* allows speakers to set their interlocutors straight, whether it is just a simple correction in real-world references—for example, *No, you!*—providing bewildered interlocutors with an answer to a query, or identifying and confronting interlocutors with their faulty assumptions or actions. In all cases, the use of *sha* helps to set interlocutors straight in some way by revealing the truth or reality of a situation, while also dealing them some level of derision or matching their heightened emotional state.

3.2.2.4 *da*

Mystery particle *da* is nicknamed here the "clarification particle," since it has a clarifying function. When speakers use this particle, they are asking for information that they missed in previous conversation. Its use is similar to the use of *again* in English for the same function, for example, *What is your name **again**?* Though *da* in Ojibwe and the use of *again* in English have similar functions, their individual meanings are not the same: *da* does not mean *again* in Ojibwe. It is the clarifying nature of *da* that allows this reading. The clarifying function can be seen with the two examples that follow. When I asked one of the elders a question, she initially did not know that I was speaking to her. Once she realized that I was, she uttered the question in (100b). The example in (100a) gives the common interrogative form for *what*.

(101) Clarification particle *da*

(a)   *Wegonen?*
      INTER

      'What?'

(b)   *Wegonen*   ***da?***
      INTER   DM

      'What now?' (asking for a repeat of the question)

Mystery particle *da* may be used with other interrogatives as well, having the same function. This is shown in the following examples provided by the elders.

(102) *da* with interrogatives

(a)   *Aaniin*   ***da***   *ezhinikaazoyan?*
      how   DM   what you are named

      'What is your name again?'

(b)   *Awenen* **da** *gaa-ojiimad?*
    who   DM   who you kissed
    'Who did you kiss again?'

As do other mystery particles, clarification particle *da* also appears in discourse marker clusters. These discourse marker clusters will be discussed in section 3.2.2.7.1, but an individual accounting of *da* here will help in understanding their usage within clusters.

3.2.2.5   *bina*

Mystery particle *bina* has a core function of strengthening the illocutionary force of imperatives, having the force of the English *damn it!, you had better do it!*, and so on. When it is used with imperatives (which appears to be its most common usage), the speaker is usually urging (almost berating) an interlocutor to do something that interlocutor knows she or he should do. The following example shows this type of usage.

(103) *bina*

(a)   *Ojibwemotawishin*   **bina!**
    speak Ojibwe to me   DM
    'Speak Ojibwe to me **damn it!**' (feeling: *since you speak the language*)

(b)   *Ojibwemon*   **bina** *naa!*
    speak Ojibwe   DM   DM
    'Speak Ojibwe **damn it!**'

While the imperative form *ojibwemotawishin* in (103a) is quite direct in itself, its propositional content is strengthened even more by the use of *bina*. One of the elders recounted to me once that he would use the imperative (with *bina*) in (103a) with other Ojibwe speakers when they would use English with him instead of Ojibwe. I have personally heard one of the elders use the imperative (with *bina naa*) in (103b) with another elder who complained that no one speaks Ojibwe anymore (discourse marker *naa* will be discussed in detail in section 3.2.2.7). For both of these examples, since it is well known among Ojibwe speakers that Ojibwe is an endangered language, the general expectation is that it should be used whenever possible, *especially* between native speakers. In essence, the speaker sees the interlocutor's actions as contradictory to general expectation (or at least, to the speaker's expectation) and tries to correct that action by using an imperative expression, accenting it with *bina*.

When used with Ojibwe jussive expressions, *bina* has the same effect, increasing the illocutionary force of the jussive expression. A jussive, according to Trask, is like a "third-person imperative" in that it is an imperative expression such as the English *Let them eat cake!*, where an imperative form is interpreted as being directed at someone other than the addressee (see Trask 1993, 150). In Ojibwe, jussive constructions usually involve the use of *maanoo* 'let it be', as in the following examples.

(104) Ojibwe jussives

(a)   (Mille Lacs sessions)

    Maanoo   *wiin*   *da-wiisini.*
    let it be   him/her   he will eat

    'Let her eat!'

(b)   (Mille Lacs sessions)

    Maanoo   *wiin*   *oga-amwaan.*
    let it be   him/her   she/he will eat him/her

    'Let him eat it [something animate]!'

(c)   (text communication)

    Me: *Can I transcribe your story?*
    Marge: *Maanoo.*

    'Me: Can I transcribe your story?
    Marge: Go ahead.'

On one occasion Virginia Davis used *bina* with the jussive *maanoo*. At the time of this utterance, Virginia was arguing with another elder at our meeting, and the elder angrily left the room. After that elder left, Virginia made the following statement, accenting it with *bina*.

(105) *bina* within jussive constructions

> *Maanoo* **bina***!*
> let it be DM

> 'Let him (leave)!' (feeling: *I don't care, it's okay that he leaves*.)

The statement in (105) was not uttered to the angry elder who left but to us, the other interlocutors in the room. Here, *bina* appears to signal to interlocutors that she does not care, against the expectation that one would *normally* care in situations such as this. Virginia was known to be a scrapper in her younger days and so it was no surprise that she would make such a comment. In short, the use of *maanoo* in her utterance tells us (the interlocutors) to *let him (leave)*, and *bina* strengthens that imperative. It is important to note that the *I don't care* attitude emanating from this utterance is pragmatically inferred, since *bina* does not have any meaning in and of itself. It is *bina*'s strengthening function that allows the pragmatically inferred attitude of *I don't care* to be obtained.

While *bina* quite often strengthens the illocutionary force of imperatives (which are inherently confronting), *bina* may also strengthen, or reinforce, expressions that are not imperative in nature. For example, *bina* occurring with words such as *ahaaw* 'alright' or *aawaaw* 'go ahead' has the effect of quashing any fears, hesitations, or unfounded expectations by interlocutors. In the following example, Speaker A asks whether it would be okay to come and sing at a ceremony (something that someone might think is inappropriate to ask about, especially at ceremonial dances); the use of *bina* with *aawaaw* 'go ahead' shows that his or her presupposed fear or hesitation was unfounded. The elders suggested that the following exchanges are common.

(106)

Speaker A:	*Indaa-bi-nagam* *ina?*	(unsure of appropriateness)
	can I come sing INTERR	
Speaker B:	*Aawaaw* **bina***!*	
	go ahead DM	
Speaker A:	'Can I come sing?	
Speaker B:	Go ahead!' (feeling: *Yes, it's okay, it's no big deal*.)	

In (106), the particle *aawaaw* has the meaning 'go ahead' and is being used by the speaker to respond to Speaker B's question. Because *bina* strengthens the proposition 'go ahead' represented by *aawaaw*, the fear-quashing attitude *it's no big deal* can be pragmatically inferred, and Speaker B's hesitations about asking are quashed.

Mystery particle *bina* is also seen within declarative-type expressions, where *bina* strengthens the propositional content of its containing utterance. This usage appears to be less common than its occurrence with imperatives, but its function remains the same, strengthening the illocutionary force of its containing proposition. The following example shows the use of *bina* with the particle *ahaaw* 'okay, alright', which is commonly used to show receipt of information.

(107) *bina* (text communication)

(a) Marge: *Zoogipon   omaa   bangii.*
        it's snowing   here   a little

(b) Me: *Indaa-dibaabandaan   the   weather   report.*
        I should check it   the   weather   report

(c) Me: *Niwii-pi-izhaamin.*   (later)
        we are coming

(d) Marge: *Ahaaw   bina.*
        okay   DM

(a) 'It's snowing here a little.

(b) I should check the weather report.

(c) We're coming.

(d) Okay **go ahead and do it**.'

In (107a), Marge informs me that it is snowing a little up at Mille Lacs (the reservation where we had our meetings), thereby implying that it might be better not to come up. I then tell her that I will check the weather report, and after doing so, I text her back sometime later saying that we will be coming. To this, she responds with *ahaaw* **bina** 'Okay go ahead and do it'. *Ahaaw* shows a receipt of information, and *bina* strengthens that receipt. What the speaker appears to mean by this statement is that she is really indifferent and could go either way. In other words, the attitude that can be pragmatically inferred by the use of *ahaaw bina* is, *okay, whatever you want to do, it doesn't matter to me.*

What all these examples have in common is the use of *bina* to strengthen the illocutionary force of its containing proposition. If *bina* is used with a confronting imperative, then that imperative is given more force. If *bina* is used with a nonconfronting imperative, then a more positive result may be obtained. If *bina* occurs with an ambivalent proposition, then ambivalence is strengthened. The various resulting attitudes or attitudinal meanings are then pragmatically inferred depending on the proposition that is strengthened.

3.2.2.6   *goda*

Mystery particle *goda* is like *bina*, since it too is used to accent imperatives. Its function is a little different, however. When used with imperative forms, *goda* has a function similar to the English temporal adverb *then* within the following English exchange.

(108) English temporal adverb *then*

(a)   Speaker A: *I don't have any money.*

(b)   Speaker B: *Get a job* **then***!*

What is essentially going on here is that Speaker B is providing a *temporal* solution to Speaker A's problem of not having any money and uses the temporal adverb *then* to suggest that the next step *in time* is to get a job. In Ojibwe, while *goda* is used for this same solution-giving function, it is not a temporal adverb and does not appear to have a temporal function elsewhere in the language that would parallel the English temporal adverb *then*, for example, *and then, she was a linguist then.* Therefore, *goda* in Ojibwe is analyzed here as an option marker, since when it is used, possible options are always being offered without reference to time (although time is an inescapable, inherent part of the solution). The point here is that the two languages handle this type of solution-giving exchange in different ways. English uses a temporal adverb, Ojibwe does not. This usage is illustrated in the following example, where one elder, who is notorious for complaining about people not using the language anymore, came into one of our meetings and said that we should meet more so that people can speak

Ojibwe, all the while speaking English himself. One of the other elders present then said the following to him:

(109) *goda*

> *Ojibwemon* **goda!**
> speak Ojibwe DM
> 'Speak Ojibwe **then**!'

Here, using *goda*, the other elder provided the complaining elder with the obvious answer to his perceived problem, that is, to speak Ojibwe himself.

Goda may also appear within declarative statements, where it appears to maintain its option marker feature. In the following example, I had asked Marge Anderson via email to listen to some sound files. Later that day and after having not been able to listen to my audio files, she texted me the following bilingual statements, one occurring with *goda* (I have kept Marge's original orthography as it appeared within her text message).

(110) *goda*

> *Sorry been a long day. I'll look at it wabang* **goda.**
> sorry been a long day I'll look at it tomorrow DM
> 'Sorry been a long day. I'll look at it tomorrow okay.'

After apologizing for having not been able to listen to my audio files, she offers up a plan (i.e., a resolution to the problem at hand) to look at them the next day. It is this phrase that is accented by *goda*, having the force of *tomorrow, then (I'll do it)*.

3.2.2.7 *naa*

Mystery particle *naa* strengthens or magnifies the overall propositional content of a speaker's utterance by increasing the attitudinal force of the speaker toward that utterance. In many contexts, the illocutionary force resulting from the use of *naa* is quite strong, so strong in fact that Marge Anderson used to translate *naa* as the English swear *damn it*, for example, *Shke* **naa** *wewiib* 'Hurry up damn it!' While the use of *naa* in some contexts results in this level of emotional tug

(albeit without the social stigma of swear words), the data also show that resulting nuances from the strengthening effect of *naa* are entirely dependent upon
the actual semantics of the uttered proposition or discourse. *Damn it* is not
always indicated by the use of *naa*. Other nuances exist also, albeit the attitudinal tug is ever present. For example, if an utterance functions to acquire information for the speaker, an increase in the attitudinal force of the petition is signaled to listeners, or to oneself in the case of self-talk. This can have a resulting
nuance of *I wonder* (usually accompanied with the expectation of a response).

(111) Propositional strengthener *naa*

(a)   *Aaniish*   **naa?**
     what   DM

    'How's that?'

(b)   *Aaniish*   **naa**   *ba-onji-dagoshinzig.*
     what   DM   why she/he does not come

    'I wonder why he doesn't show.'

(c)   *Ambe*   *sa*   **naa**   *wiisinidaa!*
     come on DM   DM   let's eat

    'Shall we finally go eat?'

The utterances in both (111a) and (111b) begin with the information-seeking particle *aaniish* 'what', and the utterance in (111c) begins with the exhortative particle *ambe* 'come on, let's'. The example in (111a) comes from Mary Ann Corbiere
(a native speaker of Odawa, a sister dialect to Ojibwe), who said that her mother's
initial query to Mary Ann about the length of a hem on her pants was *aanii*
'How's that?' Mary Ann, as a little girl, mistakenly understood *aanii* to be the
common greeting *aanii* 'hello!' and so responded in kind to her mother with
aanii 'hello!' as well. Frustrated, her mom exclaimed, *Aaniish* **naa?** *indikid* 'I'm
asking, "How's that?"!' (Corbiere 1997, 84). In this example, we can see that the
use of *naa* with *aanii* clarified to Mary Ann what her mother was actually saying: responding to her query, not offering a greeting. Only after *naa* was added
was the query finally clear to Mary Ann. In (111b), the bare proposition without
naa is *why doesn't he show up?*, but the use of *naa* allows the more evaluative

nuance *I wonder why he doesn't show up.* In (111c), the proposition without *naa* would be *let's finally go eat,* but the use of *naa* elevates this exhortative proposition to the level of a query to which a yes/no response is elicited.

If an utterance entails a lack of knowledge or commitment to a proposition, the use of *naa* increases the emotional tug associated with that lack of knowledge or commitment. This results in an increased degree of hedginess. According to Trask (1993, 128), a hedge is an "expression added to an utterance which permits the speaker to reduce her/his commitment to what she/he is saying: *I think, I suppose, I fancy, I would guess, I take it, it seems to me.*" A good example of this is shown by an utterance made by Millie Benjamin at one of our weekly meetings. After making a guess on how to spell a word, she immediately said the following, accenting it with *naa.*

(112) Hedgy *naa*

    Ganabaj **naa.**
    probably DM
    'Probably **I guess**.'

What accompanied the utterance in (112) was both a facial expression and a tone in her voice that signaled to us that she was making a guess and that she was not entirely sure of the accurateness of her answer. The attitude in this context was not a harsh one. Rather, it was quite the contrary. It was hedgy. This reading resulted from the use of *naa* to extenuate the already hedgy proposition encoded within the word *ganabaj* 'I think, probably'. Therefore, in this example a stronger *damn it* nuance is not indicated. This magnified hedginess perhaps can be seen more easily in the following examples with one control sentence without *naa* and another with *naa.* When queried, the elders felt that the sentence containing *naa* was the weaker statement, weaker in the level of surety on the part of the speaker.

(113) Hedgy *naa*

(a)   *Ganabaj* *niimi.*
        probably dance
        'He's probably dancing.'

(b) *Ganabaj*   **naa**   *niimi.*
     probably   DM   dance

     'I think he's dancing.'

The fact that the elders judged the sentence containing *naa* to be weaker in terms of speaker commitment toward the proposition *I think he's dancing* (i.e., with the use of *naa*, the speaker seems even less sure whether the subject is dancing) confirms nicely the magnifying function of *naa*. In essence, *naa* allows speakers to contribute an attitudinal amplification to their proposition, but this amplification does not always entail anger or frustration to where an ipso facto *damn it* reading might result. In (113b), for example, *damn it* is not indicated precisely because the basic proposition is not one of anger or frustration. The speaker is also not expecting a response with the use of *naa* since the proposition is not seeking information. Rather, because the hedginess is already inherent in *ganabaj* 'probably, perhaps', the use of *naa* allows the speaker to emphasize that hedginess.

Within larger spans of discourse, *naa* may frequently occur to signal a heightened sense of emotion, but the type of heightened emotion is largely dependent on what's going on at the time of the utterance(s) of *naa*. For example, in the following excerpt, a little girl, Maude Kegg, mistakenly plunges a deer hide into boiling water, shrinking and ruining the hide. She had no idea that boiling water could ruin a hide, and she was quite bewildered to see that the hide shrank so dramatically. Her recounting and her statements to her grandmother are replete with tokens of *naa*.

(114) *naa* (Kegg 1993, 160–63)

(a) *Gaawiin*   *ingii-wiindamaagosiin,*   *mii*   *i'iw*   *eta*   *go*   *gii-izhid*
     not   she didn't tell me   DP   that   only   EMPH   she tells me

     ji-ningizwag   *a'aw*   *goon,*   *ji-agonjimag*   *a'aw*
     to melt him/her   that   snow   to soak him/her   that

     waawaashkeshiwayaan.
     deer hide

(b) *Waa,   mii   azhigwa   gegaa   go   ondeg   nibi,   miish   imaa*
     wow   DP   when   almost   EMPH   it is boiling   water   then   there

   agonjimag.
   I soak him/her

(c) *Mii   go   **naa**   ezhi-odaapishkaad,   ezhi-odaapishkaad.*
     DP   EMPH   DM   then she/he shrinks   then she/he shrinks

(d) *Enda-agaashiinyi.*
   she/he is really small

(e) *"Gaawiin   wiikaa,   aaniin   **naa**   izhiwebizid,"*   *indinendam.*
     not   ever   what   DM   is happening with him/her   I think

(f) *"Nimaamaanaan,"   indinaa,   "mii   go   **naa**   gaa-izhi-odaapishkaad*
     grandma   I tell her   DP   EMPH   DM   then she/he shrank

   a'aw   waawaashkeshiwayaan."
   that   deer hide

(a) 'She didn't tell me much about it; she just told me to melt the snow to soak
     the deer hide in it.

(b) The water was about to boil and I put it in to soak.

(c) It [**naa**] just shrank and shrank.

(d) It got real small.

(e) "Well, I never, what's [**naa**] happening to it," I thought.

(f) "Grandma," I said to her, "the deer hide [**naa**] shrank."'

As a little girl in this story, Maude was told by her grandmother to melt some
snow and soak a deer hide in it. Not ever having done this before, or ever having
watched her grandmother do it, she melted the snow to a near boil and threw
the hide in, shrinking and ruining the hide. At the time, the little girl had *no idea*
what could happen to a hide if it was plunged into near-boiling water. The result
was a complete surprise to her.

   Her statements in (114 c, e, f) describing the dramatic and mysterious shrinking of the hide are all accented by *naa*, marking the little girl's heightened state
of bewilderment and wonder.

In the following example, *naa* appears again when a surprising or unexpected event occurs. The little girl in the story acquired about twenty mud turtles that were taken off the lake for her. They were frozen solid and possibly sleeping, so she thought. When she put her mud turtles in a kettle of warming water, they began to move. It was when she saw the mud turtles start to move that she made the utterance in (115c), accenting it with *naa*.

(115)   *naa* (Kegg 1993, 164–65)

(a)   *Mashkawaakwajiwag.*
      they are frozen

(b)   *Gaawiin   mamaajiisiiwag,   biina'wagwaa   miskwaadesiwag,   mii*
      not   they are not moving   I put them in   mud turtles   DP

      imaa   akikong.
      there   in the kettle

(c)   *Mii   go   **naa**-sh   mamaajiiwaad,   ganawaabamagwaa.*
      DP   EMPH   DM-DM   they are moving   I watch them

(d)   *"Aaniin   ezhiwebiziwaad?"*
      what   what is happening to them

(a)   'They were frozen.

(b)   Those turtles weren't moving when I put them in the kettle.

(c)   As I watched them, they started [**naa**] moving.

(d)   "What's happening to them?"'

In this story, as the water warmed up, the turtles began moving, and as the water got really hot, the mud turtles started trying to get out of the pail. They all eventually got out and ran away. This scared Maude so badly that she ran away too. This was obviously a dramatic and unexpected event for the little girl. It is when she recounts this dramatic event that she uses *naa*, magnifying her surprise, inherent within the story. We can tell also that Maude was completely caught off guard seeing the turtles start to move, because of her wondering statement in (115d). She apparently did not realize that the warm water would bring the mud turtles out of their dormant state. It is the mystery particle *naa* that accompanies this recounted confusion brought on by the unexpected movement of the turtles.

In some instances where there are temporal adverbs (i.e., words representing time frames) occurring within utterances, *naa* strengthens the temporal aspect of a proposition.

(116) *naa*

Gegapii	*naa*	*da-nibaa.*
finally	DM	will sleep

'She's finally [**naa**] gonna go to sleep.'

In (116), one of my traveling companions was leaning back in her chair, with her eyes closed, acting like she was tired and sleepy. There was visible relief on her face that we had ended our meeting (as we usually ended late in the evening). Upon seeing this, Millie made the statement in (116), accenting it with *naa*. This usage is not a hedge, since Millie was pretty sure that my traveling partner was tired. The usage does not have the emotional tug of frustration or anger, nor is there any surprise or wonderment, as we saw with the little girl in previous examples. Rather, it is the attitudinal force toward the proposition *finally* that is amplified.

This usage can also be seen in the following utterance, which was made by Marge's mother (according to Marge) in regard to some kids she saw playing outside in the sun all day. In this example, Marge's mother states that the kids are going to get darker and darker from being out in the sun all day, and the use of *naa* allows her to emphasize the temporal adverb *genapii* 'as time goes by'.

(117) *naa*

Genapii	*naa*	*ani-makadewaasowag*	*ongow.*
as time goes by	DM	they are getting dark	these

'They are getting darker as time goes by.'

Within imperative constructions (i.e., command statements), *naa* has a strengthening effect, adding a feeling that the speaker is urging or pleading with interlocutors. Therefore, when speakers use *naa* to accent imperatives, mystery particle *naa* typically increases the overall illocutionary force of the imperative by increasing the emotional tug of the imperative. In the following examples, the elders suggest that the imperative with *naa* is the stronger one.

(118) Pleading function of *naa*

(a) *Daga   bi-naazhishin!*
     please   come get me

     'Please come get me!'

(b) *Daga   naa   bi-naazhishin!*
     please   DM   come get me

     'Come on, please come get me!' (Polite but stern)

The basic imperative force of the imperative expression in (118) is *please come and get me!*, but *naa* in (118b) contributes an emotional tug on the interlocutor, having the force of a polite (because of *daga* 'please') but stern feel to it. It increases the overall emotional urgency of the situation, allowing the speaker to increase the urgency of his or her plea. Larry Smallwood (a native speaker from Mille Lacs; personal communication) reports that imperatives utilizing exhortative particle *daga* 'please' accented with *naa* may sound less stern if said in a more neutral tone. Indeed, less stern nuances occur, especially in cases where nonimperative words like the conditional particle *iishpin* 'if' are utilized to create a petition.

(119) *naa* (from Smart 2004, 11)

(a) *Iishpin   sa   naa   giizizimawiyan   waawanoon   miinawaa   gookoosh*
     if   DM   DM   you cook for me   eggs   and   bacon

     gemaa   gaye   ozhaashi-manoomin.
     or   also   oatmeal

     'If you would cook some eggs for me and bacon and maybe some oatmeal.'

The example in (119) represents a less stern use of *naa*, but this lessened sternness in this case appears to be because of the propositional content of the conditional particle *iishpin* 'if'. The bare proposition in (119) is *if you cook for eggs for me (and bacon)*, and the use of *naa* allows the speaker to elevate this conditional proposition into a petition.

3.2.2.7.1 *Second-position discourse clusters with* naa

Mystery particle *naa* also frequently appears within particle clusters *da naa, sha naa, bina naa*, and *sa naa*. When emphatic particle *go* appears within some of these clusters, it usually occurs as the second member within the combination, with *naa* occurring last, for example, *sa go naa* and *sha go naa*. Combinations that put *naa* first in the particle cluster, such as **naa da**, **naa sha**, **naa sa**, **naa bina**, have not been observed within the data, nor elsewhere. Within the observed particle clusters, however, each particle appears to contribute to the overall collective meaning of the cluster, resulting in nuances tailor-made for each context. So while both *da naa* and *sha naa*, for example, have similar emotional loads because of *naa*, *da naa* is clarification seeking while *sha naa* usually signals reproach toward someone. They have an emotional tug similar to the English expression *damn it* or *[what] the hell*, but without the stigma of swear words. What this essentially means is that, though both combinations *da naa* and *sha naa* have the semantic weight of the English *damn it*, they can be appropriately used with children (or by them), since these words are not considered to be profane. Examine the examples that follow.

(120) "damn it" particle clusters *da naa* and *sha naa*

(a) *Wegonen* **da** **naa?**   (said to themselves while searching)
     what   DM   DM

     'What **the hell** is it now?'

(b) *Biboon* **sha** **naa!**   (said to a group)
     winter   DM   DM

     'It's winter **damn it!**'

While both expressions carry an increased emotional load, we can tell that each particle cluster is tailor-made for each respective context. In (120a), the context is information seeking. Elfreda Sam was trying to recall a word from memory when she uttered this phrase, accenting it with the information-seeking particle *da*. In (120b), the context is one of reproach. Here Elfreda was pointing out the fact that it was too mild for the dead of winter (i.e., January) in Minnesota, accenting her utterance to the people in the room with *sha*. Recall that *sha* usually accompanies contexts where speakers want to *get after* someone by way of revealing their illogicalness or the illogicalness of a situation (i.e., revealing the actual state of things). Here she is revealing the illogicalness of the weather to the people in the room. In both examples, *naa* amplifies the respective functions of the individual markers *da* and *sha* in order to increase the overall emotional state of each situation.

Cluster *sha naa* also appears in a story about Maude Kegg as a little girl and her grandma who were traveling to go weed a garden for someone, further showing *naa*'s emotional amplification function. On the way to their destination, they got hungry. They then saw a duck, killed it, plucked it, built a fire, and then singed it. After all this work and effort, they realized they had no knife to clean it with, at which point the following phrase was uttered by Maude's grandmother.

(121) *sha naa* (Kegg 1993, 60–61)

"*Oo,*	*yay,*	*gaawiin*	**sha**	**naa**	*gegoo*	*mookomaan*
oh	no	not	DM	DM	something	knife

gibimiwidoosiimin,"	*ikido.*
we do not bring it along	she says

'"Oh no, we haven't [**sha naa**] even got a knife along," she said.'

Although the broad translation does not appear to capture the discourse cluster usage, one interpretation might be, *Oh no, we haven't even got a knife along* **damn it**. This interpretation is also supported by the fact that the situation was already one of a heightened state of excitement, evinced by the grandmother's previous statement in regard to having just killed a duck: *Oo, Naawakamigook, mii ji-wiisiniyang* 'Oh, Naawakamigook, we're going to eat'. The amount of excitement that existed in killing the duck and the amount of time and effort that was invested in preparing it for cleaning, only to find out that they did not have a knife, appear to make the use of *sha naa* in (121) indicated. By *sha*, the little girl's grandma is revealing the actual state of things, that is, they did not have a knife when they desperately needed one; accenting *sha* with *naa* adds the emotional tug evident in the situation.

Recall that *sha* also had a feeling of eliciting pity from interlocutors, for example, *ingii-wiindamawaa sha* 'I told her' (getting after herself and eliciting pity from interlocutors). This sort of pity-invoking usage is also seen with *sha naa* when speakers feel left out and want others to include them. The use of *sha naa* in the following examples provided by the elders are equivalent to the use of rising tone in English for this same self-pitying effect.

(122) *sha naa*

(a) Niwii-odaabii'iwe **sha** **naa**.
     I want to drive   DM   DM

     'I wanna drive.'

(b) Niwii-namadab **sha** **naa**.
     I want to sit   DM   DM

     'I want to sit.'

(c) Nibakade   **sha** **naa**.
     I am hungry DM   DM

     'I'm hungry.'

In these examples, pity is invoked by the speaker's use of *sha*, and its illocutionary force is increased by *naa*.

One of the elders suggested that *sha naa* can also be used in cutting people off midsentence. This is shown in the following example provided by one of the elders.

(123)

     Niwii-o-ganawaab   **sha** **naa**.
     I am gonna go watch DM   DM

     'Excuse me, but I'm gonna go watch.' (cutting them off)

This usage is quite forward and imposing. This meaning appears to derive from the getting-after particle *sha*.

The last two clusters involving *naa* are *bina naa* and *sa naa*. With the *naa* clusters just discussed, we saw that particle *naa* is the component that heightens emotional intensity or that amplifies the function of the individual marker occurring with it. Note the use of *naa* in the following example.

(124) *bina* and *bina naa*

(a) *Noongom* **bina**
      today   DM

      '(Do it) today.' (today, not yesterday)

(b) *Noongom* **bina** **naa**
      today   DM   DM

      'Do it today!' (today, not yesterday, but stern)

Recall that *bina* increases the illocutionary force of propositions and *naa* increases the attitudinal force on the part of the speaker toward propositions. In (124a), though *noongom* 'today' is not an imperative word per se, the use of *bina* allows the speaker to emphasize the proposition *today*, resulting in a feeling of temporal urgency. In (124b), *bina* again increases the temporal force of *noongom* 'today', and the addition of *naa* increases the attitudinal force of *bina*, resulting in an increased emotional tug over the whole proposition.

The cluster *sa naa* is heard a lot in valedictions, or saying goodbye. Recall that mystery particle *isa* (or its clitic form, *sa*) is commonly used in conclusory situations such as this. In valedictions, *naa* has a pleading function, allowing the speaker to increase the attitudinal force of his or her valediction.

(125) *isa* in valedictions

(a) *Agana* **sa** **naa**
      easy   DM   DM

      'Take it easy!'

(b) *Weweni* **sa** **go** **naa**
      carefully DM   EMPH   DM

      'Take care!'

In these examples, the individual contributions of each mystery particle is clear. Marker *sa* is conclusory, *go* is emphatic, and *naa* shows a wishing or urging function, strengthening the overall proposition in *weweni* 'carefully'.

In sum, what these various clusters suggest is that when mystery particles cluster together, each particle typically contributes some meaning or function to the overall meaning of the particle cluster. The individual meanings of the individual markers remain largely transparent, allowing speakers to use particle clusters tailor-made for specific contexts. For example, in valedictions, while *sa* in the cluster *sa naa* signals that a visit has come to an end, the urging function of *naa* allows the speaker to increase the attitudinal force of the goodbye.

What is also important to point out here is the consistent use of mystery particles in Ojibwe, either individually or within clusters of particles, to increase the illocutionary force of discourse in general. Listening to an Ojibwe story in an audio recording quickly reveals to listeners the relatively (at least in comparison to English) flat intonation contours inherent in Ojibwe discourse. In English, it is usually the combination of stress, word lengthening, and more varied intonational contours over sentences that result in increased illocutionary force. Though English discourse is not devoid of discourse particles either, the particles that serve to strengthen illocutionary force in English are usually in the form of swear words, and their use is quite stigmatized. Of course, the use of stress and tone may accomplish the same effect without the use of swear words, especially for some English speakers who insist upon not swearing. Over the years, I have noticed that language learners have a tendency to overwrite their English stress, tone, and intonation onto their Ojibwe language, resulting in language that is largely devoid of Ojibwe mystery particles. I have been reminded, though, that many speakers at Red Lake (in northern Minnesota) have a wider array of intonational contours in their language. Indeed, I have also observed this in my own experience. However, Red Lake speakers also show a very robust usage of mystery particles within their speech, revealing that it is not intonation contour that is providing nuance in their dialect, but the use of mystery particles. What I have hoped to show in this section is that Ojibwe speakers use an array of particles and particle clusters to accomplish a lot of the same work that intonation contours do in English. For example, in rebuking an accusation of being old, one might say *I'm not that old*, with the use of stress and a rise in intonation over the demonstrative *that* (e.g., *I'm not thaaat old*). Ojibwe speakers, on the other hand, do not make productive use of stress and intonation in this way but rather use mystery particles to accomplish the same rebuking function. This is shown in the following example that was personally said to me. I don't remember what I said, but I must have implied that Jim Clark was old (not intentionally, but through a faux pas from which we all can learn), to which he replied with the following utterance.

(126) *sha go naa*

> *Gaawiin* **sha** **go** **naa** *inde-apiitizisiin.*
> not   DM   DM   DM   I'm not that old
>
> 'I'm not **thaaat** old.'

FOUR

Conjunct order as a discourse-marking device

It is well known that for Ojibwe, as well as for other Algonquian languages, there are three major verb orders (or sets of paradigms): INDEPENDENT, CONJUNCT, and IMPERATIVE. As their respective labels indicate, independent-order verbs function as independent clauses or sentences (sometimes called "A-form verbs"), conjunct-order verbs ("plain conjuncts" or "B-form verbs") function as dependent, subordinate, or embedded clauses, and the imperatives are the command forms.[1] Examples of these orders follow. Note that for independent verbs, agreement is accomplished by the utilization of both prefixes *and* suffixes, whereas the conjunct and imperative orders utilize only suffixes.

(127) Ojibwe verb orders

(a) **gi-*maajaa-m*[2]**　　　(independent order → independent clauses)
　　2-leave-2P

　　'You all are leaving.'

(b) *maajaa-yeg*　　　(conjunct order → dependent clauses)
　　leave-2P

　　'When you all leave ...'

(c) *maajaa-g*　　　(imperative order → commands)
　　leave-IMP.2P

　　'Leave (all of you)!'

A snag that this characterization runs into, however, is the observation made by Rhodes for a related dialect of Ojibwe, OTTAWA (or ODAAWAA), that plain conjunct verbs may be used as independent clauses in certain contexts (Rhodes 1979, 103; Rhodes 2006, 6). These contexts include the use of plain conjunct verbs as independent verbs (i.e., B-form verbs used as sentences) when those verbs are marking THEMATIC content (i.e., content that moves the plot forward) within a text, in marking what he calls "thematic futures," or in the consequent of *if* constructions (Rhodes 1979, 112–13). An example of the use of plain conjunct verbs as independent, thematic verbs is given in (128).

(128) Plain conjunct as independent verbs (Rhodes 1979, 110–11)

(a) **Gii-pagdosed**   *iidig*   *gaa-dbikak.*
     that she/he walked/CONJ   must have   after it got dark

(b) *Mkoon   iidig   gaa-zhi-nkweshkwaad.*
     bear   must have   IC.and so met him/her/CONJ

(c) *"Aabii-sh   ezhaayan?"   wdigoon-sh   ge.*
     where   are you going   she/he tells him/her   also

(d) *"Ann Arbor,"   odinaan   ge.*
     Ann Arbor   she/he tells him/her   also

(e) *"Gga-ni-waawiidsemi,"   kido   giiwenh   wa   mko.*
     we will walk together   she/he says   apparently   this   bear

(f) **Bbaamsewaad**   *giiwenh*   *nshaawi-dbik.*
     that they walk around/CONJ   apparently   through the night

(a) 'After it had gotten dark, **he set out walking**.

(b) That's how he came to meet this bear.

(c) "Where ya headed?" the bear asked him.

(d) "Ann Arbor," he replied.

(e) "Let's walk together," the bear suggested.

(f) So **they walked around** through the night.'

The verbs in bold type in (128a) and (128f) are plain conjunct verbs, evident by their exclusive use of suffixes (i.e., *-d* 'third person', *-waad* 'third person plural') to mark agreement for number and person and by the absence of initial change. As Rhodes points out, rather than acting as dependent clauses as the traditional rule would dictate, they instead carry thematic content, acting as independent clauses instead.[3] It is precisely this behavior that leads Rhodes to say, "This traditional characterization of verb forms as independent versus dependent can be quite misleading to a non-Algonquianist syntactician because of the great variety of syntactic contexts in which dependently inflectioned verbs appear, some of which are not obviously subordinate" (2006, 6, 110–13).

While early on it was known that plain conjunct verbs may sometimes pose as independent clauses within certain contexts, the question remains: Why? No work to date gives an explanation of the exact mechanism at work that makes such behavior possible. Rhodes (1979) highlights this phenomenon with only a few examples, devoting only one section to the phenomenon. Jones and Coleman (1979) provide a more detailed description of this phenomenon in Kickapoo in which they show that the conjunct order in Kickapoo serves to mark eventline structures, but they do not account for it either. This is obvious in their conclusion, where they state:

In light of our analysis here, it seems strange (at least from the perspective of narrative) that the mode that carries the eventline material is called *conjunct* in Algonquian literature, whereas the mode that primarily serves to carry background material is called *independent*. Undoubtedly these labels, which have been long-established in Algonquian studies are due to the fact that isolated sentences were the primary objects of study, where the conjunct was not so apt to occur except in its more idiomatic and rather subordinate uses, e.g., locative and temporal expressions. *Conjunct* was thus adopted as a term to indicate its supposedly subordinate nature. It is not surprising that the more important eventline use of the conjunct was not even apparent then, since such use would only be recognized in the context of an entire text. (Jones and Coleman 1979, 91)

It is this behavior, however, that is relevant to our discussion of discourse markers, since what is really going on, I argue, is that the conjunct order of inflection itself is being borrowed, or exploited, for work at the discourse level in much the same way that individual lexical or grammatical items are exploited for use within discourse. Therefore, based upon what we know about the behavior of discourse markers, there is no need to try to reconcile both uses into one category. In short, within sentence grammars, conjuncts are dependent clauses, but in discourse (as we will see), they may be used to mark eventline structure.

Now, it should also be noted here that the selection of the conjunct to carry eventline structure is not random, just as the selection of many lexical or grammatical items at the sentence level is not random. Recall that for many of the discourse connectives it was their specific lexical or grammatical use at the sentence level that was exploited for work at the discourse level—for example, coordinating conjunction *miinawaa*, which functioned at the sentence level to conjoin similar grammatical categories—but it also was shown to conjoin larger discourse units above the sentence level. In this way, the conjunct is being exploited as well, since, as we will see, it is the conjunct's connective and temporal immediacy features that lend themselves for work at the discourse level.

In the following sections, both the sentence-level and discourse functions of the conjunct will be discussed. This discussion will show that it is the plain conjunct verb that is borrowed to mark the eventline structure of a story or narrative within discourse. Ultimately, I will show that the same mechanism that allows exploitation of sentence-level grammatical/lexical forms for discourse work is also at work to allow the use of TAM forms (or morphological forms such as the conjunct) to be exploited for discourse work.

4.1   SENTENCE-LEVEL USE OF CONJUNCTS

4.1.1   *Dependent clauses*

Within sentence grammars, plain conjunct verbs usually function as dependent clauses, or subordinate clauses. For example, plain conjuncts may serve as temporal subordinate clauses (e.g., *wiisinid* 'when she/he eats'), serve as complements of predicative words such a *begish* 'I wish I could' (e.g., *Begish wiisiniyaan.* 'I wish I could eat'), or as embedded clauses (e.g., *Gaawiin ingii-gikenimaasiin gii-wiisinid* 'I didn't know that she ate'). The point here, though, is that conjunct verbs such as *wiisiniyaan* 'when/that I eat' are syntactically subordinate and usually do not function as full sentences on their own within sentences. The following examples show these uses. For clarity, the conjunct verbs in question have been glossed to show more morphological structure than the other words around them.

(129) Various uses of the conjunct in sentence grammars

(a)   Conjuncts as temporal subordinate clauses (Benjamin 2006)

*Mewinzha   omaa   **gii-maajii-anokiiyaan**   gegaa   nisimidana*
long ago   here   PAST-start-work.1/CONJ   almost   thirty

daso-biboonagad   iw   wapii,   onzaam   niibowagiziwag   ingiw
be so many years   that   time   too much   they are a lot   those

bakaan   gegoo   ezhichigejig.
different   thing   those who did things

'A long time ago **when I started working** here almost thirty years ago, there would be too many people who did things differently.'

(b)   Conjuncts as complements of predicative words (text communication)

*Mii   **ji-bi-de-dagoshinaan**   oodi   Waashtanong*
DP   FUT-come-enough-arrive.1/CONJ   there   Washington DC.

nidizhaa.
I am going there

'I will be back by then as I'm going to Washington DC.'

(c)   Conjuncts as embedded clauses (Mille Lacs session)

*Gego   anaamimishiken   **maanaadiziyan.***
don't   don't blame me   ugly.2/CONJ

'Don't blame me **that you are ugly.**'

In (129a) there is no temporal word meaning *when*. It is the use of the conjunct here that gives it this temporal meaning. In (129b) the conjunct verb *dagoshinaan* appears with the predicative element *mii*, which normally dictates the use of conjunct verbs. In (129c) the conjunct *maanaadiziyan* functions as an embedded clause.

The subordinate nature of the conjunct allows for an array of adjunct clauses, some of which are cause-and-effect, benefactive, or just clausal elaborations. As a translation effect, the translation of such clauses varies widely. The following examples show these functions.

(130) Adjunct clauses

(a)   *Nigii-makadewaas*   **abaasandekeyaan.**
      I got sunburned   bask in the sun.1/CONJ

      'I got black **from basking in the sun**.'

(b)   *Onzaam*   *ina*   *gidaadawin*   **nitaa-ojibwemoyaan.**
      because   INTERR   I have you beat   know how-speak Ojibwe.1/CONJ

      'Just because I got you beat **in speaking the language**.'

(c)   *Miigwech*   *wiidokawiyan.*
      thank you   help.2>1/CONJ

      'Thank you **for helping me**.'

(d)   (Kegg 1993, 94–95)

      Mii   *dash*   *ezhi-gagwejimagwaa,*   "*Aaniin*   *dash*   *i'iw*   *ezhichigeyaan,*"
      DP   DM   and so I ask them   why   exactly   that   what I am doing

      waabamaawaad   *iniw*   *nimanidoominensiman.*
      see-3>4/CONJ   that   my beads

      '**As they looked at my beads**, I asked them, "Why am I doing this?"'

Note that many of the grammatical relations displayed between the plain conjunct and the independent verb in these sentences are established by asyndetic connection. For example, in (130a) there is nothing in that sentence that means *from* or *as a result of.* Rather, it is the asyndetic connection between the plain conjunct verb and the independent verb within context that allows a resultative relation to be selected and displayed between clauses.

4.1.2   *Temporal immediacy and the connective feature of the conjunct*

Conjunct verbs may appear within sentences in conjunction with independent verbs to show TEMPORAL IMMEDIACY between actions (following Rhodes 1979). This means that the use of the conjunct indicates that the action denoted by the conjunct verb occurs immediately after the action denoted by the preceding independent verb. This is illustrated in the following example provided by Millie Benjamin.

(131) Temporal immediacy

> *Ingii-kanoonaa*   *Sara,*   *gii-pabanaazomag.*
> 1.PAST-call.DIR/INDEP   Sara   PAST-chew out.1>3/CONJ

> 'I called Sara and chewed her out.'

There are a few things to note in this example. First, the independent-order inflected verb *ingii-kanoonaa* is juxtaposed with the conjunct-order inflected verb *gii-pabanaazomag.* Second, there is no connective word conjoining the two Ojibwe clauses, such as the one conjoining the English clauses within the accompanying translation, *and.* The plain conjunct *gii-pabanaazomag* is not acting as a subordinate clause, however (as we would expect), but as an independent clause, showing temporal immediacy. In other words, the juxtaposition of the plain conjunct *gii-pabanaazomag* 'I chewed her out' with the independent clause *ingii-kanoonaa* 'I called her' denotes that the *chewing out* occurs immediately upon calling Sara, not sometime after calling her. This behavior is perhaps demonstrated better in an example cited by Rhodes for a related dialect of Ojibwe. In the following example, there are two actions: *going to bed at night* and *getting up in the morning*, actions that cannot occur one immediately after another.

(132) Rhodes's (1979, 111) example

(a)   **Miin'waa   dash   nbaagning   gii-gwishmo,*   *ge*   *ggizheb*
      and   DM   in bed   PAST-lay down/INDEP   also   morning

      gii-nishkaad.
      PAST-get up.3/CONJ

      'Next he went to bed, and got up the [next] morning.'

(b)   *Miin'waa   dash   nbaagning   gii-gwishmo,*   *ge*   *ggizhe.*
      and   DM   in bed   PAST-lay down/INDEP   also   morning

      gii-nishkaa
      PAST-get up/INDEP

      'Next he went to bed, and got up the [next] morning.'

These two examples are identical except that the verb in the second clause of (132a) is inflected as a conjunct, while its counterpart in (132b) is inflected as an independent verb. Note that the conjunct-order inflected verb *gii-nishkaad* (evinced by its conjunct suffix *-d* 'third person') in (132a) is pragmatically un-grammatical precisely because, as Rhodes explains, the act of *getting up* cannot be both "immediate and in the morning" (Rhodes 1979, 111). According to the elders, these facts are also true at Mille Lacs.

While the Rhodes example in (132) occurred with a connective, *ge* 'also', the following example suggests that such occurrences of connective particles are sometimes optional, revealing a connective feature of conjunct verbs. In fact, the connective feature of the conjunct may be demonstrated in the following excerpt from a story in which a series of actions are conjoined, all without the use of a connective particle.

(133) Connective feature of the conjunct (Clark 2003b, 55, audio)

Shke,	*wa'aw*	*nookomisiban*	*mii-ko*	*gaa-paa-izhi-mamood*
look	this	my grandmother	used to	went aroundpicking

o-mashkiki	*gekendaagwadinig*	*ge-inikaagod*	*a'aw*	*anishinaabe,*
this medicine	known	to be used for	that	Indian

gii-agoodood	*endaad,*	***gii-paasang,***	***gii-na'inang.***
she hung it up	her house	she dried it	she put it away

'You see, my grandmother used to pick medicine known to be good for people, and **would hang it** in her house, **dry it**, and **put it away**.'

In the passage in (133), we find a string of three conjunct verbs linked together without a connective word or coordinating conjunction, such as *miinawaa* 'and' or *gaye* 'also'. While the English gloss can tolerate some absence of a connector (except with the last verb), the Ojibwe sentence shows that it may tolerate a total absence of any connectors at all and still remain grammatical. This suggests, then, not only that the conjunct denotes the immediacy of actions in relation to one another but that the conjunct also possesses a connective feature that allows the stringing together of the very verbs denoting those actions.

4.1.3   Situational immediacy

There is a very restricted context in which plain conjunct verbs are uttered in isolation, without a predicating word or element, to show what I call SITUA-

TIONAL IMMEDIACY. I use the term *situational* here because speakers usually make these comments or remarks in response to an event, action, or situation that has just occurred, either in real time or within a conversation. The term *immediacy* is used here since the use of plain conjuncts within these contexts is usually grammatical only when said *in the moment* to describe or make reference to the event or situation at hand; otherwise, the use of conjunct becomes awkward. For lack of a better comparison, the use of plain conjuncts in this fashion appears to be akin to the English usage of lone adjectives in the same type of situations. For example, in English, when people see or hear something they perceive to be beautiful, they might say, "Beautiful!" In the moment, the lone utterance of the adjectival word *beautiful* is grammatical and appropriate, but once taken out of that moment (i.e., telling a friend later that you saw a beautiful portrait), its use becomes awkward if not supported by other periphrastic content, that is, *it was beautiful*.

Also, these statements may be accompanied by a heightened sense of emotion, in either a dismissive, joking, or surprising manner. In a way, this is similar to the temporal immediacy described previously except that the preceding clause is not an independent clause but a real-world event or situation. The following examples were uttered by the elders at one time or another in relation to *in the moment* events.

(134) Situational immediacy

(a) *Chi-gagaandenimag.*   (after talking about someone who got hurt)
    very-take pleasure in his/her pain.1>3/CONJ

    *Ingichi-gagaandenimaa.
    1.great-take pleasure in his/her pain.DIR/INDEP

    'It's well enough for him!'
    'He got what he deserved!'

(b) *Gii-wawaanimigooyang.*   (after having been asked a hard question)
    PAST-stump him/her.X>21/CONJ

    *Ingii-wawaanimigoomin.
    1.PAST-stump him/her.X>21/INDEP

    'They stumped us!'

The use of conjuncts in this way is striking, especially given the traditional view that conjunct-order verbs function only as subordinate clauses. In these examples, however, conjunct verbs, not independent-order verbs, are able to function as independent clauses, even *without* a predicating element, if said immediately upon the occurrence of the anteceding event or situation. Once the moment is lost, the use of plain conjuncts becomes awkward. This is also evinced by the fact that when some of these phrases were elicited out of context, the elders provided independent forms rather than the conjunct forms. For example, when I elicited from them the phrase *he got what he deserved*, I got the independent form *nigagaandenimaa* rather than the attested conjunct form in (134a). In short, the use of the conjunct in these restricted situations appears to signal the immediacy of an event or situation, possibly allowing speakers to mark these events as being more salient or foregrounded. As we will see in the sections to come, this is one of the features that makes the conjunct a prime target for work at the discourse level.

4.2   DISCOURSE USE OF CONJUNCTS

The conjunct also has uses at the discourse level. Though conjuncts at the sentence level function largely as subordinate clauses or adjunct clauses (except for the limited cases of the situational immediacy examples), they also have connective and temporal immediacy features. It is perhaps no surprise then that the conjunct would be exploited for these features, since connectivity and immediacy are both features that are well suited to create cohesion within narratives. Though largely syntactically subordinate in nature at the sentence level, at the discourse level, conjuncts may function as independent clauses. This was also the case with Rhodes's example for a related dialect of Ojibwe. Given that independent-order verbs already serve this function (at least at the sentence level), the question becomes, then, if both independent-order verbs and conjunct-order verbs may function as independent clauses within discourse, what roles do they each play within discourse? As we will see, both the conjunct and the independent order have distinct functions within discourse. In short, conjuncts carry the eventline structure of a narrative, while independent order verbs carry background and quotation phenomena. Background content is defined here as anything that gives contextualization to eventline structures. Recall that the eventline is defined as content that moves the story along, the backbone of the story (see also Longacre 1976, 468; Salser and Salver 1976, where they also talk about this *backbone* structure in some Amazonian narratives). What it is meant by "backbone" is that if you were to make a list of only the eventline verbs, you would get a basic, albeit rudimentary, summary of the story in general. Note that this is also true for many of the Amazonian languages that utilize individual lexical items to mark the eventline structure. For example, recall that for the Amazonian language Yagua, the individual lexical items *jį́įta* or *jį́į* mark a progression through a discourse along a main eventline or a progression from one thematic paragraph to the next (see Payne and Thomas 1990, 427). Ojibwe, rather than utilizing individual lexical items to mark eventline structures, utilizes the general morphological form of the conjunct order of inflection to mark them, leaving independent-order verbs to perform other discourse functions.

A summary listing of the conjunct verbs in the following story shows indeed that it is the conjunct that carries the eventline. In this story, a young boy and his friend are talking and laughing on the side of a road when an old man walks by and thinks that they are laughing at him. While a few conjuncts occur within the quotations as sentence-level conjuncts, all the other conjuncts are otherwise eventline verbs. Note also that all discourse conjuncts are glossed more narrowly than their surrounding words. This is intended to give the reader who is unfamiliar with Ojibwe the ability to see the morphological makeup of each discourse conjunct.

(135) Conjunct marking eventline structure (Eagle 1998, 16–18, audio)

(a) *Aabiding   imaa   **naaniibawiyaang***   *jiigikana.*
    one time   there   standing around.1P/CONJ   near the road

(b) ***Gaa-izhi-bimosed***   *aw*   *Zhimaaganish.*
    IC.PAST-RR-walks by.3/CONJ   that   Zhimaaganish

(c) ***Bimosed***   *akiwenzii.*
    walks by.3/CONJ   old man

(d) ***Chi-ayizhinoo'oyangid***   *iw.*
    very-pointing.3>21/CONJ   that

(e) ***Gaa-pi-zhi-maajiiba'iweyaan***   *endaayaan*   ***gii-kiiweyaan.***
    IC.PAST-come-RR-flee.1/CONJ   my house   PAST-go home.1/CONJ

(f)   ***Gaa-izhi-wiindamawagwaa***   *indedeyiban*   *nimaamaa,*   "*Wayaa,*
       IC.PAST-RR-tell.1>3P/CONJ   my late dad   my mother   wow

       akiwenzii   niinawind   a'aw   Biindigegaabaw   ingaagiigidomin   di
       old man   we   that   Biindigegaabaw   we are talking   over there

       jiigikana   imbaapi'idimin   niinawind   bimosed   a'aw
       near the road   we are laughing   we   when he walks by   that

       Zhimaaganish   i'iw.   Ingii-inenimigonaan ji-baapi'angid   gii-ikido."
       Zhimaaganish   that   he thought of us to be laughing at him   he said

(g)   ***Gaa-izhi-wiindamawid***   *nimaamaa,*   "*Ambe   wiib,   wiib   a'aw*
       IC.PAST-RR-tell.3>1/CONJ   my mother   come on   quickly   quickly   that

       asemaa   oodi   o-miizh   akiwenzii,   wiindamaw   gaawiin
       tobacco   over there   go give it to him   old man   tell him   not

       baapi'aasiwad."
       that you are not laughing at him

(h)   *Apane-go   **inaabamid**   wa'aw.*
       always   looks.1>3/CONJ   this

(i)   ***Gaa-wiindamawag,***   "*Hey,   Zhimaaganish,   gaawiin   giin*
       IC.PAST-tell.1>3/CONJ   hey   Zhimaaganish   not   you

       gigii-paapi'igoosiin   oodi,   indinaa.
       we were not laughing at you   over there   I tell him

(j)   *Mii   akiwenzii   **gii-paapid**   i'iw,   "Ho,   ho,   ho,   ho   noozis.*"
       DP   old man   PAST-laugh.3/CONJ   that   ho   ho   ho   ho   grandson

(k)   *Ke-go   miish   **gii-wiindamawid**   indedeyiban   naa*
       you see   and then   PAST-tell.3>1/CONJ   my late father   and

       nimaamaayiban,   "Gego   wiikaa   aapiji   gego   ji-niibawiyan
       my late mother   don't   ever   very   don't   to be standing

       baapi'aaken   ingiw   akiwenziinyag   naa   mindimooyenyag,"
       don't laugh at him/her   those   old men   and   old women

       gii-ikido.
       she/he says

(a) 'One time **we were standing around** near the road.

(b) And then **Zhimaaganish walked by.**

(c) **He walks by.**

(d) **He was really pointing** that thing [his cane] around **at us.**

(e) **And so I started running** to my house and went home.

(f) **And I told** my dad and mom here where they were: "Me and Biindigegaabaw were laughing near the road, laughing it up, when Zhimaaganish walks by, he thought we were laughing at him he said."

(g) **And my mom told me,** "Come, hurry, hurry and go over there and give him tobacco, tell him you weren't laughing at him."

(h) **He was** constantly **looking at me.**

(i) **And then I told him,** "Hey Zhimaaganish, we weren't laughing at you," I told him.

(j) The old man **laughed** about that, "Ho, ho, ho grandson."

(k) **And my mom and dad told me,** "Never ever stand around laughing at old men and old women," she said.'

When we include the portions of the story that give setting or background information, or that give contextualization to the eventline, we find the use of independent verbs along with conjunct verbs. This is shown from the following excerpt from this same story. For easy visibility, the discourse conjunct verbs appear in bold type and the independent verbs are underlined. Note also that the independent verbs are glossed more narrowly than their surrounding words in order to show their independent-order morphological structure in more detail.

(136) Independent verbs carrying background information (Eagle 1998, 16, audio)

(a) *Bezhig   oshki-inini   gwiiwisens   gaa-wiijiiwag   apane,*
one   young man   little boy   who I was with   always

ingii-wiijiindimin,   *ingii-gikinoo'amaa-goomin*   *di.*
1.PAST-with each other-1P/INDEP   1.PAST-teach him/her.X>1P   over there

(b) *Aabiding   imaa   **naaniibawiyaang**   jiigikana.*
one time   there   standing around-1P/CONJ   near the road

(c)   *Haaw   niinawind   imbaapi'idimin*   *gaagiigidoyaang   imaa,*
       okay   we   1.laugh together.1P/INDEP   talking   there

       imbaapi'idimin.
       1.laugh together.1P/INDEP

(d)   **Gaa-izhi-bimosed**   *aw   Zhimaaganish   gii-izhinikaazo*
       IC.PAST-RR-walks by.3/CONJ   that Zhimaaganish   PAST-be named so/INDEP

       akiwenzii.
       old man

(e)   *Aaniish naa   imbaapi'idimin*   *niinawind   imbaapi'idimin*   *imaa*
       well......... 1.laugh together.1P/INDEP we   1.laugh together.1P/INDEP there

       anooj   ikidoyaang.
       various us saying

(f)   *Waa!   **Bimosed**   akiwenzii.*
       man!   walks by.3/CONJ   old man

(a)   'One young boy that I was always with, we were together, going to school
       over there.

(b)   One time we were standing around near the road.

(c)   We're just laughing and talking, laughing it up.

(d)   And then Zhimaaganish walked by, his name was Zhimaaganish.

(e)   Well, we were just laughing with each other there saying various things.

(f)   Man, he walks by.'

What this example shows very nicely is the distribution of independent verbs
alongside conjunct verbs. Though both conjunct and independent verbs are
acting as independent clauses, or as sentences, their functions in discourse are
different. For example, in this excerpt, the independent verbs in (136a, c, d, e)
all carry information about background and provide contextualization for the
eventline. The type of background information provided in (136a, c, e) is largely
setting information, while the type of background information in (136d) is participant information, for example, the name of the old man in the story. This distribution of independent and conjunct verbs continues in this manner through-

out the story and is a common distribution seen in all the stories examined for this book.

There are complications, though. While showing a nice distribution of independent and conjunct verbs within discourse, example (136) also reveals that there are two types of conjuncts being utilized: PLAIN CONJUNCTS and CHANGED CONJUNCTS. The difference between these two types of conjuncts is in the use of initial change, an ablaut process that changes, mutates, replaces, or alters the initial vowel of a conjunct verb (see Bloomfield 1958, 23; Nichols 1980, 146–48; Mithun 1999, 41). By definition, plain conjuncts do not exhibit initial change, while changed conjuncts do (hence their name). Changed conjuncts have specific functions within sentence grammars: (1) showing completive aspect and (2) functioning as nominalized verbs, or participles (Fairbanks 2008; see also Nichols 1980, 200). The changed conjuncts in (136), however, are not serving these functions. Rather, their occurrences *appear* (at least on the surface) to be triggered by the mere presence of the relative root *izhi*. Recall that *izhi* (and other relative preverbal elements) has a peculiar syntax, in that it may cause (or appear to cause) its containing verbs to undergo initial change, while verbs within the same syntactical environment without *izhi* do not.[4] Therefore, the occurrences of the changed conjuncts within example (136) are easily explained away, since the relative preverb *izhi* appears to trigger the presence of changed conjuncts (see also Valentine 2001, 963, 969, for Odaawaa in regard to relative roots within *mii-* clauses). In other words, but for the appearance of the relative preverb *izhi*, these verbs would appear as plain conjuncts. This can be shown with an excerpt of another story. When *izhi* appears within the verbal complex, initial change occurs on the verbal complex (or on *izhi* itself if no other element precedes it), but verbs without *izhi* remain as plain conjuncts. The verbs involved with the eventline occur in bold type.

(137) *izhi* invokes initial change (Kegg 1993, 104–5)

(a) *Mii   imaa   **ani-biminizha'oyangid.***
     DP   there   start-chase.3>1P/CONJ

(b) *Wayiiba   azhigwa   imaa   **biindigeyaang.***
     soon   now   there   we come inside.1P/CONJ

(c)   *Aaniish naa*   **zegiziyaan**   **ezhi-mawiyaan**   *imaa*
      well ———   scared.1/CONJ   IC.RR-cry.1/CONJ   there

      biminizha'od.
      that she/he is chasing me/CONJ

(d)   *"Gidaano-inin   ji-wewiibishkaayan,"*   *indig.*
      I tried to tell you   to hurry up   she tells me

(e)   *Mii   go   imaa   **ba-izhi-biindiged**   a'aw   gichi-animosh,*
      DP   EMPH   there   IC.come-RR-enter.3/CONJ   that   big dog

      gaa-izhi-biindiged   *a'aw   animosh.*
      IC.PAST-RR-enter.3/CONJ   that   dog

(a)   'It **started following us**.

(b)   In a little while **we went inside**.

(c)   Well, I was **scared and crying** at being followed there.

(d)   "I told you to hurry," she said to me.

(e)   That big dog **came right in**, that dog **came right in**.'

The *mii*- clauses, *mii imaa ani-biminizha'oyangid* in (137a) and *mii go imaa ba-izhi-biindiged* in (137e) are particularly revealing, since they show similar syntactic environments from which to make a comparison. For example, in the *mii*-clause without *izhi* in (137a), the preverbal element *ani*- 'starts' is left intact, while the preverbal element *bi*- 'come' housed within the *mii*- clause in (137b) undergoes initial change to *ba*-. In short, it is the *mii*- clause containing *izhi* that shows initial change on the verbal complex.

The fact that the conjunct verb carries the eventline structures of narratives may help to explain another syntactical curiosity involving the *mii*- clauses themselves, since they too employ the use of both the conjunct-order verbs and independent-order verbs within discourse. Earlier work has characterized *mii* as primarily requiring the use of conjunct verbs, largely relegating cases involving independent verbs as rare cases or rare constructions (see Rhodes 1998, 289). While it has been well known that *mii* may sometimes occur with independent verbs, especially with independent-order negative clauses (Nichols 1980, 118; Rhodes 1998, 287), the use of *mii dash*, or its contracted form *miish*, with independent-order verbs, as it turns out, is not so rare a phenomenon within discourse.[5] In fact, these occurrences (especially those occurring with non-negative clauses) are quite consistent within discourse, even across speakers. One such case occurs within the story discussed previously about the old man who got mad because he thought a couple of kids were laughing at him.

(138) *mii dash* with independent verbs (Eagle 1998, 16–18, audio)

(a) **Gaa-zhi-wiindamawagwaa**   *indedeyiban*   *nimaamaa*   *omaa*
     IC.PAST-RR-tell.1>3P/CONJ   my late dad   my mom   here

   eyaawaad: "*Wayaa*   *akiwenzii*   *niinawind*   *a'aw*   *Biindigegaabaw*
   where they are   wow   old man   we   that   Biindigegaabaw

   ingaagiigidomin   *di*   *jiigikana*   *imbaapi'idimin*   *niinawind*
   we are talking   over there   near the road   we are laughing   we

   bimosed   *a'aw*   *Zhimaaganish*   *i'iw.*
   when he walks by   that   Zhimaaganish   that

(b) *Ingii-inenimigonaan*   *ji-baap'angid*   *gii-ikido.*"
     he thought of us as   that we were laughing at him   he said

(c) *Ke*   *gaawiin*   *gidaa-baapi'aasiig*   *chi-aya'aag.*
     see   not   you should not laugh at them   elders

(d) *Mii*   *gaa-inendamaan*   *iw.*
     DP   what I thought   that

(e) <u>*Miish*</u>   <u>*ingii-nishki'aanaan*</u>   *akiwenzii,*   *mii*   *izhinoo'oyangid*   *i'iw*
     and then   we made him mad   old man   DP   him pointing at us   that

   omitigom.
   his stick

(f) **Gaa-zhi-wiindamawid**   *nimaamaa,*   "*Ambe*   *wiib,*   *wiib*   *a'aw*
     IC.PAST-RR-tell.3>1   my mom   come on   quickly   quickly   that

   asemaa   *oodi*   *o-miizh*   *akiwenzii,*   *wiindamaw*   *gaawiin*
   tobacco   over there   go give it to him   old man   tell him   not

   baapi'aasiwad . . ."
   that you were not laughing at him

(a)   '**And I told** my dad and mom here where they were: "Me and Biindigegaabaw were laughing near the road, laughing it up, when Zhimaaganish walks by.

(b)   He thought we were laughing at him, he said."

(c)   You see, you shouldn't laugh at elders.

(d)   That's what I thought.

(e)   <u>And then we went and made the old man angry</u>, pointing his stick at us.

(f)   **And** my mom **told me**, "Come, hurry, hurry and go over there and give him tobacco, tell him you weren't laughing at him . . ."'

The eventline verbs *gaa-zhi-wiindamawagwaa* 'and I told [dad and mom]' and *gaa-zhi-wiindamawid* 'and [my mom] told me' occur in (138a, f), but nestled in between these events in (138c–e) is the narrator's commentary, which gives contextualization to these events, that is, that one should not laugh at elders, that he knew that, but that he and his friend made the old man mad anyway. Within the background commentary, *miish* occurs with independent-order verb *ingii-nishki'aanaan* 'we made him mad' instead of conjunct-order inflection. Note, however, that when *miish* is involved with verbs functioning within the eventline structure the conjunct is triggered. This can been seen later on in this same story. Examine the following:

(**139**)   miish with conjunct-order verbs (Eagle 1998, 18, audio)

(a)   *Mii   bijiinag   gii-minwendamaan.*
        DP   finally   that I was happy

(b)   *Ingii-ni-giiwe,   wahaa,   **gii-ni-baapaapiyaan**   naa   **ni-nagamoyaan***
        I went home   wow   PAST-start-laugh.1/CONJ   and   start-sing.1/CONJ

        gaa-ni-maajaayaan.
        after I left

(c)   *Mii   bijiinag   gii-minwendamaan   gii-miinag   asemaan.*
        DP   finally   that I was happy   that I gave him tobacco

(d)   *Ke-go   **miish**   **gii-wiindamawid**   indedeyiban   naa   nimaamaayiban,*
        see   and then   PAST-tell.3>1/CONJ   my late dad   and   my late mom

"Gego	wiikaa	aapiji	gego	ji-niibawiyan	baapi'aaken
don't	ever	very	don't	be standing around	don't laugh at him

ingiw	akiwenziinyag	naa	mindimooyenyag"	gii-ikido.
those	old men	and	old women	she/he said

(a)   'I finally felt good about it.

(b)   I started home, man, and **I started laughing** and **started singing** after I left.

(c)   I finally was happy when I gave him tobacco.

(d)   **And then** my mom and dad **told me**, "Never ever stand around laughing at old men and old women," she said.'

What these examples involving *miish* show is that when the verbs connected to the *mii* complex are carrying background information, the verb appears as an independent-order verb. If it is carrying eventline information, the verb appears with conjunct-order inflection.[6] This same sort of process can be also seen with another *mii* complex, *miish i'iw*, which has a narrative-advancing function similar to that of *miish* (see also Fairbanks 2008). When the verb connected to *miish i'iw* is involved with the eventline, it occurs with conjunct inflection. When the verb occurs within background commentary, it occurs with independent-order inflection. This is shown in the following excerpts from two stories. In the excerpt in (140), the narrator, Maude Kegg, lists the events that occurred during a trip to set a net for tullibees. In (141), before telling a story about her encounter with a "Mooniyaa-Lady," the narrator provides a rather lengthy background explaining what a Mooniyaa-Lady is (only partially given here).

(140) *miish i'iw* within eventline structures (Kegg 1993, 80–81)

(a)

Gaawiin	igo	gichi-gisinaasinoon,	mii	**ezhi-gawishimoyaang**
not	EMPH	not very cold	DP	RR-lay down.1P/CONJ

imaa	jiigibiig,	**ezhi-gawishimoyaang**	imaa	jiigibiig
there	shore	RR-lay down.1P/CONJ	there	shore

ganawenimaad	iniw	odasabiin,	**jiichiigawiganebinag**	imaa
as she watches him/her	that	her net	scratch.1>3/CONJ	there

      zhingishinaang,   *apane*   *go*   *ezhi-anoozhid*   *ji-jiichiigawiganebinag.*

      as we lie there   always   EMPH   has me do   to scratch her back

(b)   *Miish i'iw,*   **miish i'iw**   **maadaajimod.**

     and then . . .   and then . . .   start telling stories.3/CONJ

(a)   'It wasn't very cold **so we lay down** there on the shore where she could watch the net and **I scratched her back** as we lay there; she always had me scratch her back.

(b)   Then **she started to tell stories.**'

(141) *miish i'iw* within background structures (Kegg 1993, 142–45)

(a)   *Mewinzha*   *dash*   *iwidi*   *ayi'ing*   <u>*ingii-izhaamin,*</u>

     long ago   DM   over there   that one place   1.PAST-go.1P/INDEP

     iwidi   *akeyaa*   *ayi'ing,*   *waasa*   *go*   *iwidi,*

     over there   way   that one place   far   EPMH   over there

     amanj   *iidog*   *ezhinikaadegwen*   *anishinaabewinikaadeg.*

     I don't know   DUBIT   what it must be called   what it is called in Indian

(b)   <u>*Ingii-o-manoominikemin*</u>   *iwidi.*

     1.PAST-go and-rice-1P/INDEP   over there

(c)   <u>*Miish i'iw*</u>   <u>*ingii-pi-waabamigonaanig*</u>   *iko*   *ingiw*   *anishinaabeg*

     and then . . .   1.PAST-come-see.3P>1P/INDEP   used to   those   Indians

     ini-onaagoshig,   *bi-mawadishiyangidwaa.*

     towards evening   to come visit us

(d)   <u>*Bimishkaawag.*</u>

     go by boat.3P/INDEP

(e)   *Gaawiin*   *gaye*   *awiiya*   *odaabaanan,*   *gaawiin*   *gegoo*   *miikana.*

     not   also   someone   car   not   something   road

(f)   *Miish*   *a'aw*   *bezhig*   *ikwe*   **babaa-naaniibawid.**

     and then   that   one   woman   around-stands.3/CONJ

(g)   <u>*Enda-onizhishi*</u>   *a'aw*   *mindimooyenh.*

     very-pretty/INDEP   that   old woman

(h) *Mii* **gaa-pi-izhi-nawadinid,**   "*Awenen* *gidoodem,*" *indig.*
    DP IC.PAST-come-RR-grab.3>1/CONJ who your clan she tells me

(a) 'Long ago we went over there, a long way, I don't know what it is called in Indian.

(b) We went over there to rice.

(c) The Indians came to see us for a visit in the evening.

(d) They got around in boats.

(e) There were no cars and no road.

(f) There was one lady **standing around**.

(g) That old lady was nice-looking.

(h) **She came and grabbed me**, asking me, "What is your totem?"'

As expected, when the verb occurring with *miish i'iw* occurs within the eventline structure, the verb appears with conjunct-order inflection, but when it occurs within background structures, it appears with independent-order inflection.

Overall, what these data show is that while the conjunct has very specific roles at the sentence level in marking subordinate clauses, it also has a very major role within discourse, to carry the eventline structure of a story or narrative. This is evident even where the use of the *mii-* complexes *mii dash, miish,* or *miish i'iw* are involved. With them, too, the conjunct carries the eventline, while the independent carries background information. This elevation of the conjunct for work at the discourse level shows that it is not only individual lexical or grammatical items that are targets for discourse work, but entire inflectional systems as well.

FIVE

Conclusion

I hope to have accomplished two things in this book. First, I have identified and characterized many of the common discourse markers occurring in Ojibwe, which heretofore have been largely unexplored. For example, while both linguists and second-language learners have known about the existence of the Ojibwe marker *isa*, its exact function within discourse has largely been unknown or misunderstood. Many of the Ojibwe mystery particles like *isa*, such as *sha, gosha, goda,* and *naa,* share a similar fate. We know they exist and that native speakers use them, but their functions as mystery particles have been exactly that, mysteries. As a result, many listings for mystery particles within dictionaries and pedagogical grammars have labeled them simply as "emphatics," "particles," or "fillers," or they have no label at all. When a translation *is* attributed to these elements within dictionaries, the translation usually cannot give language learners too many clues as to their overall usage and meaning. They are just too difficult to define within the confines of a dictionary entry. Ojibwe discourse connectives such as *inashke*, though more transparent in their meaning, also have their fair share of mysteries. For example, if you were to ask an Ojibwe language teacher in our community what the word *inashke* ('see!, look!, hear!') means, the answer you might normally hear is, "It means *behold!*" The immediate difficulty that arises from this definition is first figuring out what the meaning of the archaic word *behold* is and how it is used within English, and then figuring out how to correlate that usage back into Ojibwe, which may or may not coincide with its usage within English. In the end, such explanations based upon archaic English words are no explanation at all. Many Ojibwe discourse markers are just misunderstood, and this appears to be the reason why discourse markers do not appear much in second-language-speaker speech (at least from my vantage point). Therefore, one of the objectives in writing this book was not only to document and describe these elements (which in itself is an important endeavor) but to begin to bring to light the various meanings and functions of these elusive elements so that they may start to become common knowledge among the second-language-speaker community. Once these markers become common knowledge and are commonly taught, they then can start to make their way into the speech patterns of the second-language speakers, who in turn may start to use them with their babies in the home or in the immersion classroom. Otherwise we risk losing (in a very short amount of time, mind you) a whole array of markers that provide nuance and color to the language.

The second thing that I hope to have accomplished is the expansion of Schiffrin's initial characterization of discourse markers to include the nature of discourse markers cross-linguistically. This has revealed that a variety of elements may function as discourse markers across languages—including individual words, lexicalized phrases, clitics, affixes, and preverbs—and that markers may occur in a host of positions within an utterance or sentence: utterance initially, utterance internally, utterance finally, and in second position. Ojibwe has been especially instructive in regard to cross-linguistic evidence, since it not only employs the use of utterance-initial words for discourse work (such as *inashke, awenh, aaniish*) but also employs second-position clitics and particles (such as *idash/-sh, isa, sha, gosha, naa*) and a relative preverb (*izhi*). Other languages with rich morphological structures like Ojibwe also show a tendency toward the use of clitics and affixes as discourse markers. What this indicates is that speakers may use the linguistic and grammatical machinery available to them in their own language in order to accomplish discourse work. This is also supported by the fact that some speakers of indigenous languages of the Americas such as Tojolab'al and Yucatec Maya have even incorporated the use of markers from contact languages (such as Spanish) alongside the use of their own indigenous markers. Other machinery exploited for discourse use is the lexical or grammatical inventory existing in language itself. The cross-linguistic data have consistently shown that many lexical or grammatical items are exploited for their sentence-level use for work at the discourse level. This sort of raiding of the grammatical shelf is not restricted to individual words, affixes, clitics, or preverbs, however, but also applies to entire inflectional systems. Recall that Ojibwe makes regular use of conjunct-order verbs as *sentences* in order to mark the eventline of narratives or stories at the discourse level, a seemingly contradictive result given that conjunct verbs normally act only as subordinate clauses at the sentence level. This is a striking example of the exploitive nature of the discourse marking mechanism within languages, and ultimately of the robust language mechanism existing within the human brain.

While I have analyzed a wide range of elements as discourse markers in Ojibwe, more research is necessary in order to determine the full range of uses for each marker described in this book. For example, the section on mystery particle *goda* is quite short. This is because the data exhibiting this discourse marker are scanty. More data exhibiting the use of *goda* might reveal a broader function not noticed here. Still, a whole paper could be devoted to the exposition of each one of these markers, and I hope that further research will either confirm or provide further elaboration (or even corrections) on the various functions and meanings that I have described here. Also, one of the difficulties that I encountered in describing the various functions of Ojibwe discourse markers was trying to reconcile the *seemingly* unrelated functions that some of them have. For example, I have characterized the particle *mii* as having various functions (e.g., deictic particle, aspectual marker, veridical marker, and command softener) that, on the surface, do not appear to emanate from a single underlying core function or meaning. Indeed, if such a core function existed (and it might), it would be a more accurate characterization to identify that underlying core meaning or function, which then might account for *mii*'s various surface functions. For *mii* (no pun intended), I have not been able to reconcile its various surface functions as emanating from a single underlying function. I suggest a few possible reasons for this. First, my descriptions might be inadequate, either because of a scarcity of data (which might not show the full picture of *mii*'s distribution), or because I just inaccurately described the data. Inadequate descriptions could mask the underlying core function. Second, there might be more than one *mii*, in which case we are dealing with homophones—a situation that might result from two (or more) words that sound alike today but have different origins historically. This could also undermine an accurate description. Third, *mii* might have different surface functions that are not reconcilable with one single underlying function per se, but whose various surface functions might be typical for deictic particles like *mii*. In other words, our current linguistic knowledge of deictic particles might not be at a level sufficient to be able to account for what seem to be unrelated functions. Future discourse marker research would need to try to reconcile seemingly unrelated functions that a single discourse marker might have, either through more accurate description based upon more language data or by accounting for them with new available research.

There are still a great many elements in Ojibwe that I consider to be discourse markers that I did not describe in this book. Among these are the interjective-type words that I am only beginning to grasp. These include *aapidekamig* 'what in the world', *poh* or *powaj* 'gotcha', *chaningee* 'yuck, ew' (a female's term), and *oy yoy* 'there, there' (said to or about babies crying). While I have supplied various translations for these interjectives, they need more exploration to get a better idea of their general use and meaning. I also did not include the description of the temporal discourse marker *azhigwa* 'now, and then', which has various sentence- and discourse-level uses. This is another marker that is still largely unexplored. The exposition of these various markers (as well as others not mentioned here) will have to await further research.

NOTES

1. INTRODUCTION AND BACKGROUND

1. To my knowledge, the term *mystery particle* was coined by Longacre (1976). He used this term to describe certain verbal and nominal affixes and sentential particles that "defy analysis even at a relatively advanced state of research." He goes on to say that "the native speaker uses such affixes and particles with complete assurance but is unable to verbalize anything very concrete as to their meaning and function" (Longacre 1976, 468). I am using *mystery particle* to describe the type of markers in Ojibwe that share this difficulty. In other words, they have no, or very little, referential meaning. While it is quite easy for speakers to come up with a definition of the discourse connective *miinawaa* 'and', speakers usually cannot do so for markers such as *sha*, which have no meaning in and of themselves and can only be defined by their use within a certain context. As it turns out, all the Ojibwe mystery particles that I describe in this book happen to serve an interpersonal or pragmatic function. Many of the mystery particles described by Longacre for Amazonian languages, however, have a textual function rather than an interpersonal or pragmatic one, e.g., marking the backbone structure of a discourse. Therefore, my division between discourse connectives and mystery particles here is not meant to suggest that all mystery particles serve a pragmatic function in all languages. They just happen to do so in Ojibwe, and organizing them in this fashion is only a matter of convenience.

2. Goddard states that he did this as a convenience measure for the sake of discussion but also concedes that it was "clear that the conventional group labels just listed do not correspond well to the linguistic divisions" (1978, 583).

3. William Jones, a Fox Indian and a native speaker of Fox who transcribed many Ojibwe stories in the early 1900s, often adjoined what may be analyzed as clitics to their host words. Here are some random examples from his transcriptions, followed in parentheses by the convention I use: *mīsa'* (*mii-sa*), *mīdạc* (*mii-dash*, although the convention has been to leave separated, as *mii dash*), *migu* (*mii-go*), and one not involving *mii*: *cigwasa* (*zhigwa-sa*). See W. Jones 1919 for further investigation. I have to admit, though, that my hyphen usage may not be entirely consistent, as aesthetics also play a role in my decision making about hyphen usage. For example, if adherence to my convention for hyphens would result in what I see as an unattractive expression, such as in *mii-sa-go namaj* 'I have no idea', I usually minimize the number of hyphens that occur, preferring instead *mii-sago namanj*. Note that the traditional method would leave all elements separated, as *mii sa go*

namanj. In short, the general orthographical conventions for written Ojibwe are far from standard.

4. Function words, such as the Ojibwe demonstratives, may occur as mono-moraic, but they are truncations of bimoraic words, e.g., *aw* from *a'aw* 'that (animate)' and *iw* from *i'iw* 'that (inanimate)', and many times may cliticize to their head nouns, e.g., *i-mashkiki* 'that medicine' from full form *i'iw mashkiki*.

2. WHAT IS A DISCOURSE MARKER?

1. Both Brinton (1996) and Jucker and Ziv (1998) also give sizeable lists of names for these elements.
2. This book, in fact, will expand the known word classes or categories from which discourse markers may be drawn.
3. An "operational definition" allows readers who are not yet familiar with the identification and designation of discourse markers to be able to follow Schiffrin's analysis.
4. These are only the discourse markers she considered in her analysis, but she acknowledges the existence of others, e.g., the perception verbs *see, look*, and *listen*; the locative deictics *here* and *there*; the adverbial *why*; the interjections *gosh* and *boy*; the verb *say*; metatalk such as *this is the point* and *what I mean is . . .* ; and the quantifier phrases *anyway, anyhow*, and *whatever* (Schiffrin 1987a, 327–28).
5. In her chapter 2, Schiffrin (1987a) provides an "operational" definition of discourse markers to aid the reader in identifying discourse markers on a rudimentary level. Then, in the last chapter (chapter 10), she offers a refinement of that operational definition based upon the behavior of the English discourse markers she describes throughout the book. This refinement is the set of "tentative suggestions" provided in (3). In a later work, Schiffrin refers to that set of tentative suggestions as "theoretical definitions of markers" (2003a, 58), and so the designation of her "tentative suggestions" as "theoretical" is her phrasing, not mine.
6. Early on, Grimes also recognized this tendency, stating, "The kinds of relationships that are involved once we go beyond the sentence are different from those that operate within sentences" (1975, 4). Schiffrin too has observed this tendency in regard to the use of conjunctions within discourse: "But we have also seen several features of discourse that point to differences between discourse grammars and sentence grammars, and thus suggest that the principles governing [the] use of conjunctions in discourse do not totally parallel those for conjunctions in sentences" (Schiffrin 1987a, 320; see also Schourup 1985, 123).
7. Fraser appears to disagree with this, suggesting, "In short, discourse markers are not adverbs, for example, masquerading as another category from time to time" (1990, 388). Oddly, before and after that statement, he seemingly contradicts it by recognizing that discourse markers are indeed drawn from various grammati-

cal sources and proceeds to give examples of both grammatical and discourse uses of various items, such as *now, well,* and *however.* The cross-linguistic literature is replete with this sort of behavior by discourse markers: see, for example, Maschler (1997, 197–98) for Israeli Hebrew, in which discourse marker *ta yode'a* 'y'know' may occur with the literal meaning 'you know'; Biq (1990, 205) for Mandarin, in which discourse connective *na* and *name* also have grammatical functions as demonstratives; Jucker & Smith (1998, 183–84) for English, in which discourse marker *like* has lexical uses as a verb, preposition, suffix, and conjunction; Shloush (1998, 62) for the Hebrew discourse marker *bekicur* 'in short', which has a function as an adverbial; and Ariel (1998, 226) for the Hebrew discourse marker *harey* 'after all', which has a grammatical function as a sentence adverbial. So there is ample cross-linguistic evidence in support of the primary and secondary features of discourse markers.

8. This natural divide is observed in Ojibwe discourse and explains the organization of this paper into textual and interpersonal discourse ("mystery particles") markers.
9. She uses the term *pragmatic marker* as synonymous with the term *discourse marker.*
10. In this way, linguistics serves the Ojibwe language learning community, and not the other way around. While it is nice to know what makes discourse markers work, knowing *how* they work is much more useful for language stabilization and revitalization purposes.
11. Unfortunately, the following examples were not accompanied by word-by-word glosses in their original sources. I therefore could not provide them here.
12. Schwenter (1996) states that *o sea* is a connective and is often translatable as English *that is,* but because this translation is not always a felicitous reading for *o sea,* he leaves *o sea* untranslated in his examples.
13. Both Park and Zavala left the discourse markers unglossed in the translations, preferring to define their use in the body of the text. This appears to be the practice of some authors when speaking about various discourse marker functions. In making requests in Korean, Park suggests that marker *nuntey* is used to set up an "accountability relevance point, inviting the interlocutor to figure out what the speaker is implying" (1999, 198). In Andean Spanish, Zavala (2001, 1006) suggests that marker *pe* (or *pues*) is used to confirm a request for confirmation or clarification based upon an inference from a previous utterance.
14. For Latin, Kroon (1998) appears to have examples that show second-position clitics acting as discourse markers, albeit she never refers to them as second-position markers per se. Latin is famously reputed to have second-position clitics, but this widely accepted analysis has recently come under attack by Agbayani and Golston (2010), who argue that a proper understanding of conjunction in early IE ("Indo-European") undercuts the traditional notion of *second position* in IE. According to

Agbayani and Golston, what have been traditionally analyzed as second-position elements in Latin (including Ancient Greek and Hittite) are more correctly analyzed as clause-initial elements. Even with Latin, despite this recent controversy, the literature on second-position discourse markers is scanty, and further scholarship on this subject would help to enrich the already growing knowledge of discourse markers.

15. The Yagua marker *jĩíta* does not appear to be well known, as I can find no references to it in the literature.

16. Thomas Payne (1997) states that the second-position clitic *jĩíta* is written as a separate word for orthographic reasons.

17. It is interesting to note that McGloin and Konishi describe one of the functions of discourse marker *shi* as being "precisely in between the connective use and the final-particle use" (2010, 574), since *shi* in one particular example did not coordinate two propositions as a connective per se but was also not semantically subordinate to preceding utterances, as most of the examples with discourse marker *shi* showed. In that example, the *shi* utterances, they explain, function to elaborate, support the general feeling, and move the dialogue forward by giving additional elaborations. This is not surprising, however, given the multifunctionality of discourse markers. Grammatical elements within sentence grammars are usually targeted *precisely* for their grammatical facility, which might accomplish *similar* work at the discourse level. Given the grammatical function of connective *shi* in Japanese to coordinate propositions at the sentence level, it appears that *shi* is being exploited in order to coordinate larger chunks of discourse. This is supported by the fact that it was "difficult to find a main assertion in the text to which these *shi* utterances relate back, either as reason or supportive evidence" (574). I believe that *shi*'s function to support general feeling and to move the dialogue forward to allow additional elaboration is an extension of its grammatical use as a connective at the sentence level.

18. What I mean by "word shape" is a word that might be changed in form by morphological or inflectional processes.

19. Rhodes noticed that in Ojibwe, too, conjunct verbs may sometimes act as independent clauses, stating, "This traditional characterization of verb forms as independent versus dependent can be quite misleading to a non-Algonquianist syntactician because of the great variety of syntactic contexts in which dependently inflectioned verbs appear, some of which are not obviously subordinate" (2006, 6; originally stated in 1998 in a lecture at the University of Manitoba).

20. Although I would prefer to provide a word-by-word gloss, the original author does not provide one. Therefore I cannot do so here.

21. But see Altenberg 2006, which shows that certain exemplifying connectors, such as *for example* and *for instance*, and certain contrastive connectors, such as *how-*

ever, often occur in parenthetic second position in order to "highlight the initial element, syntactically and prosodically, thereby indicating a significant break or shift in the development of discourse" (35–36). This sort of second-position work, I argue, differs fundamentally from languages like Ojibwe, which have discourse markers that are syntactically restricted to second position and that must always occur there. Altenberg's data show that connectors such as *for example, for instance*, and *however* clearly show a proclivity for initial position, but when they occur in second position, they "create specific discourse-related orientations" (12, citing Smits 2002, 135).

22. Still, in a small number of languages, the movement of discourse markers is more free, allowing them to float within host clauses. Italian and Finnish, for example, show examples of individual discourse markers that may appear in various locations throughout the clause (Bazzanella 1990 and Hakulinen and Seppänen 1992, respectively). English has discourse markers that may move freely within utterances as well, e.g., *y'know*, but the overall preference for English discourse markers is still initial position.

23. I am using the term *discourse marking* as a way of making a distinction between *discourse markers* (individual items or lexicalized phrases) and the use of inflectional morphology for discourse work.

24. Unless what Schiffrin meant by her observation that a marker may "have a range of prosodic contours" (1987a, 328) is that discourse markers *show* or *exhibit* a range of contours, such as appearing as stressed or not stressed. The cross-linguistic data do support this. It is unclear to me, however, how this helps to determine whether an expression is a discourse marker or not. This was not made clear in Schiffrin's original work (1987a) either. In my research, whether or not a significant pause occurred directly after markers did not appear to be diagnostic either. For languages like Ojibwe, which make heavy use of affixes, pauses would not be a significant factor in their determination as discourse markers, nor have I found any differences between those markers that exhibited pauses and those that did not.

25. Not accounting for such social, interactional, or cultural aspects of discourse markers may be the reason why RT accounts of discourse markers have not been totally successful in accounting for the differences between the coherence relations of the discourse markers *nevertheless, although, however, whereas*, and *yet*. As Blakemore points out, these coherence relations "are not captured in an analysis which links them to a contrastive or adversative relation" (2004, 235). In other words, to say that they mark a contrastive or adversative relation is not sufficient to explain why one contrastive marker would be used over another. While I provide no analysis here that would account for the subtle differences between these contrastive markers (an analysis that would require the examination of actual language data and not made-up examples), I venture to say that such differences

might be accounted for if viewed not just in light of their mechanical "contrastive" or "adversative" function (which RT theorists appear to do) but also in light of the social, interactive, and cultural motivations that speakers might have in using them.

3. OJIBWE DISCOURSE MARKERS

1. There might be some doubt whether forms such as *inake*, or *ina*, are actually variations of *inashke*. My consultants tell me that they are, so I have listed them together here with *inashke*.

2. It is unclear whether the *inashke* function in Ojibwe fully mirrors the English *you see*, since it is unclear exactly what all the functions of *you see* are in English.

3. The particle *mii* in these narratives will be glossed as DP for "deictic particle." This particle is discussed in section 3.1.1.5.

4. In other words, those that had the same *clan*. The elders prefer the use of the term *clan* here, rather than *totem* (as published).

5. The elders were not familiar with the word *wegwaagi* as it appears in Kegg 1993, which is a compilation of stories collected in the 1970s. This term appears to have gone out of use with modern speakers.

6. There is much to be explored in regard to conjunctions in Ojibwe, however. While the examples in (30) showed that the two coordinated clauses were identical in category, i.e., *NP miinawaa NP*, *VP miinawaa VP* (for independent and conjunct-order verbs, respectively), examples can be found in which verbal modes are mixed, e.g., *Asemaan gii-izhiwidamoonangwaa*, **miinawaa** *ogii-ni-apenimonaawaa miigwanigikiwe'on*. 'They carried tobacco for us, **and** relied on an eagle staff'. For this example, while the two coordinated clauses (underlined) are verb phrases, the first is a conjunct-order verb and the second is an independent-order verb.

7. The verb here might actually be *da-izhaasiin* (with the use of the future tense marker *da-*, rather than the modal marker *daa-*), as this would be more fitting of the translation 'don't let Naawakamigookwe go anywhere'. I have not been able to confirm this against the original audio recordings, however, and so I am only noting it here.

8. A distinction must be made here regarding topics that are semantically related and those that are not. The discourse topics spoken of here are those that are semantically related. For example, in the upcoming example, the two topics being coordinated are semantically related to the main topic of the story, *an old man and his daily traveling habits*. Schiffrin does not make a distinction, since English may mark both semantically related topics and unrelated ones with *and*. As we will see, this is not the case for Ojibwe, since the broad topics that make up a narrative in Ojibwe and that are not semantically related are marked by contrastive marker *idash*. In this way, it is *idash* that allows speakers to move on to new topics within

narratives. The point here is, however, that Ojibwe appears to make more use of asyndetic connections in coordinating expanded event structures than English does. This is true for asyndetic connections in Ojibwe in general.

9. This is supported by the general use of asyndetic connection (i.e., juxtaposition of two constituents without a connector) in the language as a whole, where a multitude of grammatical relations may be selected and displayed by the use of asyndetic connection. One example is in the displaying causality, e.g., *Miish ezhi-mookawaakiiyaan wii-pimishkaayaan*. 'I started crying because I wanted to go paddling' (Kegg 1993, 134). In this example, there is nothing within this sentence meaning *because*. It is the asyndetic connection within context that allows the grammatical relation of causality to be displayed.

10. The unmarked word order for the nominal predicate construction "that is George" (no emphasis on *that*) would be *Jaaj a'aw*, putting the noun first, followed by the demonstrative *a'aw* (with no copula). Switching the demonstrative *a'aw* to a position before the noun results in a focus construction that puts emphasis on *a'aw*, the initial element, e.g., ***a'aw** Jaaj* '**that** is George' (emphasis on *that*). See Fairbanks 2008 for a full discussion.

11. I'm using the term *topic marker* very loosely (and cautiously) to mean a marker that signals a break from prior discourse to a new topic (which may be simply the introduction of a new character, theme, or subject). It basically marks topic shifts. As we will see, this is one of the major functions of *idash* within discourse. It is merely a label of convenience.

12. I also noted this fact in my earlier work on *mii* (Fairbanks 2008). There I provided examples from a northern dialect of Ojibwe, Northwestern Ojibwe, where *mii dash* (or *miihsh* for that dialect) occurred exclusively with independent-order verbs in an environment where conjunct verbs would be expected to occur for southern dialects of Ojibwe like Mille Lacs.

13. The fact that *mii dash* may occur with both conjunct and independent-order verbs is intriguing. The literature to date has opted to treat cases where *mii dash* occurs with independent forms as exceptions or as rare cases, rather than to offer an explanation for these occurrences. As it turns out, there is a discourse explanation. This explanation is provided in section 8.2.

14. I have transliterated the original story into the Double Vowel orthography and have reworked the placement of periods under the guidance of the elders at Mille Lacs. Also, the original publication gives authorship to "a Mille Lacs Band Elder." The elders and I suspect that it was James (Jim) Clark who wrote the story and provided it to the newspaper. I subsequently asked Jim for myself if he knew who wrote the story, to which he jokingly replied, "a Mille Lacs Band Elder!" So I never quite got a straight answer, but I think he was implying that it was indeed him.

15. It is very difficult to accurately provide a translation for the words *mii* and *idash* in

these examples. Deictic particle *mii* can have various translations depending on its use, and while *idash* may be translated as "but" in sentence-level uses, this translation is many times infelicitous in its discourse use. For this reason, I have chosen to gloss *mii* as DP (deictic particle) and *idash* as DM (discourse marker).

16. The term *event* is being used broadly here to include such actions as providing background information, actual event processes, or elaborations.

17. There are six such elements, one of which is *izhi*: *ako-* 'so long, so far, since', *apiichi-* 'such intensity, such extent', *izhi-* 'thus, thither', *onji-* 'thence, therefore', *daso-* 'so many', and *dazhi-* 'there'. Their root variants are *akw-*, *apiit-*, *iN-*, *ond-*, *dasw-*, and *daN*, respectively (Nichols 1980, 142; Valentine 2001, 160, 421–23).

18. Valentine defines a preverb as an "element which may [be] compounded to the front of a verb, to signal information such as tense, direction, etc. For example, in *gii-ni-giiwe*, 'Ansg [animate singular] went back home', *gii-* and *ni-* are both preverbs. Each preverb is set off with its own hyphen" (2001, 1050).

19. Initial change is an ablaut process that changes, mutates, replaces, or alters the initial vowel of a conjunct verb (see Bloomfield 1958, 23; Nichols 1980, 146–48; Mithun 1999, 41).

20. I have kept the original orthography for this example as it appears in the original document. These examples come from a handout prepared by Millie Benjamin. As you can see, she preferred not to use hyphens when using the Double Vowel orthography.

21. I left the word-by-word glosses as represented in the original letter, although I have disagreements with his glosses for *mii*. I would gloss them as generally VER for "veridical marker," since this appears to be its function in this example. The glosses were presumably made by Reverend Gilfillan himself (a non-native speaker of Ojibwe) before he donated his letters to the Indiana Historical Society (and which later apparently ended up at the Minnesota Historical Society). I also transliterated the original orthography of the letter to conform with the orthography used in this book.

22. Although scholars often refer to consultants by their surname, I have chosen to use first names in this work, believing that it makes the work less formal and more personable.

23. The elders were unfamiliar with the term *zaagidon*. It perhaps is a term that has gone out of use for modern speakers.

24. I am, of course, not suggesting that *sa* and *uh* are equivalent in every way. *Uh* in English has other functions too that *sa* does not appear to parallel, e.g., *Uh . . . yes*. Here, with continuing tone on *yes*, *uh* signals that the answer provided should be obvious to the interlocutor, but for some reason it isn't.

25. It is unclear who the author of this story is, as the original publication lists three people as the authors for a set of stories from whence this story came: Timothy

Dunnigan, Rose Barstow, and Angeline Northbird. I have cited Nichols, who was the editor for this collection.

4. CONJUNCT ORDER AS A DISCOURSE-MARKING DEVICE

1. More specifically, plain conjuncts are conjuncts that do not show INITIAL CHANGE, an ablaut process that changes the initial vowel of plain conjunct verbs. Those that do show initial change are referred to as CHANGED CONJUNCTS and may serve a variety of functions, i.e., showing completive aspect or forming nominalized verbs.
2. For independent-order AI verbs, there is no personal prefix for third person singular, e.g., *maajaa* 'she/he leaves'.
3. The verb *gaa-zhi-nkweshkwaad* 'that's how he came to meet this bear' in (128b) appears to me to be thematic as well, since it too moves the plot forward. In fact, this verb is actually quite pivotal to this passage of the story. Rhodes does not include this, however, in his analysis. As we will see, syntactical factors come into play that may affect the shape of plain conjuncts within discourse, i.e., conjuncts that appear with initial change, etc. In short, this verb is underlyingly a plain conjunct but must appear with initial change due to the presence of the relative root *izhi*. Therefore, verbs such as *gaa-zhi-nkweshkwaad* may carry the eventline of a narrative as well, acting as independent clauses.
4. To say that a plain conjunct verb *undergoes* initial change assumes that speakers start with a plain conjunct in their heads and then apply a rule of initial change to form (or derive) changed conjuncts. The label *initial change*, a common term in Algonquian linguistics to refer to ablaut forms, also appears to imply a derivational process. It is unclear, however, whether speakers are actually deriving anything. Speaking about the distribution of plain and changed conjuncts in this way is only a matter of convenience, as it is sometimes helpful to talk about changed forms as being derived from unchanged forms.
5. This use of *mii dash* or *miish* with independent-order verbs can be found quite commonly in older texts such as those originating from Bois Fort (a Minnesota reservation) within the 1919 William Jones collection of stories. These occurrences are not limited to the Bois Fort texts, however, as *mii dash* or *miish* can be found to occur with independent verbs quite frequently in modern texts as well. Many of these examples occur within this book.
6. Lone *mii* occurs in (139a, c) and is connected to conjunct-order verbs as well. These, however, are sentence-level functions of the deictic particle *mii* (see Fairbanks 2008 for a detailed discussion on the functions of *mii*).

GLOSSARY

ablaut: A process that changes, mutates, replaces, or alters the initial vowel of a conjunct verb.

anaphoric: Usually when some linguistic element refers back to some referent, word, or group of words in prior discourse.

asyndetic: The absence of a conjunction, such as *and*, between propositions or other linguistic units.

bimoraic: Refers to the idea in linguistics of syllable weight. Some syllables are "light syllables" and some are "heavy syllables," depending on how many mora they contain. In other words, short vowels may be analyzed as having one mora, or being mono-moraic, and long vowels as having two mora, or being bimoraic.

clitic: Refers to words that tend to be shortened or get reduced in form, sometimes so severely that they lose their own stress and attach to another word. In English, an example is the word *is*, which sometimes reduces to its clitic form *-'s* and attaches itself to a preceding word, e.g., *Where's mom?* vs. *Where is mom?*

conceptual representation: Usually referring to what is actually being said. This is opposed to procedural representations, which are words like *because, or, so*, etc., which give instructions on how to organize what is being said.

conjunct order: In Ojibwe, one of three conjugational systems where "person" is exclusively marked on the end of the verb as a suffix.

corpus: A collection of data.

cross-linguistic: Across different languages.

declarative sentence: A sentence that merely makes a statement or comment, as opposed to performing some other function such as asking questions.

deictic: A word or particle with pointing, focusing, or indexing functions within discourse.

demonstrative: A word that can stand in for people or things, e.g., ***This*** *is red*, where *this* serves as a demonstrative since it is standing in for a noun. In Ojibwe, the particle *mii* may act as a demonstrative if it stands in for something or someone, e.g., ***Mii*** *gaa-ikidoyan* 'That's what you said', where *mii* stands in for the noun phrase *what you said*.

determiner: In English, words like *a, an, the*, which modify or specify referents, e.g., *a car,* **the** *car.* Sometimes demonstratives may act as determiners, as in the sentence **This** *car is red,* where *this* is specifying *car,* rather than standing in for it. In Ojibwe, *mii* may act as a determiner, e.g., **mii** *a'aw Jaaj* 'That's George', where *mii* specifies *a'aw* 'that one'.

dialogic discourse: Discourse or conversations between two or more people.

discourse marker: In English, words like *oh, because, so,* etc., which function either to relate sentences or larger spans of discourse to one another or to provide some attitudinal or emotional tug to the overall discourse. In Ojibwe, these are words like *isa, gosha,* and *onzaam,* just to name a few.

distal: In a three-way distinction between *here, there,* and *over there,* the distance farthest away from the speaker is distal.

dubitative: A mode in Ojibwe that allows (either by the use of inflectional suffixes or by the use of hedge words such as *iidog*) speakers to make assertions without expressing total certainty about a situation or action.

epenthetic: The process in which a vowel or consonant is inserted into words, usually to prevent prohibited vowel or consonant sequences in languages. For example, in Ojibwe, the *-i-* in *diitibingwaam* 'she/he falls out of bed while sleeping' is epenthetic, separating root *diit-* 'fall out' from final *-ngwaam.*

epistemic: In linguistics, usually having to do with the interpersonal or cognitive properties within discourse.

first person: Referring to *me* or *I.*

fortis: The set of consonants in Ojibwe that are pronounced with more energy, such as with the Ojibwe fortis consonant set *p, t, k, ch, s, sh.*

gloss, interlinear: In linguistics, this is the practice of providing linguistic labels or codes for words or sentences so as to reveal their linguistic makeup.

illocutionary: Having to do with the linguistic act being accomplished by an utterance.

imperative order: Command forms.

independent order: In Ojibwe, one of three conjugational systems in which "person" is represented by both prefixes and suffixes attached on a verb.

inflectional system: A conjugational system.

interlinear gloss: See *gloss, interlinear.*

interlocutor: A listener, or listeners, or those participating in a conversation or dialogue.

interrogative sentence: Sentences that function as questions.

lenis: The set of consonants in Ojibwe that are pronounced with less energy, such as the Ojibwe lenis consonant set *b, d, g, j, z, zh*.

lexical: Pertaining to words.

lexicalized: Usually some linguistic item that has become a word.

metalinguistic phrase: Phrases or expressions that speakers use to talk about language. An interjection such as *or whatever that word is*, for example, is a metalinguistic phrase, which talks about language rather than using language as a communicative act per se.

monologic discourse: Discourse involving one person.

morphological: Having to do with the different units of meaning within a word and how these units interact with each other in form and function.

narrow gloss: When an interlinear gloss is exposited in more detail so as to show all the morphological or phonological details of word or sentence.

nominalize: The act of changing a verb or some other linguistic form into a noun.

nominal predicate construction: A linguistic construction that acts as a sentence but where there is no verb such as *is*. Some languages like Ojibwe do not require the use of a verb to form sentences, e.g., *Ozhibii'igan o'ow* 'This is a pencil'.

orthography: A writing system.

periphrastic: Words or phrases occurring in the periphery of, or around, what is being spoken of.

phonological: Having to do with the sounds of a language.

pragmatic: What may be inferred or implied by a given utterance.

preverb: Preverbal units that may be stacked on the front of a verb and that provide nuance or deictic information about the verb to which they are attached, e.g., *nitaa-niimi* 'she/he knows how to dance' (where *nitaa-* 'know how, likes to' is the preverb).

procedural representation: Words or expressions that instruct listeners how to interpret sentences or larger spans of discourse with one another.

prosodic contour: The stress and intonation patterns of utterances.

proximal: In a three-way distinction, *here, there,* and *over there*, proximal refers to the distance closest to the speaker.

referential meaning: Referring to words where the definition of the word has a referent in the real world, and the meaning does not have to be inferred by context. For example, *dog* has referential meaning, but the word *oh* does not.

second person: Referring to *you*.

semantic: Referring to meaning.

sociolinguistics: The field of linguistics that looks at social factors that might influence the linguistics of a particular language.

subordinate clause: A clause that usually does not represent a full sentence on its own.

syntactic: How words, phrases, or sentences interact and occur in relation to one other to express various meanings and functions.

temporal: Referring to time or time frames.

text: Referring to discourse in texts. Sometimes the larger spans of discourse are referred to as *text* also.

third person: Referring to *she, he, her, him,* etc.

token: An example or instance of a phenomenon.

REFERENCES

Abraham, Werner. 1991. *Discourse Particles: Descriptive and Theoretical Investigations on the Logical, Syntactic and Pragmatic Properties of Discourse Particles in German.* Amsterdam: Benjamins.

Agbayani, B., and C. Golston. 2010. "Second-Position Is First-Position: Wackernagel's Law and the Role of Clausal Conjunction." *Indogermanischen Forschungen* 115: 1–21.

Aijmer, Karin, and Anne-Marie Simon-Vandenbergen. 2006. Introduction. In *Pragmatic Markers in Contrast,* edited by Karin Aijmer and Anne-Marie Simon-Vandenbergen, 1–10. Boston: Elsevier.

Altenberg, Bengt. 2006. "The Function of Adverbial Connectors in Second Initial Position in English and Swedish." In *Pragmatic Markers in Contrast,* edited by Karin Aijmer and Anne-Marie Simon-Vandenbergen, 11–37. Boston: Elsevier.

Andersen, Gisle. 1998. "The Pragmatic Marker Like from a Relevance-Theoretic Perspective." In *Discourse Markers: Descriptions and Theory,* edited by Andreas H. Jucker and Yael Ziv, 147–70. Philadelphia: Benjamins.

Anderson, Marge. 1999. "The Circle of Great Conversation." Unpublished translation of Mille Lacs 1999 State of the Band Address.

Ariel, Mira. 1998. "Discourse Markers and Form-Function Correlations." In *Discourse Markers: Descriptions and Theory,* edited by Andreas H. Jucker and Yael Ziv, 223–60. Philadelphia: Benjamins.

Baraga, Frederic. 1992. *A Dictionary of the Ojibway Language.* Reprint, St. Paul: Minnesota Historical Society Press. First published 1878, reprinted 1880.

Bazzanella, Carla. 1990. "Phatic Connectives as Interactional Cues in Contemporary Spoken Italian." *Journal of Pragmatics* 14: 629–47.

Benjamin, Millie. n.d. "Ikido nimaamaanaan indizhitwaawininaan." Unpublished document.

———. 2006. "Elderly Advisory Council." Unpublished story.

Biq, Yung. 1990. "Conversation, Continuation, and Connectives." *Text* 10(3): 187–208.

Bishop, Ruth G. 1979. "Tense-Aspect in Totonac Narrative Discourse." In *Discourse Studies in Mesoamerican Languages 1: Discussion,* edited by Linda K. Jones, 31–68. Summer Institute of Linguistics Publications in Linguistics 58. Dallas: Summer Institute of Linguistics and the University of Texas at Arlington.

Blakemore, Diane. 1987. *Semantic Constraints on Relevance.* Oxford: Blackwell.

———. 2004. "Discourse Markers." In *The Handbook of Pragmatics,* edited by Laurence R. Horn and Gregory Ward, 221–40. Malden MA: Blackwell.

Bloomfield, Leonard. 1958. *Eastern Ojibwa: Grammatical Sketch, Texts and Word List*. Edited by Charles F. Hockett. Ann Arbor: University of Michigan Press.

Brinton, Laurel J. 1996. *Pragmatic Markers in English: Grammaticalization and Discourse Functions*. Berlin: Mouton de Gruyter.

———. 2003. "Historical Discourse Analysis." In *The Handbook of Discourse Analysis*, edited by Deborah Schiffrin, Deborah Tannen, and Heidi E. Hamilton, 138–60. Malden MA: Blackwell.

Brody, Jill. 1987. "Particles Borrowed from Spanish as Discourse Markers in Maya Languages." *Anthropological Linguistics* 29(4): 507–21.

———. 1989. "Discourse Markers in Tojolabal Maya." In *Papers from the Annual Regional Meeting of the Chicago Linguistic Society*, 15–29. Chicago: Chicago Linguistic Society.

———. 1995. "Lending the 'Unborrowable': Spanish Discourse Markers in Indigenous American Languages." In *Spanish in Four Continents: Studies in Language Contact and Bilingualism*, edited by C. Silva-Corvalán, 132–48. Washington DC: Georgetown University Press.

Bruti, Silvia. 1999. "In Fact and Infatti: The Same, Similar or Different." *Pragmatics* 9(4): 519–33.

Cadiot, A., O. Ducrot, B. Fraden, and T. Nguyen. 1985. "Enfin, marqueur métalinguistique." *Journal of Pragmatics* 2(3): 199–239.

Catricala, M. 2010. "The Formative Element Pseudo- in the Metalinguistic Universe." *Studi Italiani Di Linguistica Teorica e Applicata* 39(1): 27–46.

Clark, James. 1998a. "Dibaakonigewinini Miinawaa Anishinaabe." *Oshkaabewis Native Journal* (Bemidji State University) 5(2): 8–9.

———. 1998b. "Gaa-ina'oonind Anishinaabe." *Oshkaabewis Native Journal* (Bemidji State University) 5(2): 54–59.

———. 1998c. "Inday." *Oshkaabewis Native Journal* (Bemidji State University) 5(2): 18–23.

———. 2003a. "Inwewin." *Oshkaabewis Native Journal* (Bemidji State University) 6(1–2): 50–53.

———. 2003b. "Mashkiki." *Oshkaabewis Native Journal* (Bemidji State University) 6(1–2): 54–57.

———. 2003c. "Oshki-aya'aag." *Oshkaabewis Native Journal* (Bemidji State University) 6(1–2): 58–60.

[Clark, Jill?]. 2006. "Mii Giitagoshing Ziigwanike." *Ojibwe Inaajimowin* (Mille Lacs Band of Ojibwe, Onamia MN) 8(3): 13.

Cook, Haruko. 1992. "Meanings of Non-referential Indexes: A Case Study of the Japanese Sentence-Final Particle *Ne*." *Text* 12(4): 507–39.

Cook, J. 1990. "An Indexical Account of the Japanese Sentence-Final Particle *Ne*." *Discourse Processes* 13(4): 507–39.

Corbiere, Mary Ann. 1997. "Gaawii wi Kidwin Miiksesnoo: Semantic Rules for Selection of Some Ojibwe Adverbs." In *Papers of the Twenty-Eighth Algonquian Conference*, edited by David H. Pentland, 71–84. Winnipeg: University of Manitoba.

Cunha, G. X., and J. H. Chaves Marinho. 2012. "The Connector 'Quando' and Chaining Episodes of Journalistic Narrative." *Cadernos de Estudos Linguisticos* 54(2): 187–203.

Cyr, D. 1991. "Algonquian Orders as Aspectual Markers: Some Typological Evidence and Pragmatic Considerations." In *Papers of the Twenty-Second Algonquian Conference*, edited by William Cowan, 58–88. Ottawa: Carleton University.

Dajko, N., and K. Carmichael. 2014. "But Qui C'est la Difference? Discourse Markers in Louisiana French: The Case of *But* vs. *Mais.*" *Language in Society* 43(2): 159–83.

Davidsen-Nielsen, Niels. 1996. *Discourse Particles in Danish*. Pre-publications of the English Department 69. Odense, Denmark: Odense University. August.

Do, A. H. 2006. "Contrastive Discourse Markers: An Examination of Their Characteristics in Korean." PhD diss., Boston University.

Eagle, Melvin. 1998. "Gekendaasojig." In *Oshkaabewis Native Journal* (Bemidji State University) 5(1): 8–85.

Fairbanks, Brendan. 2008. "All about *Mii.*" In *Papers of the Thirty-Ninth Algonquian Conference*, edited by Karl Hele, 166–221. London: University of Western Ontario.

Fleischman, Suzanne. 1985. "Discourse Functions of Tense-Aspect Oppositions in Narrative: Toward a Theory of Grounding." *Linguistics* 2: 851–82.

———. 1986. "Evaluation in Narrative: The Present Tense in Medieval 'Performed Stories.'" *Yale French Studies* 70: 199–251.

Fraser, Bruce. 1990. "An Approach to Discourse Markers." *Journal of Pragmatics* 14: 383–95.

———. 1996. "Pragmatic Markers." *Pragmatics* 6(2): 167–90.

———. 1998. "Contrastive Discourse Markers in English." In *Discourse Markers: Descriptions and Theory*, edited by Andreas H. Jucker and Yael Ziv, 301–26. Philadelphia: Benjamins.

———. 1999. "What Are Discourse Markers?" *Journal of Pragmatics* 31: 931–52.

Fuji, S. 2000. "Incipient Decategorization of MONO and Grammaticalization of Speaker Attitude in Japanese Discourse." In *Pragmatic Markers and Propositional Attitude*, edited by G. Andersen and T. Fretheim, 85–118. Amsterdam: Benjamins.

Goddard, Ives. 1978. "Central Algonquian Languages." In *Handbook of North American Indians*, vol. 15, *Northeast*, edited by Bruce G. Trigger, 583–87. Washington DC: Smithsonian Institution.

———, ed. 1996. *Languages*. Vol. 17 of *Handbook of North American Indians*. Washington DC: Smithsonian Institution.

Goldberg, Julia. 1980. "Discourse Particles: An Analysis of the Role of *Y'know, I Mean, Well,* and *Actually* in Conversation." PhD diss., Cambridge University.

Grimes, Joseph E. 1975. *The Thread of Discourse.* The Hague: Mouton.

Hakulinen, Auli. 1998. "The Use of Finnish *Nyt* as a Discourse Particle." In *Discourse Markers: Descriptions and Theory,* edited by Andreas H. Jucker and Yael Ziv, 83–97. Philadelphia: Benjamins.

Hakulinen, Auli, and Eeva-Leena Seppänen. 1992. "Finnish Kato: From Verb to Particle." *Journal of Pragmatics* 18: 527–49.

Hansen, Mosegaard. 1998. *The Function of Discourse Particles: A Study with Special Reference to Spoken French.* Amsterdam: Benjamins.

Hayes, Bruce. 1995. *Metrical Stress Theory.* Chicago: University of Chicago Press.

Hyun-Oak Kim, A. 2011. "Rhetorical Questions as Catalyst in Grammaticalization: Deriving Korean Discourse Marker KETUN from Conditional Connective." *Journal of Pragmatics* 43(4): 1023–41.

Iu Otoshki-kikindiuin au Tebeniminung gaie Bemajiinung Jesus Christ: Ima Ojibue Inueuining Giizhitong [The new testament of Our Lord and Saviour Jesus Christ translated into the language of the Ojibwa Indians]. 1875. New York: American Bible Society.

Jensen, E. S. 2000. "Sentential Adverbials and Topology, with Connective Adverbials as a Starting Point." *RASK,* supplement, 11: 141–54.

Jones, Linda Kay, and Ned R. Coleman. 1979. "Towards a Discourse Perspective of Modes and Tenses in Kickapoo Narratives." In *Discourse Studies in Mesoamerican Languages, 1: Discussion,* edited by Linda Kay Jones, 69–95. Summer Institute of Linguistics Publications in Linguistics 58. Dallas: Summer Institute of Linguistics and the University of Texas at Arlington.

Jones, William. 1917. "The Birth of Nänabushu." In *Ojibwe Texts,* vol. 7, pt. 1, edited by Truman Michelson, 2–7. New York: American Ethnological Society.

———. 1919. *Ojibwe Texts,* vol. 7, pt. 2. Edited by Truman Michelson. New York: American Ethnological Society.

Jucker, Andreas H. 1993. "The Discourse Marker *Well*: A Relevance Theoretic Account." *Journal of Pragmatics* 19: 433–52.

Jucker, Andreas H., and Sara W. Smith. 1998. "And People Like Just You Know Like 'Wow': Discourse Markers as Negotiating Strategies." In *Discourse Markers: Descriptions and Theory,* edited by Andreas H. Jucker and Yael Ziv, 171–201. Philadelphia: Benjamins.

Jucker, Andreas H., and Yael Ziv. 1998. "Discourse Markers: Introduction." In *Discourse Markers: Descriptions and Theory,* edited by Andreas H. Jucker and Yael Ziv, 1–12. Philadelphia: Benjamins.

Katayama, A. 2012. "Effects of Instruction on Japanese Discourse Marker *N Desu*." MA thesis, University of Alberta.

Kegg, Maude. 1993. *Portage Lake: Memories of an Ojibwe Childhood.* Edited by John D. Nichols. Minneapolis: University of Minnesota Press.

Koike, Dale A. 1996. "Functions of the Adverbial *Ya* in Spanish Narrative Discourse." *Journal of Pragmatics* 25(2): 267–79.

Kroon, Caroline. 1998. "A Framework for the Description of Latin Discourse Markers." *Journal of Pragmatics* 20(2): 205–23.

Kwong, Luke. 1989. "The Cantonese Utterance Particle *La* and the Accomplishment of Common Understandings in Conversation." *Papers in Pragmatics* 3(1): 39–87.

Landone, E. 2009. "Discourse Markers and Verbal Politeness in Spanish." *Linguistic Insights — Studies in Language and Communication* 116: 1–390.

———. 2012. "Discourse Markers and Politeness in a Digital Forum in Spanish." *Journal of Pragmatics* 44(13): 1799–820.

Longacre, Robert E. 1976. "'Mystery Particles' and Affixes." In *Papers from the Twelfth Regional Meeting of the Chicago Linguistic Society*, 468–75. Chicago: Chicago Linguistic Society.

Macario Lopes, A. C. 2011. "The Multifunctionality of the Discourse Marker 'Afinal' in European Portuguese." *Oslo Studies in Language* 3(1): 131–40.

Maschler, Y. 1997. "Discourse Markers at Frame Shifts in Israeli Hebrew Talk-in-Interaction." *Pragmatics* 7(2): 183–211.

———. 1998. "Rotse Lishmoa Keta? Wanna Hear Something Weird/Funny? Segmenting Israeli Hebrew Talk-in-Interaction." In *Discourse Markers: Descriptions and Theory*, edited by Andreas H. Jucker and Yael Ziv, 13–60. Philadelphia: Benjamins.

Massam, Diane, Donna Starks, and Ofania Ikiua. 2006. "On the Edge of Grammar: Discourse Particles in Niuean." *Oceanic Linguistics* 45(1): 191–206.

Matsumoto, Y. 1988. "From Bound Grammatical Markers to Free Discourse Markers: History of Some Japanese Connectives." In *Proceedings of the Fourteenth Annual Meeting of the Berkeley Linguistics Society*, edited by S. Axmaker, A. Jaisser, and H. Singmaster, 340–51. Berkeley CA: Berkeley Linguistics Society.

McGloin, N. H., and Y. Konishi. 2010. "From Connective Particle to Sentence-Final Particle: A Usage-Based Analysis of *Shi* 'and' in Japanese." *Language Sciences* 32(5): 563–78.

Mille Lacs Band of Ojibwe. 1998. *Baswewe "echo."* Nay Ah Shing Schools Mille Lacs Band of Ojibwe.

Mithun, Marianne. 1999. *The Languages of Native North America*. New York: Cambridge University Press.

Moose, Lawrence L., Mary Moose, Gordon Jourdain, Marlene Stately, Leona Wakonabo, Eugene Stillday, Anna Gibbs, Rosemarie DeBungie, and Nancy Jones. 2009. *Aaniin Ekidong: Ojibwe Vocabulary Project*. Edited by Anton Treuer and Keller Paap. St. Paul: Minnesota Humanities Center.

Na-gan-i-gwun-eb. 1893. Letter to Reverend Gilfillan. March 26. Red Lake. Gilfillan letters, 1883–1913. Minnesota Historical Society.

Nakao. 1995. *Japanese-English English-Japanese Dictionary.* New York: Ballantine Books.

Nichols, John D. 1980. "Ojibwe Morphology." PhD diss., Harvard University.

———, ed. 1988. *An Ojibwe Text Anthology.* London ON: Centre for Research and Teaching of Canadian Native Languages, University of Western Ontario.

———. 1995. "Weak of Heart—Strong of Heart: Approaching the Narrative Art of Dedaakam of Mille Lacs." *Oshkaabewis Native Journal* 2(1): 49–68.

Nichols, John D., and Nyholm, Earl. 1995. *A Concise Dictionary of Minnesota Ojibwe.* Minneapolis: University of Minnesota Press.

Ningewance, Patricia M. 2004. *Talking Gookom's Language: Learning Ojibwe.* Lac Seul ON: Mazinaate Press.

Onodera, Noriko Okada. 1994. "Pragmatic Change in Japanese: Conjunctions and Interjections as Discourse Markers." PhD diss., Georgetown University.

———. 1995. "Diachronic Analysis of Japanese Discourse Markers." In *Historical Pragmatics,* edited by Andreas H. Jucker, 393–437. Amsterdam: Benjamins.

Or, W. 1997. "Chinese Temporal Adverbs of Succession and Overlap." Paper presented at the annual convention of the Midwest Modern Language Association, Chicago.

Pak, D. 2013. "A Study of the Korean Clausal Connectives '-oso' and '-ko' of Temporal Sequence." *Acta Koreana* 16(1): 5–21.

Park, Yong-Yae. 1999. "The Korean Connective *Nuntey* in Conversational Discourse." *Journal of Pragmatics* 31(2): 191–218.

Payne, Doris L., and E. Thomas. 1990. "Yagua." In *Handbook of Amazonian Languages,* edited by Desmond C. Derbyshire and Geoffrey K. Pullum, 2:249–474. Berlin: Mouton de Gruyter.

Payne, Thomas E. 1997. *Describing Morphosyntax: A Guide for Field Linguists.* Cambridge: Cambridge University Press.

Redeker, Gisela. 1990. "Ideational and Pragmatic Markers of Discourse Structure." *Journal of Pragmatics* 14(3): 367–81.

Rhodes, Richard. 1979. "Some Aspects of Ojibwa Discourse." In *Papers of the Tenth Algonquian Conference,* edited by William Cowan, 102–17. Ottawa: Carleton University.

———. 1985. *Eastern Ojibwa-Chippewa-Ottawa Dictionary.* Trends in Linguistics, Documentation 3, edited by Werner Winter. New York: Mouton.

———. 1998. "The Syntax and Pragmatics of Ojibwe *Mii.*" In *Papers of the Twenty-Ninth Algonquian Conference,* edited by David H. Pentland, 286–94. Winnipeg: University of Manitoba.

———. 2006. *Clause Structure, Core Arguments and the Algonquian Relative Root Construction.* Belcourt Lecture series. Paper originally delivered before the University of Manitoba on March 20, 1998. Winnipeg: Voices of Rupert's Land.

Richardson, Peter. 1991. "Tense, Discourse, Style: The Historical Present in 'Sir Gawain and the Green Knight.'" *Neuphilologische Mitteilungen* 92: 343–49.

———. 1995. "Tense, Structure, and Reception in Þorsteins Þáttr stangarholggs." *Arkiv för nordisk filologi* 110: 41–55.

Sadler, Misumi. 2006. "A Blurring of Categorization: The Japanese Connective *De* in Spontaneous Conversation." *Discourse Studies* 8(2): 303–23.

Salser, J. K., and Neva Salser. 1976. "Some Features of Cubeo Discourse and Sentence Structure." In *Discourse Grammar: Studies in Indigenous Languages of Colombia, Panama, and Ecuador*, 2:253–72. Summer Institute of Linguistics Publications in Linguistics and Related Fields 52(2). Dallas: Summer Institute of Linguistics.

Schiffrin, Deborah. 1987a. *Discourse Markers*. Cambridge: Cambridge University Press.

———. 1987b. "Discovering the Context of an Utterance." *Linguistics* 25(1): 11–32.

———. 2003a. "Discourse Markers: Language, Meaning, and Context." In *The Handbook of Discourse Analysis*, edited by Deborah Schiffrin, Deborah Tannen, and Heidi E. Hamilton, 54–75. Malden MA: Blackwell.

———. 2003b. "Discourse Markers." In *International Encyclopedia of Linguistics*, 2nd ed., 458–67. New York: Oxford University Press.

Schourup, Lawrence. 1985. *Common Discourse Particles in English Conversation*. New York: Garland.

Schwenter, Scott. 1996. "Some Reflections on *O Sea*: A Discourse Marker in Spanish." *Journal of Pragmatics* 25: 855–74.

Shemesh, Rivka. 2006. "Direct Discourse Markers in Mishnaic Hebrew." *Journal of Semitic Studies* 51(1): 45–58.

Shloush, Shelley. 1998. "A Unified Account of Hebrew *Bekicur* 'In Short': Relevance Theory and Discourse Structure Considerations." In *Discourse Markers: Descriptions and Theory*, edited by Andreas H. Jucker and Yael Ziv, 61–82. Philadelphia: Benjamins.

Silva, Giselle, and Alzira de Macedo. 1992. "Discourse Markers in the Spoken Portuguese of Rio de Janeiro." *Language Variation and Change* 4: 235–49.

Smart, Sonny. 2004. *Ojibwe Language*. Vol. 2. Ringle WI: Otter Trail Multimedia.

Smits, Aletta. 2002. *How Writers Begin Their Sentences: Complex Beginnings in Native and Learner English*. Utrecht: LOT.

Solomon, Julie. 1995. "Local and Global Functions of a Borrowed Native Pair of Discourse Markers in a Yucatan Maya Narrative." In *Proceedings of the 21st Annual Meeting of the Berkeley Linguistic Society, February 17–20: General Session and Parasession on Historical Issues in Sociolinguistics*, edited by J. Ahlers, 287–98. Berkeley: Berkeley Linguistics Society.

Staples, Lee. 2007. *Miigwanens*. Unpublished story.

Tchizmarova, Ivelina K. 2005. "Hedging Functions of the Bulgarian Discourse Marker *Xajde*." *Journal of Pragmatics* 37: 1143–63.

Torres, Lourdes. 2006. "Bilingual Discourse Markers in Indigenous Languages." *International Journal of Bilingual Education and Bilingualism* 9(5): 615–25.

Trask, R. L. 1993. *A Dictionary of Grammatical Terms in Linguistics.* Routledge: New York.

Treuer, Anton, ed. 2000. *Omaa Akiing.* Princeton NJ: Western Americana Press.

———, ed. 2001. *Living Our Language.* St. Paul: Minnesota Historical Society Press.

Valentine, J. Randolph. 1994. "Ojibwe Dialect Relationships." PhD diss., University of Texas at Austin.

———. 2001. *Nishnaabemwin Reference Grammar.* Toronto: University of Toronto Press.

Vaskó, Ildikó. 2000. "The Interplay of Hungarian *De* (but) and *Is* (too, either)." In *Pragmatic Markers and Propositional Attitude*, edited by G. Andersen and T. Fretheim, 255–64. Amsterdam: Benjamins.

Vincent, Diane. 1993. *Les ponctuants de la langue et autres mots du discours.* Quebec: Nuit blanche.

Wilson, Deirdre. 1994. "Discourse Markers: Social and Cognitive Approaches." Paper delivered at conference on Linguistic Processes in Communication, University of Wales, Bangor.

Wilson, Deirdre, and Dan Sperber. 1993. "Linguistic Form and Relevance." *Lingua* 90: 1–25.

———. 2004. "Relevance Theory." In *The Handbook of Pragmatics*, edited by Laurence R. Horn and Gregory Ward, 607–32. Malden MA: Blackwell.

Wouk, Fay. 1998. "Solidarity in Indonesian Conversation: The Discourse Marker *Kan.*" *Multilingua* 17(4): 379–406.

Zavala, Virginia. 2001. "Borrowing Evidential Functions from Quechua: The Role of *Pues* as a Discourse Marker in Andean Spanish." *Journal of Pragmatics* 33: 999–1023.

Zhou, J. 2013. "On Discourse Perspective Marker 'X shuolai.'" *Shijie Hanyu Jiaoxue / Chinese Teaching in the World* 27(4): 512–22.

Ziv, Yael. 1998. "Hebrew *Kaze* as Discourse Marker and Lexical Hedge: Conceptual and Procedural Properties." In *Discourse Markers: Descriptions and Theory*, edited by Andreas H. Jucker and Yael Ziv, 203–22. Philadelphia: Benjamins.

INDEX

situational immediacy by, 158–60; showing of temporal immediacy by, 156–58

planes of discourse, 16–17, 20–22, 42, 104, 105

Portage Lake (Kegg), 7

positional distribution: cross-linguistic data on, 29–31, 40, 181nn21–22; in Deborah Schiffrin's characterization, 18; of English discourse markers, 18, 38, 39, 180n21, 181n22; options for, 1–2, 38–39, 40, 43. *See also* initial position; second position

position-strengthening markers, 52–54, 110–15

pragmatic markers, 25–27, 37, 179n9, 189

preverbal elements: definition of, 88, 184n18, 189; discourse functions of, 1–2, 88–90; hyphen usage with, 9–10; and *izhi*, 88–91, 165; in the Ojibwe language, 34

procedural representation, 24–25, 189

profanity, 137–38, 145, 149

prosodic contours, 40, 181n24, 189. *See also* intonation contours

qualifying markers, 101

Quechua language, 44

Red Lake Ojibwe reservation, 5, 63, 149

reformulation markers, 65–66

relative preverbs, 88–90, 165

relative roots, 88–90, 184n17

relevance theory, 23–28, 181n25

relinquishment markers, 105–6

resolution markers, 101–3

resultant action markers, 108–10

resultant interjections, 117–19

Rhodes, Richard, 151–53, 157–58, 180n19

Rice, Lillian, 122

role reversal markers, 32–33

sa (mystery particle). See *isa* (mystery particle)

sa go (particle cluster), 117–19

Sam, Dorothy, 128–29

Sam, Elfreda, 95, 99, 145–46

sa naa (particle cluster), 145, 148–49

Saulteaux (Ojibwe dialect), 4

Schiffrin, Deborah, 14–22, 26–28, 35–36, 40–42, 61, 91, 178nn3–6, 181n24

Schourup, Lawrence, 13

Schwenter, Scott, 36–37, 179n12

second position: cross-linguistic data on, 31, 33–34, 38, 179n14; discourse markers at, 1–2, 43; and mystery particle *bina*, 126–31, 132–36; and mystery particle clusters, 117–19, 129–30, 145–50; and mystery particle *da*, 131–32; and mystery particle *goda*, 136–37; and mystery particle *gosha*, 120–25; and mystery particle *naa*, 137–45; in Ojibwe, 72. See also *idash* (discourse connective)

self-pity-invoking markers, 128–29, 147

Severn Ojibwe (Ojibwe dialect), 4

sha (mystery particle), 126–31, 146–47

sha naa (particle cluster), 145–47

short vowels (Ojibwe), 8

Simon-Vandenbergen, Anne-Marie, 27

situational immediacy, 158–60

Smallwood, Larry, 144

Spanish language, 29–30, 36–38, 43–44, 179n13